DRIVING DOWN
THE COST OF DRUGS

DRIVING DOWN
THE COST OF DRUGS

Battling Big Pharma
in the Statehouse

Ramón Castellblanch

FIRST**FORUM**PRESS

A DIVISION OF LYNNE RIENNER PUBLISHERS, INC. • BOULDER & LONDON

Published in the United States of America in 2012 by
FirstForumPress
A division of Lynne Rienner Publishers, Inc.
1800 30th Street, Boulder, Colorado 80301
www.firstforumpress.com

and in the United Kingdom by
FirstForumPress
A division of Lynne Rienner Publishers, Inc.
3 Henrietta Street, Covent Garden, London WC2E 8LU

Library of Congress Cataloging-in-Publication Data
A Cataloging-in-Publication record for this book
is available from the Library of Congress.
ISBN: 978-1-935049-45-6

British Cataloguing in Publication Data
A Cataloguing in Publication record for this book
is available from the British Library.

This book was produced from digital files prepared by the author
using the FirstForumComposer.

Printed and bound in the United States of America

∞ The paper used in this publication meets the requirements
of the American National Standard for Permanence of
Paper for Printed Library Materials Z39.48-1992.

5 4 3 2 1

To my spouse, Eleanor Prouty,
who steadily helps her union to stay on track and
who makes my life as wonderful as it could possibly be

And to our sons, Carlos and Leo Castellblanch,
our pride and joy

Contents

Preface   *ix*

Acknowledgments   *xi*

1   David, Goliath, and Prescription Drugs   1

2   How Drugs Got So Expensive   9

3   Vermont Raises the Cry   27

4   As Goes Maine   53

5   PhRMA Tries Stopping State Action   81

6   So Goes California   95

7   Politically Organizing for Access to Medicines   137

Appendix. Useful Websites on Health Care Policy and Politics   *151*

Bibliography   *153*

Index   *169*

About the Book   *173*

Preface

In mainstream U.S. policymaking literature, the concept of a window of opportunity is used to illustrate that it is only at certain times that policy-makers can get their proposals made into laws or regulations. These times are described as those when the window of opportunity is open. At other times, policymakers see the window as closed and cannot expect to change the way government works.

U.S. writers on policymaking often treat the matter of when a window is open as a given and do not ask why it is either open or shut. To consider that question could raise a discussion of special interest groups who often keep these windows closed. Such discussion might be seen by these groups as impolite.

But, for those who are not among the special interests, considering how others like themselves have opened these windows could help them to do it, too. Then, their chances to win policies denied by blocked policymaking processes could be improved. This book is about how grassroots leaders found a political window of opportunity closed   and opened it.

Acknowledgments

I particularly want to thank Donald Light and Theodore Marmor, without whom this book would not have been possible. For my privileged access to the stories in the book, I give special thanks to Suzanne Haviland and Deborah Socolar in New England and Bruce Lee Livingston, Jodi Reid, and Gilbert Ojeda in California. The guidance of Barney G. Glaser, Sanford Thatcher, Linda Shopes, Mark A. Peterson, Vicente Navarro, Fred Block, and Melvin Kohn was indispensable. Finally, I want to thank Lloyd Ulman for showing me the way to a career in which I could write a book like this and get paid.

1

David, Goliath, and Prescription Drugs

One of the first places where I saw someone outraged by how rising prescription drug prices could mean that she could lose her medicines was at a New England town meeting in the autumn of 2000. At the time, I was a health policy professor at a Connecticut college, Quinnipiac University, and a member of a Connecticut legislative task force looking into the availability of prescription drugs. A public interest group advocating in the legislature to improve access to prescription drugs had gotten me on the task force. To learn how strongly voters felt about the problem and to see if they should do something about it, the task force held a series of hearings around the state and one was in New Britain, Connecticut, an old industrial town. New Britain was still home to Stanley Works, the toolmaker. But once there had been 5,000 jobs in the Stanley Works factory. By the year 2000, most of those jobs were gone.

Our task force was meeting in the old town's senior center, hearing what its retirees had come to say about access to prescription drugs. We sat on a stage at one end of the room; seniors faced us with a standing microphone in the middle aisle. Despite only low tech publicity like flyers and local newspaper articles having announced the event, all the seats were filled and more people were standing around the perimeter of the meeting hall. After we started, many seniors got in line behind the standing microphone waiting to speak. I was surprised to see that the room was packed; I imagine everyone else on the task force was as well.

After waiting her turn, one elderly woman slowly walked from her place at the head of the line to the mike and explained to the panel that she could only walk one day out of three. She told us that she had saved her "walking day" for the day of this hearing so that she could tell us about her problems in getting access to prescription drugs. As did many other witnesses we were to hear, she had brought along all her pill bottles in a paper bag. She took them out of the bag and held each one of them up for us to see. She told us what was in each bottle, what each medicine was for, and what the drugs cost, individually and cumulatively. She told us what her income was and what portion of it she was already spending on prescription drugs. Next, she explained that, if the price of the medicines in her bag were increased another five or ten percent, then she'd have no choice but to discontinue one of the medicines she had showed us. She finished by asking us on the panel which medicine we thought that she should give up first.

For those of us on the panel, the story she told was not to turn out to be unusual. In hearings around the state, at least one witness would start out by showing us all her pill bottles. At the end of these unrehearsed presentations, each speaker would finish by asking the panel the same question that we heard in New Britain: which medicine should she give up first, if prices went up?

As these witnesses testified at the task force's hearings around Connecticut, they were always observed by drug industry representatives who stood around the edges of the rooms. The representatives' stylish clothes and constant use of cell phones, which were not so common in 2000, made them easy to spot. The industry had a spokesperson on the panel, sometimes a dapper gray-haired woman flown in from Washington, DC, especially for these town meetings. She would make comments that appeared to have been developed using industry focus groups and polls. She used words and catch phrases that sounded as if they were carefully tailored by highly paid wordsmiths. High prices make possible wonderful research, she would argue. She asserted that many diseases could be cured. She warned that, if prices were lowered, cures in the research pipeline would be cut off and many in the room would suffer.

I expected that some in the room would be dazzled by this industry logic; legislators often were. But the seniors defied these expectations: they were unimpressed, and many in the audiences would actually hoot. They didn't seem to care even if the claims were true. Elderly and facing the prospect of losing vital medicines in a few months, many had little interest in possible new cures available in a decade. At each hearing, while the expensively developed messages from the industry representatives bombed, the testimony of plain seniors speaking from the heart about their personal crises carried the day. The industry's message-makers did not expect seniors to dismiss their arguments. Normally, these kinds of persuaders are able to influence US voters with carefully crafted messages that are relentlessly repeated. But, at these meetings, they were met with righteous indignation. People knew high prices were threatening their access to essential medicines, and they were getting a chance to say so.[1]

Fifteen years earlier, I had heard a discussion of the economic logic that led to the high prices that were outraging the seniors around Connecticut and, as is explained in this book's next chapter, around the rest of the United States. In those earlier days, I was getting my start in public policy as a student at the Kennedy School of Government at Harvard. Along with some other students at the Kennedy School, I was able to take a few courses outside of the public policy program. At the time, I was interested in getting involved in what was called "social investing." So, I took the investment course at the Harvard Business School. The course professor presented us with a series of investment experts espousing various strategies. We had a contrarian, we heard about derivatives, and we were given other presentations on picking winners on Wall Street.

One day, we had a guest lecturer who explained the logic by which Wall Street analysts' profit expectations affected a business's stock price. Our guest told us that the movement of a stock price for a business reflected the difference between what Wall Street analysts expected that business's profits to be and what they actually turned out to be. If a business's profits met or exceeded expectations, then its stock price should hold steady or go up. If it failed to live up to expectations, then its stock price should go down. So, a good business in which to own stock would be one with profits that consistently met or exceeded expectations. Its price should only move upward. One problem with prices based on expectations, our expert warned, is that analysts tend to raise expectations for a business each time it meets its previously set expectations. If a business's profits meet expectations once, then it seems more likely that the business will meet expectations again, driving the stock price higher. But, as expectations get higher, they become harder to meet. Eventually, the expectations are not met causing the stock price to fall and hurting the efforts of those who held it to increase the size of their portfolios.

Then, our guest told us of one set of businesses that did not have this problem—the pharmaceutical industry. These businesses kept meeting expectations and their stock prices just kept going up. To explain how they could, he told us how profit expectations are built in the pharmaceutical industry. To begin with, the industry's big profits are based on "blockbusters." In this industry, a blockbuster is basically a drug for which its owner has a patent and can charge high prices and that many patients would take for a long time. For example, in 2010, cholesterol-lowering drugs like Crestor were blockbusters. Tens of millions took them daily, many in the United States paid a high price for them (Hirschler 2010), and they would take them daily for years.

Expectations for the prescription drug industry are based on what our expert called "blockbusters in the pipeline," drugs under development that are designed to become the next blockbusters. So, to meet expectations and keep their stock prices rising, the hoped-for blockbusters must pan out to become actual blockbusters. Here, our guest told us, we could trust the top businesses in the pharmaceutical industry. As evidence of their reliability he pointed out to us one drugmaker who had had a string of so-called blockbusters in the pipeline that had met expectations: Merck. It consistently met expectations and so its stock price kept going up. To sum up his talk, our expert folded his hands as though he were praying, raised his eyes to the ceiling of the Harvard Business School lecture hall, and, in a hushed voice, invoked the name of his miracle-working stock: "St. Merck."

Unfortunately, the prices of blockbusters that led the lecturer to view his stock with such reverence also meant that some needed drugs would be too expensive for many Americans. Without high-priced drugs on which millions of paying customers were dependent, there could be few, if any, blockbusters. Without blockbusters, big drugmakers' profits would disappoint Wall Street and their prices would fall. But the requirement that made pharmaceutical investors richer also made some medicines too expensive for some who needed them, threatening their access to them. Efforts to restrain prescription drug price inflation and improve access for those unable to afford high prices would run counter to the way that the industry makes its big profits and that its investors get their big returns.

In the United States, high prices, such as those charged by the pharmaceutical industry in selling blockbusters, can be effectively challenged in the political arena. But, contrary to what many expect, relying on an argument that high drug prices would endanger the health of many would do little, if anything, to move decisionmakers in the political arena to improve access to medicines. In our country, policymaking has little to do with the quality of arguments for justice. On a day-to-day basis, policymaking is mainly driven by the pressure of competing interest groups on politicians

If policymakers were going to do something about access to medicines, then some interest group or groups would have to stand up for those in need and pressure them. But most of the competing interest groups in our political system are private interest groups like the pharmaceutical industry and have relatively simple missions: make sure that relevant policies support the highest profits possible for themselves.

To fulfill their political missions, private interests rely most heavily on campaign contributions and money generally to influence politicians.

That's where public interest groups come in. Public interest groups are different; they have much less money than private interest groups and need alternative ways to sway policymakers. With little money, they need to convince politicians that they have enough popular support that it would be politically risky for the officeholders to ignore them. They use grassroots tactics like trying to generate large numbers of letters, calls, or visits to officeholders. They include staging demonstrations. A large turnout of seniors as at the New Britain town meeting could be evidence of the kind of popular support of public interest group needs. Without such evidence, public interest groups are relatively powerless.

Even with it, they are hard pressed when confronted by powerful private interests. While a public interest lobbyist must usually wait outside politicians' offices for chances to talk to them, private interest representatives can use their contributions to gain access through closed political events and by enticing legislative and executive branch leaders into their own offices. Big businesses playing this "inside game" can also muster high-paid experts, attorneys, and media professionals to bolster their efforts. Public interest groups playing the "outside game" only have their usually modestly or unpaid supporters using grassroots tactics to press their cases. Given this disparity, public interest groups engaging in politics in the United States often find the odds heavily stacked against them. In the case of people in this country needing medicines and trying to gain greater access to them, public interest groups would have to do political battle with the pharmaceutical industry. The chances of their success would seem somewhere between slim and none, given the extraordinary political clout of drugmakers. In taking on the pharmaceutical industry, a public interest group is playing David to their Goliath. But, in spite of such a daunting situation, advocates for those needing medicines—such as some of us at the Connecticut hearings—would find in time that it was worth the effort to challenge the pharmaceutical industry over access to medicines.

This book is about the political contest between people advocating for those like the elderly woman in New Britain and those running businesses like Merck. It looks at it in three different states, one large and two small. It seeks to draw lessons from these cases as to how grassroots advocates could prevail over wealthy interest groups. In three stages, this book looks into how public interest lobbyists could beat a powerful force like the pharmaceutical industry in a legislative battle. The first part of this book outlines in greater detail the basis of how the industry generates profits and the impact of this strategy on public health. With this background, it becomes easier to understand the events described herein, in particular what prompted seniors to react the way they did to the industry's policies and what policy options were available to those who were working to increase their access to needed medicines. The second section of the book presents the stories of the three different state cases in which public interest groups challenged the pharmaceutical industry through their legislatures. The section goes on to discuss how the industry altered its profitmaking tactics in the face of these challenges. The first two cases are political battles in New England: Vermont and Maine. Vermont in 1999 and 2000 was the first state where an effort was made to do something about the rapid prescription drug price inflation of the late 1990s.

While price legislation failed in Vermont, the second case, Maine in 2000, was the archetype of success for challenging the powerful pharmaceutical industry. It is the classic David-and-Goliath story: a legislative victory inspired by local grassroots activists against the then most profitable industry in the world. The third case took place in California in 2006 where, again, prescription drug access advocates won a major legislative victory over the daunting power of the industry's political arm, the Pharmaceutical Research and Manufacturers of America (PhRMA), and enacted a bill modeled after the legislation with which grassroots leaders had defeated PhRMA in Maine.

In the years that have followed these legislative victories over drug prices, the pharmaceutical industry has been able to prevent implementation of the state laws. Nevertheless, these wins did help generate and maintain political pressure felt at the national level that is leading to increased access to medicines and that is posing a growing threat to high drug prices. As described in Chapter 5, the Maine legislation and subsequent copycat bills around the country pushed PhRMA, in 2003, to lobby President Bush and the Republican Congress to enact the Medicare Modernization Act, (MMA) a law that deeply involves the federal Medicare program in the financing of medicines for seniors. The industry hoped that the MMA would satisfy popular demands for access to medicines while leaving prices high. But, the law was so poorly designed that it initially did little to improve access to medicines. Further, federal payment for health care through such laws puts the industry in a position where more of its sales can be subjected to the purchasing power of the US government. In this time of crushing US budget deficits, it is probably only a matter of time until the federal government acts to lower its drug costs. So, the law cannot be relied upon to protect high prices and the state victories could well bear fruit in lower drug prices.

The book's third section uses its cases to address the question on which this book focuses: how grassroots advocates sometimes defeat the rich and powerful in the political arena. From this discussion, it suggests larger lessons about factors that may explain how public interest lobbyists can push the rich and powerful to better act in the interests of the communities in which they operate.

This book is written from the point of view of a health policy academic who has sided with advocates for increased access to needed medicine and who has had a ringside seat from which to view the cases under study. In New England in 2000, I was part of a multistate group demanding broader access to essential medicines for residents. Our coalition included the Vermont legislators whose work showed our multistate group that a state could take on high prescription drug prices. It also included the Maine legislators who were to beat PhRMA in 2000 and who, later, successfully defended their legislation against the industry's lawsuits. After returning to my home state of California in 2002, I ended up working with the OURx Coalition, the group that spearheaded access advocates' win in 2006. I write in the hope that this work will contribute to the efforts of activists to politically challenge the rich and powerful.

---

[1] The Connecticut legislature did later act to substantially expand its state's program aimed at helping residents afford medicines, ConnPACE (Connecticut Citizen Action Group 2010). As a result of the work of ConnPACE starting in 2000 and running over the next few years, approximately 50,000 Connecticut seniors and people with disabilities pay no more than $16.25 per prescription (Wilson-Coker 2006).

2

How Drugs Got So Expensive

To understand the policies discussed in this book's case studies, it can help to see how blockbusters came to be central to the pharmaceutical industry's strategy in the United States, the impact the blockbuster strategy has had on access to medicines, and the policies and practices to reduce prices and improve access that were tried before the time of the first case studies. This chapter traces the rise of blockbusters, starting with the steps that made them feasible. It moves through the 1980s and early 1990s, when the industry began to use blockbusters as the key to their making profits and governments and private payers first addressed the cost consequences of this development. Then this chapter describes how, in the years immediately preceding this book's cases of state policymaking, blockbusters reached the top of their market power. Finally, it provides an overview of the impact of the industry's profitmaking strategy on the US public and the prescription drug policy options under discussion when the first cases studied in this book were about to take place.

Getting Patent Privileges

One has to look at events in the decade immediately following World War II to see the first step that the pharmaceutical giants took in order to offer the miracle investment opportunities that I heard described in a Harvard Business School classroom; that step was obtaining the privilege of patenting medicines. Before the war, the most in-demand drugs, antibiotics, were not patentable because they were not discoveries of private firms. But, to promote availability of these drugs, the government subsidized private production of them.

After the war, the US government was looking to further promote private production of essential medicines and to encourage private industry to develop new medicines. A patent could create an incentive for innovation and production by reducing competition for the

9

drugmaker's patented product and thereby allowing the producer to charge a higher price and make a higher profit than a fully competitive market would allow. So, in 1948, the US Patent Office allowed domestic drugmakers to patent medicines for private profit (Thomas 1983).

While patents can reduce competition and raise prices, among medicines they do not necessarily create monopolies. There could be several patented products of different designs that treat the same disease; so, the drugs could be said to fall in the same therapeutic class. In that case, there could be an oligopoly for medicines treating that disease, that is, just a few businesses selling the lion's share of the drugs in that therapeutic class. Businesses that have an oligopoly in selling a product are in a position to charge a high price for it. They can do this by effectively agreeing with one another not to engage in price competition and by colluding in setting the price of the product so that each gains as much as possible. They maximize their profits by setting a price for a given product as high as possible without sharply lowering demand, that is, by setting what economists call an oligopolistic price. When oligopolies are based on patents, they can last as long as the patents.

The term of a drug patent gives drugmakers exclusive rights to sell a drug (possibly for a high price) for up to twenty years from the date of filing for a patent. But, in the United States, before a prescription drug is put on the market, the drugmaker must get Food and Drug Administration (FDA) approval and a drugmaker loses time between the granting of a patent and getting the FDA permission. Nevertheless, if the difference between FDA approval and patent expiration is long enough, then many patented drugs not only cover all costs, they can be highly profitable (Schweitzer 2007). So, the ability of drugmakers to patent drugs was a big step because it could allow them to charge high, oligopolistic prices for many years.

Yet it takes more than an oligopoly to make a drug a blockbuster; it must also be an oligopoly in a drug that is taken for a long time by a large numbers of patients or at an extremely high price. In the 1960s and 1970s, the search for blockbusters focused on drugs that could be taken for a long time. To be needed for a long time, drugs must address the problems of chronic diseases, conditions that pose health problems over a long period of time such as heart disease.

In the 1960s and 1970s, the FDA made it hard to get approval for medicines for chronic conditions and leave enough years left on a patent to make it profitable. In those days, the FDA was cautiously responding to the Thalidomide drug disaster of the 1950s. Thalidomide was a drug that had been widely distributed to expectant European mothers for morning sickness and had resulted in thousands of babies being born with severely stunted limbs, along with severe internal defects of the heart, genitals, kidneys, digestive tract (including lips and mouth), and nervous system (US Food and Drug Administration 2005).[1] In the wake of the disaster, the FDA reasoned that drugs that were to be taken for a long time had to be observed for a long time before they were approved and, so, it was exceptionally cautious when considering approval for drugs for chronic conditions.

The case of the drugmaker Ayerst's effort to get the beta-blocker Inderal approved by the FDA for angina pectoris illustrates the drugmakers' problem in getting approval in time to make large profits. Through the 1960s and 1970s, Ayerst had to negotiate with the federal agency under three different presidents to get Inderal approved. In the end, it took the business ten years to get the drug approved (Daemmrich 2004). So, with these kinds of delays, it was difficult for the industry to develop blockbusters in the 1960s and 1970s. In those decades, the pharmaceutical industry's share of US health care spending actually declined (Centers for Medicare & Medicaid Services 2009b). The industry needed to change the policies of the FDA for blockbusters' prospects to brighten.

Making the FDA a Partner and the Rise of the Blockbusters

In the 1970s, the industry began to lay the political groundwork to do just that and make it easier to get drug approvals and sell high-priced drugs for chronic conditions. As part of its efforts, its friends went after the FDA's approval process with hyperbolic attacks. For example, in 1975, at an American Enterprise Institute roundtable, industry ally and future president Ronald Reagan blamed the FDA's approval process for thousands of deaths. Referring to the drug Rifampin, he said, "I think something more than 40,000 tuberculars alone have died in this country who conceivably could have been saved by a drug that has been widely used for the past few years throughout Europe."[2]

After Reagan got into the White House, his administration quickly worked to lower the barrier that the FDA posed for drug approval and increase the chances that the industry could sell blockbusters. He reorganized the agency to work closely with the prescription drug industry. The administration's deputy commissioner of the FDA, John Norris, expressed the administration's position well: "We consider ourselves partners with consumers and manufacturers in providing therapies needed by people." In 1982, Reagan's vice president George H.W. Bush observed the change: "I think we've started to see this philosophical shift, the end—or the beginning of the end—of this adversarial relationship. Government shouldn't be an adversary. It should be a partner" (Molotsky 1987). Under this new neoliberal regime, the idea became that the American patient no longer needed as much state protection from the industry; she was more of a free-market consumer who deserved easier access to still-experimental drugs and could be expected to take more of a role in looking out for herself (Daemmrich 2004).

With the FDA then a "partner" of the pharmaceutical industry, it became much easier to get new drugs to market in time to make them blockbusters. One example of the new process was the way that the FDA approved the cancer control drug Proleukin, a potential blockbuster because, while it couldn't be sold to large numbers of people, it could be sold at extremely high prices. When the drug's maker, Chiron, reported to the FDA that, out of 270 patients with melanoma treated with the drug between 1985 and 1993, only 16 percent had gotten at all better and 84 percent had suffered adverse reactions without benefits, the FDA approved the drug anyway. Unlike the review of Inderal, when reviewing Proleukin, the FDA had made it much easier to get a drug to market (Daemmrich 2004).

With the FDA now acting more like a partner and blockbusters more easily coming on line, the industry turned to the economics of selling as many of them as possible. One major tactic it began to extensively employ in the 1980s was influencing the people in the United States who had the most discretion over when prescription drugs are bought, the physicians and others who could prescribe them. To reach these prescribers, the major drugmakers assembled armies of sales representatives whom they call detailers (Schweitzer 2007).

The industry trained the detailers, sent them out in cars that they provided, and oversaw regular face-to-face meetings they had with prescribers and future prescribers, particularly physicians and medical students. With scripts provided by drugmakers, detailers commonly promoted blockbusters, and often worked to build the goodwill of the drugmakers producing them. To build goodwill, they frequently provided prescribers with meals, gifts, research support, and trips to conferences (Schweitzer 2007). They also provided physicians with vast quantities of free samples to start patients on high-priced medicines.[3] Detailers would generally end each physician visit with a "close." Ideally, they closed a visit by asking the physician for a nonbinding commitment to prescribe their drugmakers' medicines (Crotty 2009).

To prod their efforts to market blockbusters, drugmakers often gave detailers "incentive payments." These incentive payments were tied to the number of prescriptions written by physicians within the detailers' territory for drugs to which the detailer is assigned. For one major drugmaker, these incentives were recently found to average between 15 percent and 25 percent of a detailer's annual salary. High-performing detailers for that drugmaker also were eligible for additional benefits such as all-expenses-paid vacations (Crotty 2009).

By the end of the 1980s, with development of drug blockbusters made much easier by the FDA, the industry had entered a new phase. Merck and the other patrons of high drug profits were then paying off stockholders as our guest lecturer at the Harvard Business School had predicted. The pharmaceutical industry no longer lagged other parts of the health industry in revenue growth. By the end of the decade, the industry's share of US health care spending had begun to rise (Centers for Medicare & Medicaid Services 2009b).

The pharmaceutical industry is based in both the United States and Western Europe, and the industry's growing share of health care revenues got the attention of governments throughout the older industrialized world.[4] In Canada, for example, because it was concerned about drugmaker abuse of patent laws to make profits, Parliament established the Patented Medicine Prices Review Board in 1987. It charged the PMPRB with making sure that prices on patented drugs were not excessive (Elgie 2002). To do this, Parliament gave the PMPRB the guideline that the price of patented drugs cannot exceed the median of the price in other industrialized countries and that prices could not increase by more than the Consumer Price Index (Elgie 2002).[5] As a result, Canadians can pay much less for blockbusters. Table 2-1 lists the percentage discount from US prices for several popular drugs sold in the United States.

As in Canada, virtually all Western European governments restrained oligopolistic prices from widely denying access to essential medicines or crippling health care programs. They either set prices to ensure broad access or they cap profits so that the resulting prices will make the medicines affordable. But the US government does not do so. Unlike its European counterparts, it didn't develop a national standard for drug prices. What the US government did at the same time that Canada was establishing the PMPRB was to develop a system for holding down drug prices just for some of its own programs. Its first noteworthy step in this area was the Federal Supply Schedule (FSS). Using pricing calculations outlined under the law, the FSS made available to Veterans Administration, the Department of Defense, the Public Health Service (Indian Health Service), and the US Coast Guard prices not unlike those paid in Canada (US Department of Veterans Affairs 2009). By the early 1990s, the schedule was a price catalog containing about 10,000 pharmaceutical and drug items (US General Accounting Office 1991).

Table 2-1
Percent Discount from US Base Price for Several Drugs (2007)

Drug	Canadian % Discount
Lipitor (lowers cholesterol)	49%
Plavix (thins blood)	32%
Prevacid (blocks stomach acid)	49%
Zocor (lowers cholesterol)	23%
Nexium (blocks stomach acid)	36%

Source: AFL-CIO 2007

In 1990, Congress moved forward on getting discounts for other federal programs. Through the Omnibus Budget and Reconciliation of Act of 1990 (OBRA 90), Congress required drugmakers to give the Medicaid program, its main government health insurance program for low-income families and people with disabilities, either the best price on patented drugs that it gave to private group purchasers or, at least, a 15.1 percent discount off of the Average Manufacturers Price (Centers for Medicare & Medicaid Services 2009a).[6]

In addition, Congress allowed individual states to use the large group purchasing power of their Medicaid programs to negotiate "supplemental rebates" in addition to the newly mandated Medicaid discounts (Smith 2002). A state can set up a Medicaid preferred drug list (PDL), that is, a list of drugs for which a Medicaid program will pay without requiring specific or prior authorization (PA) for the prescription before a pharmacy dispenses it. Because PA requires additional documentation from prescribers, they are less likely to write prescriptions for drugs that are excluded from the PDL than for those that are on it. Exclusion from the PDL can thus reduce a drug's share of the market and the threat of it is an incentive to pharmaceutical manufacturers to give supplemental drug rebates. In considering whether or not to put a drug on a PDL, while a Medicaid program looks at the clinical value of the medicine; it can also consider a supplemental rebate the drug's maker would pay.

As discussed in Chapter 6, Medi-Cal, California's Medicaid program, was the pioneer in attempting to use a PDL to win supplemental rebates. By fiscal year 2003/4, the state Department of Health Services would be obtaining approximately a half-billion dollars in supplemental rebates a year, according to the California Bureau of State Audits (Hendrickson 2005).[7] In 1992, the federal government once more saw that its programs got discounts from the pharmaceutical industry. The Veterans Health Care Act of that year set up the 340(b) program to require discounts for outpatient drugs for federally qualified health care centers, hospitals with a high proportion of patients who are poor, and similar institutions. The discounts had to be at least as low as the price that state Medicaid agencies currently paid (Richardson 2002). These discounts were known as the 340(b) discounts. A recent study shows that the 340(b) discount has turned out to be substantial, finding that the program pays 12.2 percent less than Medicaid for medicines.[8]

At the time the federal government was obtaining drug discounts for its programs, about a dozen states had established drug-purchasing programs called state pharmaceutical assistance programs (SPAPs). The SPAPs had generally been set up to provide low-income residents not eligible for Medicaid with discounts on their medicines. As part of funding these SPAPs, a number of state legislatures mandated that their SPAPs pay drugmakers the same prices as their Medicaid programs. A few SPAPs even received supplemental rebates beyond their Medicaid rebates (Carreon et al. 2000).

For private groups like employers purchasing prescription drugs, the government had no help to offer and, in the 1990s, they began to seek rebates on their own. For this purpose, they turned to pharmacy benefit managers (PBMs), businesses that had originally provided the service of prescription drug claims handling. The PBMs offered to negotiate discounts for them. By combining their clients' drug purchasing power, PBMs could organize purchasing pools with greater capacity to increase a drugmaker's market share for certain drugs than their individual clients' purchasing power could provide. In exchange for this increased market share, the PBM could ask for larger discounts from the drugmaker. Even with a larger discount, a cooperating manufacturer could still increase its overall revenue from the discounted drug. To show a drugmaker how it could increase market share, a PBM could assure the drugmaker that numerous clients would make the co-pay for its drug the lowest in its therapeutic category, giving their beneficiaries a strong incentive to request it. To strengthen their bargaining positions against drugmakers, PBMs consolidated across the country. By the end of the decade, they had gone from scores of businesses into a few large enterprises (Weber et al. 2001). But, even in consolidated form, their bargaining power was no match for that of government programs and the discounts they obtained couldn't equal those of Medicaid, let alone those of the 340(b) program of the VA (Von Oehsen 2004).

Although the industry had managed to avoid Canadian-style price controls in the United States in the 1980s and early 1990s, US budgetary concerns had given some life to government efforts to at least contain its own prescription drug costs. The growing number of US government programs restricting drug prices threatened to expand the number of people they covered and the depth of the discounts they might obtain. To keep their profits growing and to continue to keep the stock prices of their industry leaders rising, the pharmaceutical industry would have to contain US government activism in the area of prescription drug prices.

Fighting Government Oversight and Exploiting the Blockbusters

With the newly elected President Clinton promising action on health care costs, including drug costs, federal-level political spending by the pharmaceutical industry took off in the early 1990s. Table 2-2 below indicates how sharply it rose.

Table 2-2
Campaign Contributions to Federal Candidates

Cycle	Dollars (millions)
1990	$3.276
1992	$7.425
1994	$7.967
1996	$14.033
1998	$13.220
2000	$27.087

Source: Center for Responsive Politics 2009

Campaign contributions to federal candidates were only one part of industry spending aimed at keeping government aloof from the prescription drug price issue. In the 1990s, the industry would build a federal lobbying operation that would become the biggest in the nation (Ismail 2005). Apart from Congress, the industry used these lobbyists to pressure an array of agencies including the Department of Health and Human Services, the FDA, and the State Department on dozens of issues concerning its profits. For instance, PhRMA lobbied 33 federal agencies on 39 issues separately identified under the Lobbying Disclosure Act of 1995 (Ismail 2005). By 2001, the industry would have 651 federal lobbyists (Richards 2003). The industry used former government employees, especially former members of Congress, to stock its stable of lobbyists. By 2005, a third of all lobbyists employed by the industry were former federal government employees; it was found that at that time they included more than 15 former senators and more than 60 former members of the US House of Representatives (Ismail 2005).

To back up their own lobbyists, the industry not only poured millions into campaign contributions and lobbying, but also gave support to groups that could give a friendly face to industry positions in the political arena. With such groups, the pharmaceutical industry worked at creating the appearance of grassroots support for its cause. i.e., "astroturf" lobbying. There were two networks in particular that got pharmaceutical industry support: so-called disease groups and purported senior groups. One example of support for a disease group that was repaid was Wyeth's backing of a group called the Society for Women's Health Research (SWHR). SWHR claims it is "the nation's only non-profit organization whose mission is to improve the health of all women through research, education and advocacy." In April 2002, Wyeth underwrote a SWHR black-tie event in Washington, DC, billed as a salute to middle-aged women and ironically called "Coming of Age" (Integrity in Science 2003).

Shortly afterward, Wyeth needed political support. In July 2002, its profit-making strategy took a hard hit as the US National Institutes of Health (NIH) announced that it was abandoning its study of the effects of Prempro, Wyeth's market-leading hormone replacement therapy (HRT) drug. NIH had originally planned an eight-year trial of the drug, but it only took five years to accumulate conclusive evidence of increased health damage to women who use the drug over time.[9] The announcement was reported with shock in media outlets around the world, which had long been accustomed to glowing reports of HRT. The announcement precipitated a crisis for Wyeth, which had a 70 percent share of the HRT market and earned $900 million annually from sales of the drug; its share price plummeted.

SWHR came to Wyeth's aid and publicly condemned the NIH's decision. The group distributed op-eds and letters to newspapers around the country, making it appear that the NIH's finding that Wyeth's blockbuster was a threat to women's health was itself a threat to women (Burton and Rowell 2003). Thus, Wyeth got the cover of a nonprofit group supposedly dedicated to women's health. A year later, the grand benefactor for SWHR's gala dinner at the Ritz-Carlton Hotel in Washington, DC, was Wyeth (Integrity in Science 2003). Despite SWHR's help, Wyeth was unable to prevent its sales of Prempro from plummeting in the wake of the NIH study and makers of HRT have been hit with thousands of lawsuits (Alazraki 2009).

Another part of its arsenal for blocking government policies to lower drug prices is the industry's support of private pharmaceutical assistance programs (PAPs), which are drugmakers' programs to provide certain low-income people lower prices on some of their own medicines. But, generally, they are used to promote blockbusters and physicians who treat eligible patients frequently face the choice of providing a "free" PAP drug or an equally effective generic alternative. So, while the PAP drug is cheaper in the short run, it may be more expensive to both the health care system and the patient in the long run (Carroll 2007). The drug businesses can increase sales and profits, even as it appears that something is being done to ease access. More importantly, the industry can use PAPs to argue that political action is unnecessary and head it off. The ramped-up 1990s industry lobbying and campaign contributions paid off for the industry within a few years of its beginning. While President Clinton's Health Security Act proposal included prescription drug price control proposals in its earlier versions, heavy lobbying by the industry led the administration to abandon the idea as consideration of the plan proceeded (Center for Public Integrity 2009).

As the industry built its capacity to fight off political challenges, it also expanded its economic means of selling blockbusters. To minimize the chances that the FDA would see any problem during research on their drugs, drugmakers started in the early 1990s to run most clinical trials on their products (Evans et al. 2005). Running the research themselves, drugmakers can oversee the design of the research to see to it that they pose the questions most likely to present their products as effective. A recent report illustrates how this process works:

. . . a study might compare an arthritis medicine to ibuprofen when the arthritis medication has been designed not to cause stomach problems and ibuprofen is a proven stomach irritant. Then, if the outcome measures were weighted toward observing stomach-related side effects—especially at the expense of identifying other complications and determining the superiority of the new drug for arthritis treatment *per se*—the results would be misleadingly optimistic (Moon, et al. 2008).

When they conduct the research, drugmakers can also work to withhold unfavorable results from regulators and the public. The World Health Organization (WHO) has found that the results of fewer than half of all clinical trials are ever published. Further, WHO noted that many trials are never even registered on its website, especially those conducted in developing countries (Jack and Williams 2006). If they publish results, researchers reporting to drugmakers can ensure that findings are phrased in ways most advantageous to manufacturers. To foster reports that support their products, drugmakers often make academic researchers their financial "partners." For example, researchers serve as consultants to companies whose products they are studying, become paid members of advisory boards and speakers' bureaus, and enter into patent and royalty arrangements together with institutions (Angell 2004). Through these kinds of arrangements, researchers can increase their annual incomes by hundreds of thousands of dollars.

Although follow-up studies on the safety of medicines after they have been released for public sale are supposed to provide a check on this research, the industry is lax in conducting them. Drugmakers are expected to set schedules for their follow-up studies and report regularly to the FDA on their progress. But, according to an audit conducted by the Office of the Inspector General of the US Department of Health and Human Services, the industry's self-reported data are glaringly incomplete. Of 2,353 post-market study commitments reported during fiscal years 1990 to 2004, only 6 percent had listed start dates; 21 percent had projected completion dates (Chen 2007).

Increased drugmaker control of research can endanger those using the medicines involved. In the case of Vioxx, the heavily promoted pain reliever, much research was suppressed (California Healthline 2004). Meanwhile, the drug was prescribed to more than 20 million patients before its maker, Merck, pulled it from the market in 2004—after it became widely known that it doubled the risk of heart attack (Peterson 2008). FDA congressional testimony conservatively estimates that the toll Vioxx took was about 27,000 heart attacks or sudden cardiac deaths (Graham 2004).

To extend its marketing beyond using detailers to convince physicians to buy their drugs, the industry got the FDA to revise its guidance for direct-to-consumer (DTC) advertising in 1997, making it cost-effective for them to heavily engage in this form of advertising. Prior to that year, pharmaceutical companies generally had to provide all of the risk information associated with the medication during a TV advertisement. Including full risk information in a broadcast DTC advertisement increased the length of such ads to the point that it was largely impractical. After the guidance was issued, pharmaceutical companies had an alternative to the requirement that all risks in broadcast advertisements be disclosed. They could meet the regulatory requirements by presenting the major side effects, either in audio or in audio and visual form, and by telling consumers where to find additional information, including how or where to obtain the approved product labeling (US General Accounting Office 2002). In the wake of 1997 FDA ruling, the industry took DTC advertising into nearly every US living room with a TV. Between 1997 and 2001, DTC advertising spending increased 145 percent; sales of the heavily advertised drugs rose dramatically (US General Accounting Office 2002).

For 2000, it was estimated that each dollar spent on DTC advertising yielded $4.20 in additional sales (Rosenthal et al. 2003). While the industry continued to spend most of its marketing on physicians, by 2001 it was spending $3 billion a year on DTC advertising, especially on television (Brownlee 2003). From 1996 to 2005, total DTC advertising spending increased 330 percent, focusing on such drugs as AstraZeneca's Nexium for heartburn and Sepracor's Lunesta for insomnia (Donohue et al. 2007).

The FDA is supposed to regulate drug advertising. Under the administration of George W. Bush, it missed many violations such as understating the dangers of a given product. The number of letters sent by the FDA to drugmakers regarding advertising violations fell from 142 in 1997 to 21 in 2006 (Donohue et al. 2007). When the FDA did catch advertising violations, it often allowed misleading ads to run for months and enforce laws regarding inadequate warnings and unsubstantiated claims only when it was too late (Committee on Government Reform Minority Office 2005). Furthermore, of the letters FDA sent in 2004 and 2005, 19 were issued an average of eight months after the advertising first appeared. By then, drugmakers had already discontinued use of more than half of the violative materials. Further, regulatory letters did not always prevent the business from later disseminating similar advertising for the same drugs (Crosse 2006).

To address private group payers' use of PBMs to reduce what they paid for medicines, pharmaceutical businesses worked to undermine these efforts. They paid PBMs on the side to put their blockbusters on their approved list of drugs. Therefore, the PBMs had incentives to use those drugs for which they were paid the most and not necessarily drugs that were the best value for their clients (Garis et al. 2006). So, for example, a PBM might be able to get one client a good deal within a class of drugs, but pass on that deal. It might have that client buy a more expensive medicine in that class in exchange for some consideration from the maker of the more expensive drug. The drugmaker could give the PBM a good discount for a second client who more closely looks at discounts in exchange for taking advantage of the first client. So, PBMs could end up actually promoting drugmaker's high-priced products to clients.

By the end of the 1990s, the industry had begun intensively using data from electronic healthcare records (EHR) to push their products. These data could provide users with specifics on what health care treatments and medicines individual physicians prescribed. Drugmakers went to businesses that specialized in handling such data and got them to combine data from PBMs, private insurers, and national pharmacy chains to precisely view the prescribing patterns of most physicians. The data were so precise that a drugmaker like Merck could grade physicians from D to A+ for each product based on how reliably they prescribed a Merck product (Flynn 2007). Drug companies then gave the information to their detailers, who used it to tailor marketing strategies, messages, gifts, and other inducements for individual physicians (Prescription Project 2008). Presumably, in the case of Merck, the high volume A+ prescribers could expect more lavish gifts, consultancies, and speaker bureau invitations (Flynn 2007).

The Blockbusters' Toll on America

As big drugmakers entered the twenty-first century, they were the envy of the business world. But, as described below, many patients were not happy with the consequences of their profit-making strategy, giving rise to the political backlash seen in this book's case studies. Why the industry was the envy of the business world is illustrated by a check of the Fortune Global 500 for the year 2005. It shows how the pharmaceutical industry stacked up against all other industries in the world, near the beginning of the new century. Pharmaceuticals had a

17.9 percent return on revenue, ranked the highest of any industry in the world. Its profits were way ahead of those of the industry in second place at the time, securities. The securities industry had a 12.5 percent return on revenue (CNNMoney 2009). The main source of these profits was the US market (Daemmrich 2009). As US and European price control policies diverged in the end of the 1980s, the US pharmaceutical market had gone from being roughly equal to the European market to being almost twice as large in the 2000s (Pammolli and Riccaboni 2004). By 2004, the United States, with only 5 percent of the world's population, accounted for more than 40 percent of the sales in the world's $550 billion pharmaceutical market (*Economist* 2005).

What this situation meant to people living in the United States starts with the drug prices they were generally required to pay. As shown above, people in the United States can pay nearly double what Canadians pay for some blockbusters. These markups and resulting high prices are not just expensive; for many in the United States, they have put needed drugs out of reach altogether. So, the desperate situation of the Connecticut woman who could walk one day in three described in this book's introduction was not unique. In fact, it is typical of many older people all over the United States.

Not only were drugs getting more expensive, they were becoming a more common feature of health care. Since the 1980s, as managed care programs have become increasingly important in health care delivery, they emphasized ambulatory care—a venue where most contacts result in prescriptions. So, prescribing medicine has become an increasingly prominent feature of medical treatment in the United States (Weiner et al. 1991). As a result, a larger share of US health care dollars is being spent on prescription drugs. After 1997, DTC advertising had further raised the demand for medicines. From 1997 to 2004, the average annual number of prescriptions for persons age 65 and older increased from 21.9 to 30.8 (Stagnitti 2007). At the same time as the demand for drugs has been increasing, drug prices have also been sharply increasing. According to Families USA, the prices of the 50 prescription drugs most frequently used by the elderly rose by nearly two times the rate of inflation during calendar year 1999 (McCloskey 2000).

Combined, rising prices and rising volume of drugs sold have been driving the costs of medicine for individual consumers in the United States sharply upward. Between 1997 and 2004, total US expenditures for outpatient drugs increased 160 percent, from $72.3 billion to $191.0 billion. The average prescription drug expenditure for persons age 65 and older increased approximately 130 percent (from $819 to $1,914). Of these increased expenditures, older people bore much of the burden.

Their average out-of-pocket expense for prescription medicines more than doubled, from $483 to $1,027 (Stagnitti 2007).

At the same time, many seniors have very limited incomes with which to cover these rising costs. In 2001, the median annual income of men 65 years of age or older was $19,685; for women, $11,313. That year, most income for seniors was fixed; an average of 41.1 percent came from Social Security, 20.4 percent from pensions, and 16.6 percent from savings. Of people 65 and over, 68.3 percent got a majority of their income from Social Security (Wu 2003). So, for many seniors, getting by was difficult. In 2001, 42.2 percent of those age 75 to 79 lived in households with incomes at or below 200 percent of the federal poverty level (FPL). Even more (47.2 percent) of those 80 and older lived at or below 200 percent of the FPL (Wu 2003). Although 200 percent of the FPL is not technically poor, in 2003, it was below what the National Economic Development and Law Center found to be the minimum needed for basic economic self-sufficiency in urban areas like Boston or Los Angeles (Pearce and Brooks 2003b; Pearce and Brooks 2003a).

So, a large proportion of seniors had little, if any, capacity to absorb increasing prescription drug costs. As a result, many did without needed medicines. In 2001, 14 percent of those age 65 and older did not fill a prescription one or more times because of cost; 16 percent skipped doses because of cost. In total, 22 percent of seniors either did not fill prescriptions or skipped doses because of cost; some did both (Kitchman et al. 2002). Others reallocated their income to cover rising prescription drug costs, but at the expense of other items such as heat, warm clothes, or other health care (Mortimer 1998; Thomas et al. 2002). Either way, pharmaceutical industry practices have threatened the health of seniors across the country.

Up until 2000, Medicare managed care plans with drug coverage had provided seniors with some relief from the costs of prescription drugs. But, in response to rate cuts to these plans contained in the Balanced Budget Act of 1997, the percent of Medicare managed care policies with drug coverage also started to drop in 2000. In some areas, seniors lost Medicare managed care altogether. As the plans withdrew drug coverage, the number of people they covered started to drop in 2000 and fell substantially in 2001 (Achman and Gold 2002). So, at the turn of the century, the number of seniors whose health was threatened by high drug prices jumped significantly.

High drug prices not only threatened seniors, they undermined the whole financing structure of the US health care system by draining the resources of payers such as insurers that pay the high prices. Industry marketing, including the way it has used research, has swelled the volume of the sale of its blockbusters and other products. From 1997 to 2004, total number of prescription purchases increased from 1.9 billion prescriptions to 2.9 billion (Stagnitti 2007). By getting people to use more expensive drugs when cheaper alternatives are available, drugmakers further sapped the resources of public health insurance plans like Medicare Part D, Medicaid, and the State Children's Health Insurance Program (SCHIP). In 1998, public funds paid 22 percent of retail drug costs; by 2008, it was 37 percent (Fein 2010). They also undermined plans that finance health care when drugs turned out to have dangerous side effects and increased the number of people needing expensive medical care.

The industry's share of the US health care spending pie has continued to widen. When comparing 1997 and 2004, prescribed medicines' share of US health care expenditures increased from 13.1 percent to 19.8 percent (Stagnitti 2007). The blockbuster strategy had worked to perfection for the pharmaceutical industry, but it had taken a huge toll in the costs of the US health care system. Despite US government efforts before the end of the 1990s, most people in the United States were paying, far and away, the highest prices in the older industrialized countries of the world. The woman at the meeting in New Britain was the tip of the iceberg. With a Republican-dominated Congress blocking federal action on US prices at the turn of the century, the anger beneath the surface was about to prompt state policymakers into fundamentally threatening the profit strategy of the pharmaceutical industry. Vermont is where that drama first unfolded.

---

[1] Fortunately for US expectant mothers, the FDA didn't license the drug for general use before it was connected to birth defects and banned for women who were or might become pregnant.

[2] In fact, Rifampin had been approved by the FDA five months after the manufacturer submitted the application (Anrig 2007).

[3] While industry representatives claim that these free samples help poor and uninsured Americans, research shows that poor people are less likely than wealthy or insured Americans to receive free drug samples (Cutrona et al. 2008).

[4] GlaxoSmithKline (ranked third among pharmaceutical businesses in the 2009 Fortune 500) is based in the UK; Roche (fourth) is based in Switzerland; Sanofi-Aventis (fifth) in France (CNNMoney 2011).

[5] The other industrialized countries currently used to construct the median are France, Germany, Italy, Sweden, Switzerland, United Kingdom, and the United States (Gillespie 2009).

[6] The Average Manufacturer Price (AMP) is the average price paid by wholesalers for drugs distributed to the retail class of trade, net of customary prompt pay discounts.

[7] Critics of these approaches argue that they lower access to some drugs. It is true that excluding certain drugs from PDLs or formularies makes them harder to get. Requiring PA can indeed create access problems for people on Medicaid, incurring delays in obtaining needed drugs, multiple trips to the doctor or pharmacy, and insufficient information about the process itself. Problems with obtaining drugs in certain classes can be particularly critical. Evidence from one peer-reviewed study suggests that patients respond differently to psychotropic drugs within the same therapeutic class; PDLs can make it less likely that consumers will promptly get the drugs they need (Hoadley 2005).

Still, the PA process for people on Medicaid includes a number of legal safeguards. Under Medi-Cal, for example, the program must respond to authorization requests within 24 hours and requires pharmacies to provide a 72-hour emergency supply of any drug. A study supported by California's Western Center on Law & Poverty found that PA problems could be ameliorated by stronger sanctions against providers who consistently fail to observe those rights (Health Consumer Alliance 2004). So, while use of purchasing power and PDLs can make access more difficult for some, they save Medicaid programs money and increase the volume of medicines that they can purchase. To the extent that these kinds of policies are successful and incorporate practices such as fair provisions for exceptions and appeals, more people can get the medicines they need.

[8] Given these deep discounts, the pharmaceutical industry has opposed the expansion of the 340(b) program, and it includes severe restrictions on its use: 340(b) health care facilities are monitored to make sure they don't resell the drugs that they get at 340(b) prices. It is also necessary for patients getting 340(b) drug prices to get the prescriptions for those drugs only through health care professionals working at qualified health care facilities. But, as of 2008, over 13,000 health care facilities have signed up and the program buys about $5 billion of medicines a year (Scholz 2008).

[9] This study, called the Women's Health Initiative, was the largest clinical trial ever conducted of women's health. It found that participants who took certain combined hormones had an increased risk of breast cancer—as well as a higher risk of heart attack, stroke, and blood clots in the lungs—compared with those taking a placebo. Other parts of the same federal study later found that hormone drugs increased the risk of dementia in a subset of participants, those aged 65 and older (Singer and Wilson 2009).

3
Vermont Raises the Cry

Legislation introduced in Vermont's senate in 1999 to control drug prices was what first connected me to the battle for access to medicines. As described below, the bill would not get far, but it would be a prelude to a much bigger fight in 2000. I didn't get a good look at the key Vermont lawmakers behind the legislation until March 2000 when—as part of the Northeast Legislative Association on Prescription Drug Prices, a policy group working for lower prices of and broader access to medicines—I attended a New York City meeting of northeastern state legislators concerned about high prescription drug prices. This was the third in a series of regional meetings initiated by the Vermont legislators. The first had been held in Montpelier, Vermont, the smallest capital city in the United States, and the second in Boston, Massachusetts, capital of New England's most populous state. The New York City meeting, arranged by Rep. Richard Gottfried (D–New York City), took place at Manhattan College, in the Tribeca neighborhood within Gottfried's district.

Although representatives from half a dozen states were present at the meeting, the Vermont delegation was clearly the leading player. Vermont State Senate President Cheryl Rivers (D–Windsor) commanded center stage when she reported that, three weeks earlier, the Vermont state senate had shocked the pharmaceutical industry by passing a pathbreaking prescription drug price control bill, S 300, by a lopsided vote of 25–4. With not only Democratic but also many Republican votes, the bill used the classic political policy for addressing drug costs: price-setting.

The Vermont legislators were the first to come up with the idea of price controls, the first to put it in legislative language, and the first to develop arguments supporting it. At the March meeting, they presented more ideas to get lower drug prices. Vermont Senate President Peter Shumlin (D–Windham) explained that he was working with Vermont's US Republican Senator Jim Jeffords[1] to obtain Canadian prescription drugs for people in Vermont (Shumlin 2000c). Rivers talked about how she was working with Vermont's US senators to qualify the whole state as a catchment area for a federally qualified health center (FQHC) and thus qualify for the 340(b) prices available to FQHCs. She argued that there were poor people all over Vermont, not just in one or two areas. To illustrate their idea about FQHC prices, the Vermont legislators put up two maps on the wall behind the speakers. The first map showed the current FQHC catchment area—one or two small portions of Vermont. Next to it was another map of the proposed catchment area—the whole state of Vermont. The Vermont legislators exhorted their colleagues to join them in taking on the pharmaceutical industry. They argued that, since PhRMA money was blocking a national solution to the prescription drug price problem, states should at least light as many brush fires on the issue as they could (Poirier 2000).

Rivers and her Vermont colleagues also predicted that S 300 would be out of the Vermont House Health and Welfare Committee where it had been assigned after passage in the senate and back from the house in a week or a week and a half.[2] And, indeed, conditions did look promising for S 300. They had a popular proposal in pushing to lower residents' prescription drug costs. At that time, in addition to the state senate, Democrats held the leadership of the Vermont house and the governor, Howard Dean, was a Democrat. As there were nearly two months left in the legislature's session, it seemed that they would have plenty of time to get action on the bill.

But the success of S 300 was not to be. Despite rapidly rising drug costs and state senate leadership looking to rein in drug prices, the story of the effort to promote the legislation is more a story of the tremendous political influence of the pharmaceutical industry and what was missing when public interest advocates tried to counter it. As is shown below, it takes more than what Vermont's advocates for access to medicines had to defeat the pharmaceutical industry in 2000.

The Road to S 300

Vermont had been as likely as any state to be the place where a proposal to regulate prescription drug prices would arise. Vermont had a particularly progressive electorate. Its congressman at the time, Bernie Sanders (I), was a self-described "socialist." In the 2000 presidential election, Vermont would give Ralph Nader his second highest proportion of a state's presidential vote.[3] As a rural New England state, Vermont also has no large media markets to make it easy for wealthy interests to drown out progressive voices. House members in the

Vermont legislature each represented about four thousand citizens, and campaign expenditures were measured in the hundreds, not hundreds of thousands, of dollars. Most candidates visited door-to-door every household in their districts (Mackey 2001). The governor had to run every two years. The state had high voter turnout and a long tradition of town meetings. With Vermont's main source of outside revenue coming through local businesses trading on the state's charm for skiers (CareerOneStop 2010), its business lobby is not particularly strong.

On the other hand, Vermont's public interest groups did not have great political strength either. For their public interest group support, progressive politicians depended more on low-resource groups like the Vermont Public Interest Research Group (VPIRG)—a backer of S 300. These groups could do little to muster grassroots demonstrations, let alone turn out voters and thus gain easy access to officeholders. The Vermont State Employees Association was independent of the national unions representing public employees and did not have access to the political expertise, financial resources, and capacity to turn out voters that can come with such affiliations. Without the capacity to turn out voters, Vermont's progressive activists had little to hold officeholders' loyalty, if powerful forces were on the other side. But Vermont wouldn't need powerful public interest groups to raise the issue of high drug prices. When events led to state proposals on prescription drug prices, Vermont was the first to get one moving.

Vermont's effort to lower prescription drug prices can be traced back to 1998. That year, while the Republican Congress in Washington, DC, was pushing the privatization of Medicare, some congressional Democrats focused on doing something about drug prices for people on Medicare. That summer, in response to price discrimination between the United States and Canada, Rep. Tom Allen (D–ME) and Rep. Marion Berry (D–AR) had formed a congressional prescription drug task force to bring focus to issues involving the cost and availability of prescription drugs. The minority staff of the House Committee on Government Reform conducted twenty studies around the country of the prices of the best-selling drugs. They found that the prices in the United States of the five brand-name drugs with highest sales to seniors were roughly double what they were in Canada (Committee on Government Reform and Oversight 1998). The report also strongly suggested to state politicians that, if voters knew how much they were being overcharged, they would be outraged with drugmakers and supportive of lawmakers who challenged these prices. On 25 September 1998, Allen, Berry, and several dozen House Democrats introduced HR 4627, the Prescription Drug Fairness Act, which would charge pharmacies Federal Supply

Schedule prices for Medicare beneficiaries (Strongin 1999). Presumably, the drugstores would pass the lower prices on to customers. Using this issue to increase their electoral appeal, some of the members of Congress supporting HR 4627 staged events in their districts releasing versions of the House Committee on Government Reform minority staff studies tailored to their districts.[4] On 9 October 1998, Vermont's Congressman Bernie Sanders released one of these studies in his district (Olson 1999).[5]

When Senator Rivers heard about the study that Sanders had released in 1998, it occurred to her to try to do something about prescription drug prices at the state level (Rivers 2002).[6] Rivers was not the only person in Vermont who noticed the study Sanders had released. It also inspired Anthony Pollina, policy director of VPIRG. VPIRG raised funds by going door-to-door in mid-income neighborhoods and soliciting contributions to support its work. To do so successfully, it needed appeals that would quickly interest the people it was canvassing. Usually it uses issues like clear air and clean water—popular among mid-income residents (Haviland 2002).[7] Pollina and VPIRG were looking for an issue that would directly affect consumers and lower taxes. An effort to reduce the prices of prescription drugs in Vermont—both a problem for residents and a costly item in the state budget—fit these requirements (Pollina 2000).

1999

In January 1999, Pollina and VPIRG joined with a Vermont group advocating a single-payer scheme,[8] the Vermont Consumers Campaign for Health, to draft a state prescription drug price control bill—using the HR 4627 model (Davis 2000a). They took the draft to Senator Rivers and she took it to the Vermont capitol in Montpelier, a town nestled in the mountains and featuring a small state capitol and a few blocks of vintage New England shops and restaurants. There she introduced it as S 88 (Pollina 2000). The bill only mandated price controls, linking drug prices in Vermont to either those in the US Federal Supply Schedule or those paid in Quebec, the Canadian province bordering Vermont (Vermont PIRG 1999).

In February, Congressman Sanders continued to highlight prescription drug access, introducing HR 626 in the US House of Representatives. The bill would require drugmakers who obtain exclusive rights to commercialize drugs developed by federal research to first enter into a reasonable pricing agreement with the secretary of the Department of Health and Human Services (DHHS).[9] To dramatize the need for his bill, Sanders adopted a tactic that Minnesota advocates for prescription drug access had been using since 1995—a prescription drug-buying bus trip to Canada (Weil 2004).[10] For prescription drug access advocates in states near the Canadian border, bus rides are a relatively inexpensive and easy way to dramatize the stark differences between US and Canadian prices. The main expense for organizers was the bus rental—about $500 a day in the late 1990s. These trips were particularly easy for Vermont residents because, unlike the seven-hour one-way trip from Minneapolis to Winnipeg, the ride from Montpelier to Montréal took only two and a half hours. Once the Vermont bus came down from the mountains, it could quickly cross the agricultural French-speaking region of Quebec and the St. Lawrence River to reach the metropolis of Montréal. When Sanders's bus arrived in Montréal, Sanders saw women struggling with breast cancer able to buy AstraZeneca's Tamoxifen, a widely prescribed breast cancer drug, at one-tenth the price they were forced to pay at home. Recalling the trip, Sanders commented: "This . . .is nothing short of a moral outrage and if the [drug] industry had any shame whatsoever it would have discontinued such egregious price-gouging on its own years ago" (Church 2004).

In addition, the story of Sanders's bus trip was later picked up by ABC News, further publicizing the problems of access in the United States and adding to the growing public outrage over drug prices. The broadcast highlighted his Tamoxifen story, featuring Ruthmary Jeffries who took Tamoxifen to prevent a recurrence of her breast cancer. The report noted that, if she bought it at her local pharmacy in Vermont, it would cost $1.65 a pill; in Canada, the same pill costs only 17 cents. "The difference is huge," Jeffries said. "Like a thousand dollars a year difference." The same story also featured Randy Boardman. If he drove a hundred miles into Canada, he could get a year's supply of Merck's Zocor, for lowering cholesterol, for $600 less than in the United States. "You charge us the higher price," said Boardman to the drugmaker. "and yet you'll send it to foreign countries for less money—and why?" (Woodruff 1999).

After Sanders's trip, the Vermont bus rides became a regular event sponsored by the Central Vermont Council on Aging (CVCOA).11 Every six weeks or so, two vans with about ten people in each set out for Montréal from Montpelier. "It shows how we kind of don't take care of our weak links in society," said CVCOA spokesman Will Fleming. "The school of thought seems to be, '[t]hose who can afford it, fine—those who can't, well, it's not our problem'" (Cosgrove 2000). The steady stream of Vermonters crossing the border highlighted how deeply the cost of prescription drugs was affecting state residents. In New England states like Vermont, advocacy by members of Congress was distinctly helpful in developing policies to address drug costs and in mobilizing support for them. It gave the issues visibility in the local press and helped rally state legislators. Their studies provided documentation that could be repeatedly used in legislative hearings and in meetings with the local press.

Meanwhile, Rivers looked to get S 88 out of its first committee, the Senate Health and Welfare Committee. However, there was immediate opposition from the pharmaceutical industry. The industry claimed that price controls violated the commerce clause of the US Constitution. The basis of the commerce clause objection was that it reserved for the federal government the right to regulate interstate commerce. Opponents also argued that S 88 could cause many out-of-state drug wholesalers to cease selling pharmaceutical products to Vermont retailers owing to a maximum price schedule. In reviewing the constitutional objection, the state attorney general's office recommended that Rivers modify S 88 to allow the state to negotiate with drug manufacturers, using the FSS as a price benchmark (Ellis 1999).

To try to get S 88 passed, Rivers followed the recommendation. But drugmaker opposition still blocked Rivers's bill, making committee passage unlikely. She compromised by supporting a house bill, H 365, proposed by Elaine Alfano (D–Calais), which directed the Health Access Oversight Committee (HAOC) to "analyze the effectiveness of a range of options [to ensure access to necessary prescription drugs], including (1) a regulatory structure to set maximum prices; [and] (2) a [Vermont] purchasing pool" (Olson 1999). The committee was chaired by State Senator Jan Backus (D–Chittenden). Backus was running for US Senate in 2000 and was collecting large campaign contributions from the health care industry (CampaignMoney.com 2010). Not surprisingly, she was not inclined to antagonize the pharmaceutical industry and was not likely to be supportive of Rivers's effort to take on the industry. With the analysis of options going before a committee chaired by Backus, the drug industry let the bill by; it passed both houses and was signed into law by Governor Dean on 1 June, 1999 (Vermont Legislative Bill Tracking System 2000b). Thus, Rivers turned the likely defeat of S 88 into a chance to put the issue of prescription drug cost containment on the agenda of the 2000 legislative session.

At the same time, Vermont Senate President Peter Shumlin was considering his position on the issue. Shumlin had been aware for years of the high price of medicines in the United States. In his hometown of Putney, in the Green Mountains in southern Vermont, his family ran

Putney Student Travel—a business that took students abroad, often to Europe. When he had to help students get medicines in European drugstores, Shumlin was struck by how much less they paid for them abroad than in Vermont. As a legislator, however, Shumlin didn't initially see the political opportunity inherent in the drug access issue and had taken campaign contributions from the pharmaceutical industry.

But, as he later explained to a Connecticut legislative committee, Shumlin came to see that the political advantage of siding with seniors on the prescription drug issue could outweigh that of taking campaign contributions from the pharmaceutical industry. He was in a state known for its progressive politicians. If he could get a bill challenging the pharmaceutical industry through the state senate, maybe Pollina's group and its organizational allies could put enough voter pressure on legislators in the Vermont house to get such a bill through. As a Democrat, Governor Dean might sign the legislation and Shumlin would then have a major consumer victory to tout to voters. He began to think he would get more votes taking on the high prices of US medicines than by using PhRMA money to get publicity during elections.

As Rivers was pushing H 365 toward enactment, perhaps the most important development was Shumlin's warming to the idea of taking on drug prices. For legislative leadership of one or both houses to support a particular policy greatly increases its chances of enactment. Leadership has at its disposal the ability to help or hinder many legislators' careers through such means as legislative committee appointments. It also can put issues high on the legislative agenda. Leadership also has extra staff to develop policy ideas and support for them, and better contacts with the media than most legislators, allowing it to promote its agenda publicly.

In May, Shumlin started to take charge of the issue by having the senate set up a study committee to look into prescription drug pricing; the committee was set up so that he could be elected chair, and he was. That way, his committee could operate without being sharply constrained by someone like Backus. His idea was to "smoke out" the pharmaceutical industry's 2000 legislative agenda to help him determine his own course of action on the issue (Shumlin 2000a).

The HAOC began meeting in the capitol in June, but got off to a slow start. Under Backus, the committee's initial effort to analyze options promoting prescription drug access was exceptionally harried (Rivers 2000a). Pollina, meanwhile, had seen enough to surmise that one small state legislature would have a very hard time taking on the pharmaceutical industry by itself. Bringing other states into the fight, he thought, would force the industry to confront adversaries on several fronts, possibly spreading it thin enough that it could be beaten in one or more states.

To advance this idea, Pollina convened a meeting in August of about fifteen New England contacts he had from public interest groups promoting access to health care, including John Marvin of the Maine Council of Senior Citizens. Marvin was part of a Maine group that had been working on prescription drug access for a year, and that group was looking for policy options.[12] Pollina told the assembled that Vermont needed other states to become active in pressing for prescription drug price control legislation. Taking a stand on the issue, he argued, would appeal to senior voters. To dramatize this point, he took the public interest group leaders to a nearby senior center where they met about forty seniors. Pollina argued before the group to the seniors that it was time for the state to take action on drug prices. Many of the seniors strongly agreed. The health access activists saw a righteous indignation that was simmering among seniors—indignation over how much they had to pay for their medications, righteous in that they believed that the government should do something about it. After they had seen how the seniors responded to the talk, the activists came away thinking that they had an important new health access policy on which to work. Pollina gave them a model bill based on S 88 to take back to their home states (Haviland 2002).

The senate had given Shumlin's senate study committee subpoena power, but relations between him and the industry were still fairly amicable and he did not use it (Rivers 2000a). In September, the committee did hear from Judith Bello, PhRMA's vice president for policy. She attempted to explain why US prescription drug prices were often higher than Canadian prices. She argued that price controls would cut off research on life-saving medicines. If the state wanted to set its own agenda, she suggested that expanding Vermont's SPAPs—Vermont Health Access Program (VHAP) and VScript—would be good policy (Bello 1999). VHAP and VScript were §1115 federal waiver programs: the former offered discount medicines to residents living in households with incomes 150 percent of the federal poverty level (FPL) or less, the latter to seniors or people with disabilities living in households with incomes of 175 percent of the FPL. VScript had higher out-of-pocket costs than VHAP (Office of Health Care Ombudsman 2011). With its waivers, Vermont got Medicaid prices on all drugs for these programs. But both SPAPs helped relatively few people and only covered people who were quite unlikely to be able to pay for medicines otherwise.

Simultaneously with Shumlin's work, Rivers was also pressing on the issue of drug access through the HAOC. At an October hearing, the committee considered how to address the constitutional issues around state-level price controls (Hempling 1999). Among the policy ideas discussed were building market power through a multistate purchasing group and giving prescribers reliable information about the relative effectiveness of medicines. At a November legislative hearing, Stephen Schondelmeyer, director of the PRIME Institute at the University of Minnesota,[13] came to Montpelier and reviewed for the HAOC all of its options. He told members of the committee that the state could use its model of the state liquor store—through which the state purchases liquor in bulk and then sells it to its residents—and become a prescription drug wholesaler in an attempt to get lower drug prices. He agreed with PhRMA that expanding VScript and VHAP could help expand access. But he concluded that state regulation of prices could get consumers the lowest possible prices available to anyone in the United States. Whatever they did, Schondelmeyer warned the legislators, they should look out for the interests of the state's pharmacies (Pollina 1999). Particularly in a rural state like Vermont, where retail options are not easily available, it is essential that the independent pharmacies serving small towns remain viable. As 1999 ended, HAOC chair Backus was discouraging. "Everywhere [the HAOC] looked, we found a dead end." She argued that, instead of pushing for state action, advocates "had to make a political case to get change in Washington" (Goldberg 1999).

But, in December, the HAOC rebelled against Backus and backed an agenda for improving prescription drug access in Vermont that included every idea on the table. On 10 December, it listed its recommendations for action by the 2000 legislature:

> Promote PAPs (pharmaceutical assistance programs)
> Expand VScript and VHAP
> Educate physicians, pharmacists, and patients about the relative effectiveness of medicines in the same therapeutic class
> Regulate profiteering by drugmakers
> Help residents obtain Canadian medicines
> Build a multistate purchasing coalition
> Request Congress to authorize a multistate drug purchasing entity modeled on the Northeast Dairy Compact
> Establish prescription drug price controls (Olson 1999)

That same month, Peter Shumlin emulated Pollina by encouraging other New England states to become involved in taking on drugmakers. On 16 December, in what became the first of such meetings, he brought

Vermont state legislators together in a purple-curtained chamber of the Vermont state house with legislators and staff from Maine, Massachusetts, and New Hampshire to discuss the issues and possible remedies. Among those present was a staff member of Maine State Senator Chellie Pingree (D–North Haven), who was to become a key figure in that state's battles with the drugmakers. Like Pollina, Shumlin suggested that they could help advocates for prescription drug access in Vermont by raising the issue in their states. He sent them home with a draft resolution to propose in their legislatures that proclaimed that they would work together to coordinate passage of model laws (Goldberg 1999).

As 2000 approached, Shumlin and Rivers were poised to press the prescription drug issue in the next session of the legislature. Comparisons of US and Canadian prescription drug prices had dramatized the issue to voters. Grassroots support was expected from Pollina and allied public interest groups. PhRMA's relatively polite political response of proposing SPAP expansion had been signaled. The senators' lawyers had approaches to price-setting that they believed would address the constitutional issues raised by PhRMA and they were expecting the introduction of price control legislation in other states to thin the ranks of PhRMA lobbyists in Montpelier.

But, a few days later, a new item for the 2000 legislative agenda emerged, one that would come to sap energy from the fight for prescription drug access. From their chambers next to the legislature, the Vermont Supreme Court ruled that same-sex couples were being unconstitutionally denied the benefits of marriage and ordered the 2000 state legislature to seek a remedy (Shumlin 2000b). Efforts to lower drug prices could face a major competing policy initiative that could weaken its chances, as mandated civil union legislation could draw off limited legislative staff time and take up the front pages of the papers.

S 300

How policymaking on civil union might take up public attention was immediately evident at the start of the 2000 legislative session. Huge crowds turned up at the statehouse to express their views on same-sex unions. The chief of the capitol police, David Janawicz, said that in his eight years at the statehouse he had never seen crowds as large (Frothingham 2000). As the legislature was hit with the uproar, drug access advocates continued to move their agenda forward. On 5 January 2000, Senators Shumlin and Rivers, with the backing of seven other state senators, went to the small but ornate senate chamber to introduce,

S 300, the bill that would implement the last of the HOAC recommendations, establishing a board empowered to set prices drug manufacturers could charge in Vermont. The board was to act on prices after reviewing prices on the FSS and in Canada (Vermont Legislative Bill Tracking System 2000d).

However, from within the Democratic Party, Governor Dean soon began to pose a problem for S 300. Dean, a physician from an affluent New York City family, had moved to Vermont in the late 1970s and quickly moved into politics. After he had set up his practice near Burlington, he launched his political career as an advocate for a bike path along the beautiful lake from which Burlington rises, Lake Champlain. In 1982, he was elected to a seat in the state house of epresentatives and became lieutenant governor in 1986, when it was still a part-time job. In 1991, he inherited the governorship upon the sudden death of Governor Richard Snelling and distinguished himself mainly as a tax-cutting Democrat (America Votes 2004 2004). Dean scaled back Vermont's welfare program, reduced cash benefits, and imposed strict time limits on single mothers receiving welfare assistance. He also supported the death penalty and was embraced by the National Rifle Association (Farrell 2003). By 2000, he had already begun considering a run for the US presidency or, at least, the vice presidency.

A recipient of large campaign contributions from the health care industry as well as IBM, Vermont's most prominent business, Dean worked to substitute his own approach to prescription drug costs for S 300 as it went for its senate committee hearing (opensecrets.org 2004). He said he could not support price regulation unless other New England states did the same and that Vermont could not afford to defend itself if the industry sued Vermont for passing such a law. Taking a cue from a PhRMA lobbyist, the governor announced that he would apply to the Clinton administration's Health Care Financing Agency (HCFA) to expand VHAP to cover all those in households with incomes under 300 percent of the FPL (Kasprak 2001). Under the terms of the expansion, all those newly eligible would get the Medicaid discount when they purchased prescription drugs. Rather than setting drug prices with Canadian prices as a standard, Dean's proposal could have used higher Medicaid prices and his proposal would have benefited a smaller population. Shumlin and Rivers wanted to push for the lowest possible prices and for all Vermont residents. Such a signal from the governor in the same party as the bill's proponents certainly weakened their hand. Legislative leadership would need too many other bills signed and other favors from a governor in their party to make it likely they would go to war with Dean over one issue. Although Dean could hurt their bill's chances, criticisms of him would have to be muted, allowing him to play the pro-health care Democrat while using PhRMA's agenda.

Nonetheless, S 300 was heard in the Senate Committee on Health and Welfare, the first step toward passage. For support of S 300, VPIRG brought in Health Law Advocates, a Boston-based law firm specializing in health access issues to testify that, contrary to industry claims, S 300 complies with the US Constitution's commerce clause (McGorrian 2000). VPIRG also joined with the Older Women's League and the Coalition for Disability Rights to release a report on pharmaceutical industry campaign contributions to Vermont lawmakers, finding that they exceeded those of any other industry in 1998 and the first half of 1999. Industry lobbyists testified in the hearing that lowering drug prices would mean less research and fewer cures (Ptashnik 2000). But, on 10 February, both the Senate Health and Welfare and Finance committees voted out S 300 unanimously.

The next day, Shumlin along with Rivers held the second meeting with New England legislators on prescription drug prices, this time at the Massachusetts statehouse on Beacon Hill in Boston (Sneyd 2000b). Not to be outdone by Pollina and Shumlin in building alliances across New England, four days later, Governor Dean hosted a meeting in Montpelier with the governors of Maine and New Hampshire. They discussed building a tristate purchasing pool (Rich 2000). The governors also sent a letter to the Quebec Premier Lucien Bouchard on 29 February asking him to help arrange a meeting between the Quebec health minister and representatives of their legislatures (Shaheen et al. 2000); a likely topic would be the importation of medicines (Rivers 2000c). But the prime minister refused.[14]

From Burlington came several hard hits on S 300. The *Burlington Free Press*, the most influential newspaper in the state, reported that the state's attorney general had said that the prescription drug price controls would be unconstitutional when, in fact, he had not. Shumlin called the *Free Press* for a correction, but the editors refused to print it while the bill was under consideration (Shumlin 2000a). Opposition of a major state paper like the *Burlington Free Press* could make the support of S 300 appear ill-advised. It provided talking points for potential opponents in the legislative debates and upcoming elections and, along with Governor Dean's ambivalence, undermined public confidence in S 300.

When S 300 was taken up on the senate floor in late February, Vermont began to see the impact of the pharmaceutical industry's heavily financed political operations. As the bill was being decided on the senate floor, the state's only pharmaceutical wholesaler, the Burlington Drug Company, weighed in. Its board of directors had voted to develop a contingency plan to move to New York or New Hampshire if S 300 passed. Confirming the vote, Michael Mitiguy, president of Burlington Drug Company, said "we would move" (Remsen 2000). Mitiguy, who was well known to many senators, sat in the gallery closely overlooking the small senate floor as S 300 was debated (Shumlin 2000a).

Senate Republican Leader John Bloomer (R–Rutland) led the opposition in two protracted floor fights (Rivers 2000a). On 25 February and again on 29 February, opponents proposed four sets of weakening amendments that were voted down. On the same dates, an amendment to strip the price-fixing mechanism from the bill was also narrowly defeated, 14-15 (Vermont Legislative Bill Tracking System 2000c). While votes on such amendments are seldom seen by the media or the public, final floor votes are more likely to be noticed by the public. So, at the end of the day on the 29th, most Republicans did not want to be seen as opposing price controls and voted for them. S 300 passed out of the senate with the 25-4 vote noted at the New York City meeting and was sent to the house.

In addition to drawing on their legislative power, S 300 backers were counting on strong grassroots pressure on legislators to win the votes needed to get their bill through the house and the governor to sign it. Without it, S 300 backers would be hard-pressed to succeed. But public employee unions, a bulwark of support for prescription drug access in other states, were largely absent in efforts to pressure legislators. The Vermont State Employees Association had a good pharmaceutical plan, and this issue was not a priority for its leaders (Shumlin 2000b; Sanchez 2001). So, Shumlin and Rivers counted on VPIRG and similar state groups to have the resources to produce letters, e-mails, and visits to legislators.

On the first Tuesday of March, Vermont had what is called Town Meeting Day. The meetings convened on this day could debate and vote on resolutions of concern to residents, whether local, state, or national. The Vermont Consumers' Campaign for Health took advantage of Town Meeting Day to push for support of S 300 in Windham County—a southern county and one of those closest to traditionally more progressive urban centers. On 7 March, towns around the county discussed and voted on S 300 (Davis 2000b). The meeting in Brattleboro, the county's principal town, voted 2,491-130 in favor (Smallheer 2000). Rockingham voted 1,025-45 in support (Davis 2000c).

But, even at the level of the town meetings, the civil union issue competed with S 300. The town meetings generally only lasted a few hours and discussion of resolutions on state or federal matters often came at the end and had limited time. A civil union resolution could use up most, if not all, of the time needed to discuss S 300, thus effectively keep it off the agenda. At the urging of the Republicans, towns placed nonbinding questions on their local town meeting day ballots about support for marriage. The issue was considered in town meeting votes of about 50 of Vermont's 249 cities and towns during the week (Bonauto 2000).

As S 300 went to the much larger house floor, the industry was in an especially strong position to use its clout to protect its high prices. Representing its interests would be two Burlington area legislators who had formerly worked for the pharmaceutical industry: Michael Flaherty (D–South Burlington), retired from Merck, and Hank Gretkowski (D–Burlington), who had been with American Home Products, later known as Wyeth (Freyne 2000). Neither was running for reelection and so would not have to face voters angry over high drug prices (Pollina 2000). The industry used nearly every one of the lobbying firms in Montpelier to lobby the house (Sneyd 2000c). "No less than 18 statehouse lobbyists," according to a capitol reporter. PhRMA, Bristol-Myers Squibb, Pfizer, GlaxoSmithKline, Merck, and the National Wholesale Druggists all hired individual lobbying firms. Chain drugstores were represented by Otis & Meehan as was the Burlington Drug Company (Freyne 2000). Many lawmakers said they felt more pressure from pharmaceutical lobbyists than they had on any other issue in their careers, whether on prescription drugs or any other policy (Sneyd 2000c).

To generate calls and visits opposing the bill, the industry lobbyists rallied the pharmacies. Many independent pharmacies operate with small margins and are heavily dependent on the markups they can charge individual customers. They strongly fear proposals that could cut what they could charge them. A discount program like that proposed by S 300 had such a potential, for it could enable administrators to lower retail prices by limiting pharmacy income. This possibility presented a good opportunity for the industry to rally pharmacy opposition to S 300.

It was possible Shumlin and Rivers could induce pharmacies' support by increasing their Medicaid reimbursement. But Rivers thought that the dispensing fee Vermont's Medicaid program paid pharmacies was already "high" compared to the fee in other states. Senator Rivers met with the president of the pharmacies' association. She offered to have the state fund a program to import Canadian drugs, require residents using the program to consult with local pharmacists, and pay the pharmacists for the consultation (Rivers 2000a). But she only proposed $150,000 to reimburse pharmacists under the program and this idea did not appeal to them. So, the industry could line up pharmacies in loud opposition. Otis & Meehan, Burlington Drug Company's lobbyist, also represented the independent pharmacies. The lobbyist couldn't be expected to question the big clients' arguments. When PhRMA-linked lobbyists went to the pharmacists with worst-case scenarios about the impact of S 300, it scared them. The bill lost independent pharmacies' support (Sanchez 2001).

In the middle of March, the civil union bill passed out of the house and went to the senate. There considerable energy went into moving the bill. For several days, the Senate Judiciary Committee held hearings to explore whether, and if so how, to change the bill presented by the house (Bonauto 2000). A local minister and a Washington, DC-based activist group joined forces to send Vermonters more than 81,000 letters opposing same-sex civil unions (Lisberg 2000). In-state and out-of-state phone calls on the issue overwhelmed those answering phones in the state capitol (Sanchez 2001). To boot, the bill also continued to dominate page one of the state's papers, where S 300 remained on page four (Rivers 2000b). Front-page media attention could have provided a boost to grassroots efforts by groups like VPIRG, but coverage of the civil union issue kept that from happening. At the same time that the civil union bill was dominating the news, Governor Dean undercut support for S 300. In the words of Rivers, he "trash-talked" the bill while the house was deliberating on it and his statements were used by house opponents in debates (Rivers 2002). On 17 March, he pressed his competing agenda forward by requesting the federal government to allow expansion of VHAP (Elliott 2000).

Given opposition from key house Democrats and the pharmaceutical industry, and the inability of S 300 backers to counter with much in the way of letters and calls to legislators, the chances of S 300 passing in the house were looking increasingly less likely. So, senate supporters planned for the bill to come back to the senate from the house without price controls and, then, use a conference committee to restore some form of strong price restrictions.[15] In this way, they anticipated that house members could be made more accountable to voters for their votes on price controls (Rivers 2000a; Davis 2000b). The only place legislators can vote on conference committee reports is in a single floor vote. Just as a final floor vote that could be seen by the public had pushed senators to switch from voting to weaken S 300 to voting for the bill on 29 February, having to vote on a conference committee report with price controls could again pressure legislators to support it.

When Senators Shumlin, Rivers, and Paul Poirier (D–Barre City) met with their counterparts in New York City on 24 March, they were feeling the heat, but still quite hopeful. Because their bill had the support of senate leadership, they could keep it alive until the end of session. In the meantime, they could wait for the civil union hubbub to die down. Maybe the governor would come around in time to help them gain legislative support. Most importantly, they were still hopeful that their public interest group supporters could get voters to pressure house members at the critical moment.

The bill's first stop in the house was its Health and Welfare Committee, and the hearing took place as scheduled. Many of the same experts who had testified before the HAOC testified again. But pharmacists appeared before the committee, saying that they feared S 300 would put them out of business. The Burlington Drug Company said that some drugmakers wouldn't sell their medicines in Vermont if the bill's provisions for price controls were enacted. It was also at this point that the American Association of Retired Persons (AARP) Vermont offered a little help, getting an opinion piece in the *Burlington Free Press* calling for lower drug prices. As is often the case, the AARP at the state level had very little in the way of resources for generating letters and calls to officeholders.

S 300 did not come out of the house Health and Welfare Committee in early April as Shumlin and Rivers had hoped. With a 15 May deadline for legislative action approaching, time was starting to grow short. It was still stuck there in the third week of April when PhRMA tried a tactic that would give cover to house members who voted against price controls. On 19 April, the pharmaceutical industry went public with an offer to provide free medicine for low-income residents if price controls were dropped from S 300. They claimed this offer was worth $3 million.[16] Suspicious of PhRMA's offer and holding out for strong price restrictions, Shumlin said, "If they're trying to bribe the people of Vermont, it's not going to fly" (Bever 2000c). But the speaker of the house, Michael Obuchowski (D–Rockingham), responded positively and focused on negotiating a higher income level to qualify for PhRMA's offer (Bever 2000c). On 20 April, the house Health and Welfare Committee passed out S 300 without price controls, but with a plan based on the drug companies' supposed $3 million offer (Bever 2000c). Afterwards, the drug companies withdrew their offer, claiming that one of their lobbyists had misspoken (Shumlin 2000b).

Meanwhile, as April was ending, the legislature and governor finally resolved the civil union issue. On 19 April, the state senate approved H 847. On 25 April, the House gave its final approval

(Goldberg 2000b). The next day, Governor Dean signed it into law (Goldberg 2000a). In addition to being a distraction, the civil union uproar weakened the chances of S 300 in another way. For a majority of lawmakers, the H 847 vote was already a plunge into uncharted waters. Voting for strong restrictions on drug prices could antagonize pharmaceutical industry campaign contributors. As Senate President Shumlin put it, a lot of "courage" was spent on the civil union bill (Shumlin 2000a).

With the civil union bill out of the way and fifteen days left in the session, the legislature's focus shifted to S 300 at the beginning of May. As the house version of S 300 without price controls came up for a vote by the full house, Speaker Obuchowski said the house was the object of the most intensive lobbying effort he had seen in twenty years in the statehouse (Freyne 2000). Republicans used the arguments of pro-business economists to rationalize their opposition. Rep. Malcolm Severance (R–Colchester), a retired economics professor, lectured the house about the difficulties in attempting price regulation. "It sends a powerful message that is negative relative to the business community in this state," Severance said. And, he added, the private sector's response to price controls generally is to reduce the availability of its products in the regulated area. "When you regulate the price at less than market, you may have a favorable price, but you have no access," Severance said. "We don't need this. It doesn't work. It has no clout" (Meier 2001).

On 3 May, pharmaceutical industry pressure paid off as the weakened house version of S 300 carried by a lopsided 101-39 vote (Vermont Legislative Bill Tracking System 2000c). As Shumlin explained, the "legislators perceived no political price" for voting against price controls (Shumlin 2000b). The house and senate version of S 300 went to a conference committee (Sanchez 2000b). On 9 May, a conference committee of Paul Poirier, Malcolm Severance (R–Colchester), and Ann Pugh (D–So. Burlington) from the house, and Shumlin, Rivers, and Helen Riehle (R–So. Burlington) from the senate, began to meet, giving Shumlin and Rivers an opportunity to put strong price restrictions back into the bill (Vermont Legislative Bill Tracking System 2000a).

Two days later, Vermont prescription drug politics was rocked by news from Maine. One of the Maine legislators who was in the group of northeastern state legislators whom Shumlin had convened, Senator Chellie Pingree (D), had proposed a price control bill similar to S 300 in her state. On 11 May, an amended version of the bill that still contained price controls was signed by Maine's governor, Angus King (I). But the Maine bill provided for a two-step process to price controls. First, it would use Medicaid purchasing power to try to negotiate lower drug prices for all Maine residents. That would give the state the authorization to tell a drugmaker that, if it didn't give a certain discount for a particular drug to all residents, then the state Medicaid program would require prior authorization for that drug, reducing the drugmaker's overall revenue and profit. Second, if after two years prices weren't comparable to Federal Supply Schedule or Canadian prices, price controls would be imposed. The Vermont conferees amended the framework of the Maine bill into S 300, creating the same two-step process for price controls (Sanchez 2000a).

The passage of the Maine legislation alarmed the industry and led to intensification of its efforts in Vermont. Industry representatives who had been working in Maine came to Vermont to support industry lobbying. They could join their colleagues walking the Vermont state capitol's halls to put the pressure of a well-financed industry on legislators in order to get them to oppose restrictions on drug prices. Although it didn't need to be said, it was widely understood that opposition from a wealthy lobby could mean loss of substantial campaign contributions or, worse yet, substantial campaign contributions for an electoral opponent. Out-of-state phone calls opposing price controls grew to three hundred calls a day (Sanchez 2000b). Nonetheless, Shumlin and Rivers used the senate's leverage on the state budget to pressure Governor Dean into support for the amended S 300 (Rivers 2002).

On 13 May, the two-step version of S 300, starting with an effort to negotiate lower prices for an expanded VScript program, was voted out of the S 300 conference committee. Only the retired economics teacher, Rep. Severance, voted against it. The governor announced his support of the bill but, as the papers noted, he did it only after it appeared that backers "couldn't get enough votes" to pass the legislature (Bever 2000a). Leaving nothing to chance, during the last day of the session, 15 May, the pharmaceutical industry made a show of force around the statehouse. Many legislators were repeatedly confronted with reminders of what crossing a wealthy industry's representatives might mean for their political campaigns and, maybe, careers. According to Shumlin, "I saw one lobbyist get up this morning in the cafeteria and say, 'we just broke a record. Nine different lobbyists talked to an individual lawmaker before he sat down with his coffee'" (Sneyd 2000c).

The house rejected the two-step version of S 300 the conference committee had recommended and sent back another prescription drug bill, one without price controls. But the vote for the weaker bill fell to 83–62, closer than the 101–39 vote of 3 May (Sanchez 2000b). Still, business-friendly Democrats led by Representatives Flaherty and Gretkowski held the line against price controls. The houses appointed a second conference committee on S 300, made up of the same members who had been on the first committee.

By this time, the Vermont Republicans agreed to support a version of S 300 without price controls. "Moderate Democrats promised that the Senate leadership would yield," said Rivers (Rivers 2000b). That, moderates argued, could be a "win-win" resolution: the senate Democrats would get their prescription drug access bill in time for the election and the Republicans and their Democratic allies would make sure that the bill didn't seriously threaten industry profits. But the moderate Democrats were wrong. When Shumlin and Pollina discussed the idea of going along with moderate Democrats, they both agreed that they'd be better off using drug access as an electoral appeal rather than cave in to a "toothless" prescription drug bill (Davis 2000a). If the voters were asked to decide between a backer of an industry proposal versus a backer of a proposal with "teeth," progressives and senate Democrats believed that many would choose the latter. With an impasse likely, a new conference committee did not begin meeting until after 9 PM on the last day of session (Sneyd 2000a). Sen. John Bloomer stalled adjournment, saying he would prevent it until conferees agreed to the bill without price caps. But Shumlin and Rivers were in no mood to compromise.

At 11:15 PM, conferees threw in the towel. Shumlin said, "At some point we should acknowledge they've beaten us" (Bever 2000b). The senate adjourned at 1:12 AM; the house 27 minutes later (Sneyd 2000a). Things had not turned out as Shumlin and Rivers had hoped. VPIRG and the other public interest groups never produced the hoped-for public reaction to the high prices of medicines. By the time the governor came around to supporting S 300, the blue dogs had already locked the House into overwhelming opposition. The power of senate leadership and a popular proposal in a very blue state were not enough to beat the power of PhRMA.

The pharmaceutical industry had used its lobbying power to take advantage of Vermont's relatively weak grassroots infrastructure to beat down the price control threat in the state. It left the state with the only option for lower drug prices being Dean's proposed expansion of VHAP. The March élan shown by the Vermont legislators at the meeting of northeastern legislators working to cut prescription drug prices seemed more like naiveté.

Epilogue

In the wake of the defeat of price controls in Vermont, the key players developed respective policy approaches to the issue, even as they pursued their various career paths. Howard Dean continued his efforts to get a HCFA waiver to extend the Medicaid rebate to those in households with incomes under 300 percent of the FPL. Peter Shumlin and Cheryl Rivers institutionalized their alliance of northeastern legislators challenging the pharmaceutical industry by forming the Northeast Legislative Association on Prescription Drug Prices (NLARx), devoting time to institutionalizing the alliance of state legislators concerned with drug prices that they had started in Montpelier in 1999.

With price controls no longer threatened, PhRMA objected to Dean's waiver proposal. Although the industry supported SPAP expansion when tougher prescription drug prices policies were on the table, it withdrew support when there was no danger of serious restraints on prices. On 5 June, PhRMA advised HCFA that it believed HCFA had no authority to grant the requested waiver (Powell 2000). So, PhRMA argued that the program could not be approved.

Dean also pursued his proposed tri-state alliance for drug purchasing. On 17 July, the northern New England governors agreed to organize the Tri-State Drug Purchasing Coalition. To increase the visibility of this accord, they announced it at a meeting in Halifax, Nova Scotia, among the governors and the premiers of the eastern provinces of Canada (Sneyd 2000d). Dean also supported the work of the NLARx with a provision of office space and a state appropriation (Rivers 2004).

Pollina ran as the Progressive Party candidate for governor against Dean in the 2000 election, creating a three-way race (Davis 2000a). In Vermont, if one candidate in a three-way race gets a majority of the vote, then that candidate wins; but, if no candidate gets a majority, then the legislature picks the winner. To push for a majority, Dean announced in August that he was foregoing public financing and would finance his campaign with private campaign contributions.[17] A week before the November election, the Clinton administration overruled PhRMA's objections and approved the expansion of drug benefits under VHAP as Dean had requested (National Conference of State Legislatures 2009). In the election, Dean received 50.4 percent of the vote, barely achieving his majority; Pollina polled 10 percent (Markowitz 2000). That year, voters made the Vermont house more conservative than previously, electing a Republican majority.

Ultimately, Dean's efforts to lower drug prices were not successful. PhRMA sued the federal government in December (Sneyd 2000e). The industry claimed that, since the state would not actually subsidize the drug costs of those newly eligible under Dean's proposed expansion, the program was not entitled to Medicaid discounts or a HCFA waiver. In June 2001, PhRMA won its court challenge and the federal waiver to expand VHAP was disallowed (Kasprak 2003). The tristate coalition announced in May 2001 that it had chosen a private business, First Health, to manage its buying pool (Weber 2001). But the program was never implemented (Cauchi and Victoroff 2006). By then, Maine's Commissioner of Human Services, Kevin Concannon, thought a publicly run consortium would be more cost-effective. Maine was committed to trying to use its Medicaid purchasing power to get drug discounts, and Maine's representative in the alliance believed that Maine would get better discounts that way than through First Health.

In October 2001, Rivers resigned as state senator to become the first executive director of what was then called the National Legislative Association on Prescription Drug Prices (NLARx) (Rivers 2004).[18] One of the association's projects was promoting legislation that would give state officials the authority to bargain for all their prescription drug programs simultaneously, making it easier for states to combine their prescription drug purchasing power. NLARx developed model legislation for that purpose. In 2002, Shumlin integrated this model into a bill, H 31, featuring a less radical set of measures than S 300, and was able to work with Dean and his allies in the house to get it enacted that June. The resulting law, Act 127, authorized a common preferred drug list for all Vermont drug-purchasing programs (Cauchi and Hanson 2006). By providing for joint negotiations for all state drug-purchasing programs, the bill's authors hoped to give state negotiators more ability to move drugmakers' share of the market for classes of drugs and, thus, more ability to gain discounts. One provision of the act allowed for multistate purchasing, but it was not utilized owing to Maine's continued skepticism about the privately managed consortium set up to run it. However, another provision, aimed at reducing state payments to drugmakers by empowering the state to negotiate for supplemental rebates on Medicaid prescription drugs, has been successfully implemented (Padgett, et al. 2006). Act 127 also required pharmaceutical gift reporting when drugmakers provided them to physicians to promote their products. By incorporating this innovative last provision, Vermont once again provided leadership in prescription drug access policy.

In the fall of 2002, Peter Shumlin gave up his senate seat and ran for lieutenant governor. He was challenged by Anthony Pollina. Shumlin received 32 percent of the vote; Pollina, 25 percent; and the Republican,

Brian Dubie, 41 percent. Dean vacated the governor's office, and another Republican, Jim Douglas, got a plurality of the vote in a three-way race for his position. Because neither Dubie nor Douglas received a majority of votes, the legislature decided the outcome, picking Douglas and Dubie for governor and lieutenant governor respectively (Markowitz 2000).

The following June, Howard Dean brought dozens of media vans to the streets of Burlington and announced before five thousand people that that he was running for the US presidency. His 2003 claim to be of the "Democratic wing of the Democratic Party" (a phrase he borrowed from US Senator Paul Wellstone [D–MN]) helped create a national image of Dean at odds with his business-friendly record in Vermont.

In 2004, Pollina looked to run for lieutenant governor as a Democrat (Kelley 2004). But Cheryl Rivers left NLARx that year to challenge Dubie and the Democrats chose her over Pollina. Both Douglas and Dubie were reelected (Markowitz 2000). Rivers left state politics to return to her family business in horse ranching. Although Douglas and Dubie continued the Republican domination of the state's two top offices in 2006, Bernie Sanders became Vermont's newest US Senator, succeeding Jeffords.

In 2008, Anthony Pollina was once again the Progressive Party candidate for governor. He got the endorsements of the Vermont chapter of the National Education Association, the Vermont State Labor Council, and the Vermont State Employees Association (WCAX.com 2008), but only 22 percent of the vote (*New York Times* 2008). Peter Shumlin, who had left the senate in 2002 to run for lieutenant governor, was again elected state senator in 2006 and once again became senate president. Shumlin ran for governor in 2010 and was elected. Once in office, he once again took a national lead on health policy, signing a law that established a board to set the state on the path toward a single-payer medical insurance system (Shumlin 2011).

Back in March 2000, it seemed as though Vermont's advocates for access to prescription drugs were about to succeed in establishing price controls. They had codified a policy in a bill before the legislature, they had state senate leadership dedicated to their proposal, and many voters perceived the problem of access to drugs as a critical hardship. But 2000 was not their year. Too many obstacles stood in their way. Foremost was the massive political opposition of the pharmaceutical industry. In addition, leadership of the state house of representatives never joined the senate in taking on PhRMA; in fact, the house leadership promoted a PhRMA proposal instead. Howard Dean's initial ambivalence and too-late conversion didn't do much to help their chances. The civil union bill also was a major distraction, costing drug access advocates legislative time and press attention. Finally, the relative weakness of VPIRG's grassroots operations and the lack of support from the state employees association left prescription drug access advocates with insufficient means to withstand PhRMA's assault on their bill. Vermont may be a very blue state with a progressive US senator, but its progressivism may be better attuned to policy proposals that, while addressing hardships for voters, are not direct threats to powerful industries. In particular, it seems to lack the grassroots organizational infrastructure necessary to win full use of Medicaid purchasing power or price controls over the pharmaceutical industry.

But the fight for S 300 showed Vermont to be a state with political leaders determined to take on the pharmaceutical industry and fight for better access to medicines. Vermont is now a state from which ideas for challenging powerful industries can germinate to threaten these industries in political environments where public interest groups can find better-funded allies, and it continues to be a base for policy ideas challenging the pharmaceutical industry. It continues to fund NLARx, enabling it to educate state legislators across the country on how to push for greater access to prescription drugs. Its legislature continues to be the fount of proposals aimed at this objective. It has become a long-term problem for PhRMA's blockbuster strategy for high profits, one on which the industry can never turn its back. While Vermont's prescription drug policy leaders failed in 2000, they started an uprising of state legislatures against the pharmaceutical industry that would spread across the country. In fact, without S 300, it is difficult to see how this movement would ever have gotten going. Maine, the case discussed in the next chapter, may never have gone after the pharmaceutical industry as it successfully did in 2000 without inspiration and ideas from Vermont.

---

[1] In 2001, Jeffords became an Independent and put the US Senate leadership into Democratic hands.

[2] As in legislatures generally, to become law, a Vermont bill has to pass through both houses of the legislature and be approved by the governor. On the way through each house, the bill must be heard by one or more committees, the rules of each house providing which committees hear what bills. In the case of

S. 300, the house was expected to amend the senate version of the bill, which would require the senate to consider the amended version—if it were to go to the governor.

[3] Alaska gave Nader his highest proportion of a state's 2000 presidential vote.

[4] HR 4627 was referred to the Subcommittee on Health and Environment; as Republicans controlled the House committees at the time, the bill never came back out of the subcommittee.

[5] Sanders was an indefatigable Vermont politician originally from Flatbush in Brooklyn, New York. After graduating from the University of Chicago and living on a kibbutz, he moved to Vermont. Initially elected mayor of Vermont's only large town, Burlington, by 10 votes in 1981, he had started his political successes with relentless precinct walking and regular town meetings (Leibovich 2007). He has used the power of his office to serve constituents energetically and address problems that posed hardships to many voters (Bleifuss 2005). By 1990, he had learned to garner large campaign contributions and, with strong backing from the National Rifle Association, he was elected to the US House (Cummins 1991).

[6] Rivers was a legislator who had extensive experience organizing around social issues. She had come from a Vermont horse-ranching family, graduated from a state college, and had founded a homeless shelter, a battered women's program, and a farmer's market (Vermont NEA Today 2004). Her interest in these kinds of programs led her to the political arena where she thought she could win support for them (Grotke 2004). She began her career as a politician by a successful campaign for a seat on her local school board. From there, she rose to selectwoman and, then, state senator. Along the way, she developed a strong interest in health policy (Vermont NEA Today 2004).

[7] Pollina himself had grown up in rural New Jersey, but had moved to Vermont and gone to Johnson State College where he majored in political science. In the early 1990s, he worked for Congressman Sanders and was Sanders's liaison with seniors. By the end of the decade, he had become a leader at VPIRG. By then, he was also a prospective gubernatorial candidate of the Progressive Party, which had been recognized under Vermont law in 1999 (Equal Time 2005).

[8] A single payer would be a government insurance program covering all residents, replacing our private medical insurance system.

[9] While drugmakers ran most clinical research on their products, the National Institutes of Health continued major research projects of its own. When NIH research developed a useful drug, it could turn to private drugmakers to market it. However, drugmakers were known to exorbitantly mark up prices on these drugs. For example, beginning in early 1993, the NIH and Bristol-Myers Squibb were widely criticized when Bristol-Myers Squibb announced a wholesale price of $4.87 per milligram for Taxol, an important NIH-developed cancer drug that BMS acquired in bulk from a contractor for $.25 per milligram (CPTech 1999).

[10] The Minnesota bus rides had started as gambling trips to Winnipeg for seniors from Minneapolis. But, as US drug prices rose and seniors noticed the lower drug prices in Canadian pharmacies, they turned into prescription drug-buying bus trips (Wyckoff 2007).

11 Central Vermont Council on Aging is a 501(c)(3) nonprofit that relies heavily on federal funds. While, with government funding, its political work must be low-key, it can use its resources to highlight needed public policies.

[12] Marvin is a major actor in Chapter 4.

[13] Under Schondelmeyer, the Pharmaceutical Research In Management and Economics Institute produced sharp criticism of pharmaceutical industry practices limiting access to medicines.

[14] It was suggested at a subsequent meeting of the New England legislators working on prescription drug access that a threat from the pharmaceutical industry to raise drug prices in Canada in retaliation if such a meeting were held led to the refusal.

[15] When the houses of a legislature pass two different bills on the same policy, they can send the different bills to a conference committee, a group of legislators with equal numbers from each house who can prepare a report resolving the differences between the bills. A conference committee report can sometimes provide a way to enact a policy that one house, earlier, would not pass.

[16] But the industry may have overestimated the value of its offer.

[17] As governor of Vermont, Dean targeted for elimination the public-financing provision of the state's campaign finance law (Farrell 2003). In 2003, Dean became the first Democratic presidential candidate ever to abandon the Watergate-era public financing system (Zeleny 2003).

[18] The NLARx was the successor organization to the Northeast Legislative Association on Prescription Drug Prices.

4

As Goes Maine

Three months after the March 2000 New York City meeting of northeastern legislators at which Vermont legislators had expressed optimism about passage of S 300, the legislators were at another meeting on the subject; this time in Portland, Maine. As Vermont's proposal for prescription drug price controls had gone down to defeat, a Maine proposal inspired by it had been enacted. The new law, Maine Rx, took two steps toward lower drug prices: first, it authorized the state to use its Medicaid purchasing power to negotiate drug prices for Maine residents; and, second, it provided for drug price controls if the first step failed to meet the law's price goals. It was to be implemented, and Kevin Concannon, Maine's Commissioner of Human Services under Governor Angus King (I), was the state official in charge of implementation. This was the public meeting at which Concannon would announce his implementation plans.

The setting was a college campus in South Portland. The meeting was held on a beautiful June day and the Maine hosts had gotten a room with a glorious view of Casco Bay, typical Maine coastline set off sparkling blue water featuring sailboats and other boats, many moored and a few under way. Inside, at center stage, was Concannon.

A Mainer by birth, he had earned a MSW degree in Nova Scotia and had been a Maine public health official (with a hiatus in Oregon) since 1980. He had been tough on Medicaid spending and had had numerous run-ins with advocates for people on Medicaid. But, on this day, he was about to let the pharmaceutical industry know how tough he planned to be in implementing Maine Rx.

Behind the commissioner sat a dozen or so expensively dressed and neatly coiffed pharmaceutical industry lobbyists. Concannon quickly got to the point and described his plan for implementing the Maine Rx program. He described in detail the plan's mechanics, displaying the knowledge of one who had played a leading role in developing it. It was a well-developed approach to use the state's purchasing power to lower drug prices. As Concannon outlined his plan, it became plain he was determined to carry out the new law vigorously. He appeared totally indifferent to industry pressure.

As the commissioner went on, the expressions of most of the lobbyists seated behind him began to slowly change from impassive to confused. By the time he had finished, a number of them seemed as if they were in pain. A few of the older men in the group were visibly fuming. The industry lobbyists were having a rare experience: they had not only lost a major legislative battle, they were learning that the state official in charge was planning to use all his resources to fully implement the bill with which they had been defeated.

As in Vermont, the cash and power of the industry had poured in to stop the law. Yet, in the case of Maine, the industry lobbyists had lost to an unlikely group led by a retired union official and a few others with modest political resources, a legislator living on an island accessible only by boat, and the small state's health services commissioner. Rather than beating down strong legislation to contain drug prices as they had in Vermont, the pharmaceutical industry had been run over by it in Maine.

There, progressive activists working the state legislature had found the political resources and opportunity they needed to hand the pharmaceutical industry a stunning political defeat. As is shown below, when these conditions were present, then public indignation over an issue like high drug prices could become a factor in the political process.

Maine Background

There are similarities in the economics and politics of Maine and Vermont. Like Vermont, Maine tends to be a "blue state." It voted for Clinton in his two runs for the White House and against Bush in his two presidential elections. Although its two US senators are Republicans, they are among the most moderate in their party caucus. For example, they were among the five members of their party to vote not guilty on both counts against President Clinton in his impeachment trial. Maine's percentage of voter turnout in the 2000 presidential election was not only high, it was the highest in the United States.

Like Vermont, Maine has no large media markets. Legislative races are fairly affordable as Maine provides public financing for legislative campaigns. In the 2002 Maine elections, 77 percent of the candidates for the state senate and 55 percent of candidates for the state house ran with public financing (Sifry 2004). Maine also has a long tradition of town meetings and, like Vermont, its politics feature grassroots activism, but with an important difference.

Maine's state employee union, the Maine State Employees Association, was an affiliate of the Service Employees International Union (SEIU), a national union with many state affiliates that are aggressively political. As such, it had greater access than unaffiliated state employees associations like their Vermont counterpart to resources like well-trained organizers and a national affiliate with campaign funds. In MSEA's case, it had become politically energized after it became embroiled in a 1991 battle between Democratic legislators and the Republican governor over workers' compensation policy. For years, out-of-state private insurers selling workers' compensation insurance in Maine like AIG had demanded that the state weaken regulation on the rates they could charge (Kerr 1992). When the state went into the 1991 fiscal year without a state budget, Governor McKernan (R), husband of US Senator Olympia Snowe (R), demanded that legislative Democrats agree to workers' compensation reform in order to get a budget signed (*Orlando Sentinal* 1991). When the Democrats balked, the governor sought to pressure them by going after one of their backers, the state workers' union, and locked out state workers right before a payday (Dawson 1994). SEIU's national president came to their defense. "It's the first time in the 171-year history of Maine that any governor has had the heartless audacity to shut down the state in order to pander to the interests of the rich and powerful," President John J. Sweeney said (Associated Press 1991).

Shocked, state workers reacted militantly, demonstrating in front of McKernan's office. Further, led by SEIU's senior New England staffer, John Marvin, state workers took over the legislative chambers, chanting "do your job, pass the budget" and refusing to let members leave. State workers wanted McKernan to drop his insistence on linking workers' compensation to the budget. But he didn't agree to a budget until changes were made in the state's workers' compensation law. In the wake of that battle, many MSEA members became convinced of the need for MSEA to be more engaged in the state political arena. So, afterwards, it was (Leinonen 2006).

Maine's business lobby is relatively weak. Centralized industries like paper and shoes have largely left the state and the remaining industries such as tourism, fishing, and agriculture are more decentralized. Their main business lobby, the Maine Chamber of Commerce, had only two lobbyists in 2000.

Low-cost Drugs for the Elderly

The genesis of Maine's pharmaceutical access politics in 2000 went back over two decades. In 1975, Maine and New Jersey were the first of a wave of northeastern states to establish state pharmaceutical assistance programs (SPAPs) in the next decade (Carreon et al. 2000). In Maine's case, it was the Low-cost Drugs for the Elderly program (DEL). Initially, DEL covered only drugs for select catastrophic conditions, and coverage was limited to people who were eligible for property tax relief, a relatively small group (Families USA 2001).[1] Although people did not have to be eligible for Medicaid to get into DEL, the program paid for medicines the same way that Medicaid did: the pharmaceutical industry gave DEL about a 15 percent rebate from the mid-1970s to the mid-1990s.

In 1992, Chellie Pingree, a knitting business owner, school board member, and tax assessor from an island on Penobscot Bay started to think seriously about getting into state politics. She was particularly concerned about issues affecting women like access to health care, education, and support for families. She was also a strong believer in equal pay for equal work. Then she heard a speech by Rep. Pat Schroeder (D–CO); according to Pingree, "Pat said that people didn't want to run for office anymore, and I thought it's such an interesting thing to work with your friends and neighbors to balance budgets and solve problems, why wouldn't people want to do it?" When she learned the Democratic Party was looking for someone to run for state senate in her district, one that was considered to be safely Republican, she jumped in (Ross 2008). She walked door-to-door in most of the nineteen towns in the district, meeting a large proportion of the voters as well as the towns' politicians, and won.

When Republicans took over the state senate in 1994, they assigned Pingree to a subcommittee on health care (Mishra 2000). Through that assignment, one of Pingree's responsibilities was oversight of the Low-cost Drugs for the Elderly program, where she began to think lower drug prices could expand the program's capacity for covering Mainers. In 1996, the Democrats won back the senate and she rose to the position of senate majority leader, where she would have more power to pursue her ideas (Pingree for Congress 2008).

In 1997, the Maine Equal Justice Partners, a lobbying group formed by Maine's poverty bar a year earlier, had picked up on the declining access to medicines of the late 1990s and was looking for a well-positioned legislator to expand the SPAP's capacity cover residents and medicines. At that time, Pingree's mother was deteriorating to the point that she would die the next year. Remembering those days, Pingree later recounted that "I watched my mother in the last three or four years of her life—just like every other senior citizen—need about six drugs a day to stay alive." She recalled it got to the point where there wasn't enough money in her mother's checking account to pay for what she needed (Washuk 2000a). The Maine Equal Justice Partners managed to get Pingree to back a proposal to increase the program's rebate from pharmaceutical companies to 21 percent (from 15 percent), increasing the number of people and drugs it could help buy (Henderson 2001). Although she received campaign contributions from the industry, Pingree found it was difficult to have a dialogue with PhRMA about lowering DEL's drug costs; the pharmaceutical industry representatives with whom she was meeting were responsible to others in drugmakers' headquarters beyond Maine's borders. As opposed to most interest groups with which Pingree met, she felt like the PhRMA representatives were representing "outsiders" (Pingree 2000b). As such, they tended to be less responsive to Maine's concerns and more fixated on their own businesses' bottom lines. As part of this effort, she consulted with Kevin Concannon. The senator then amended the state budget to try increasing the state's rebates to the SPAP (Holzman 2000). Through her amendment, Concannon's department was requested to seek an additional $2 million from pharmaceutical businesses (Joint Standing Committee on Appropriations and Financial Affairs 1998).

Pingree quickly found out how vehemently the pharmaceutical industry would fight reductions in its income. Pingree recalled, "The next morning, there were 6 representatives of the pharmaceutical industry in my office." When a legislator gets such visits, it is only reasonable to infer that campaign contribution support may be at risk. After her "rebate" amendment, Pingree found that any fears she may have had about losing the financial support of the pharmaceutical industry were borne out: her campaign financing from the industry was, largely, terminated (Holzman 2000). The industry refused to increase the state's rebates (Pingree 2000b).

In the summer of 1998, Maine's movement for prescription drug access got support from the national level. Tom Allen (D–ME) had been elected to the Congress in 1996. He was a native Mainer who had gone to Bowdoin College (where he was captain of the football team) and Harvard Law School. He was a Rhodes scholar along with Bill Clinton and had gone from there to Portland city council and mayor by the early 1990s.

After he got to the US House of Representatives, he had started holding town hall meetings on Medicare, which the Republican

Congress was looking to reform at the time. At a town hall in Sanford, Maine, a retired firefighter by the name of Leon Currier got up to speak. To Allen's surprise, Currier didn't want to talk about Medicare; he wanted to talk about the price of prescription drugs. He said that he had to pay $100 out-of-pocket for his medicines, which he thought was high, and wanted to know what Allen was going to do about it (Allen 2008).

While Allen was aware of a buzz on prescription drug prices, it was Currier's statement that prompted him to act. Allen had his staff look for legislation on prescription drug prices that he could support and they found that there wasn't any. So, he introduced HR 4627, the Prescription Drug Fairness for Seniors Act of 1998—the bill that would give Medicare recipients the same prescription drug prices that are available to federal agencies from the Federal Supply Schedule (Allen 2008). He also led the effort of the minority staff of the House Committee on Government Reform to conduct studies on the prices of the best-selling drugs (Strongin 1999).

One of the committee's minority staff reports was released in his Maine district. Along with the minority staff report released by Rep. Sanders in Vermont, it found that local prices of the five brand-name drugs with highest sales to US seniors were roughly double what they were in Canada. When Allen released his report, the issue was picked up by the Maine papers—hinting at its political potential (Pingree 2000b). Rep. Allen had elevated the drug price issue in Maine. He had taken it from being a matter for the relatively few beneficiaries of the Low-cost Drugs for the Elderly program to begin making it the concern of all those people in Maine who were angry about the prices of their medicines.

In tandem with Rep. Allen's press conference, Maine senior activists looked to publicize the issue of high drug prices. They had already heard of the Minnesota prescription-drug-buying bus trips to Canada. The Maine activists organized a five-hour ride from their state to a Canadian pharmacy on 5-7 October (Sweet 1998). Pingree decided to join the seniors on the ride to a Canadian pharmacy (Sweet 1998).

One of the people who rode the bus was Viola Quirion. Ms. Quirion's story illustrated the situation that more and more seniors around the United States were facing. She was a single 72-year-old woman from Waterville, Maine, and had worked in the local Hathaway shirt factory from the age of 15 until 67 for a salary just above minimum wage. In retirement, her income was largely Social Security (about $1,000 a month) and her health insurance was Medicare (Wallace 1999).

Ms. Quirion's health was impaired by both arthritis and severe stomach problems. She had been forced to make some hard choices. "I had to skip my drugs and I had a lot of pain," she reported. "I tried to skip some meals, I bought the cheapest food I could." She paid more than $200 a month for the medicines she needed: Prilosec for her stomach and Relafen for her arthritis. "When I skip the Relafen, my inflammation comes back," she said. "And if I skip the Prilosec, I can't digest my food" (Noonan 2000). In Canada, Quirion found that a three-month supply of her medicines cost $400. After the bus trip, she decided to go to Canada once a year (Mishra 2000).

In April 1999, the Maine State Employees Association began to be pulled into state pharmaceutical politics. MSEA members, including retirees, were hit with an increase in their prescription drug costs. Their co-pays were increased from $5 for generic drugs and $10 for branded drugs to $10 and $20 respectively; this hike was expected to cost them $10 million a year in the aggregate.

MSEA leaders partly controlled the health plan for state employees and retirees with the state government. They were expecting there would be more health care cost inflation and prescription drug price increases to be the fastest-growing expense (Marvin 2001). Retirees retained full voting rights within MSEA, were particularly affected by the co-pay increase, and the union leadership knew that it needed to show the members that they were doing something about health care costs besides passing them on to members. If they did not, they could be vulnerable to a political challenge in subsequent union elections.

The union officials decided to take action on prescription drug cost inflation and began political organizing around the issue. Union staff circulated petitions calling for government action to contain drug prices like that proposed by Rep. Allen (Leinonen 2006). [2] MSEA staff got the petitions up on bulletin boards at country stores across the state. Advocates for lower prices brought the petitions with them to meetings; union activists went around with the petitions at state employee worksites. In the end, thousands of signatures and phone numbers were gathered. The call by so many for government action to contain the price of medicines showed that many Mainers were concerned about drug prices. MSEA leadership saw that they had an issue that strongly concerned their members.

Also seeing the success of the petition drive and looking for an issue around which to mobilize Maine seniors was John Marvin, president of the Maine Council of Senior Citizens (MCSC). After retiring as SEIU's senior New England staffer, Marvin remained highly active. He was an avid jogger and spent each summer living with his spouse in a cabin on Little Deer Isle. In the state capitol, he threw himself into organizing seniors for political action and had oriented the MCSC toward state political action.[3]

In August 1999, Marvin was among those prescription drug access activists attending the meeting Anthony Pollina had convened in Vermont in the effort to institute price controls in that state. Along with the activists, he had gone with Pollina to the senior center and had seen the indignation of many seniors over high prescription drug prices. He saw how the seniors reacted to Pollina's argument that the state should do something about it and heard Pollina's proposal that other New England activists open fronts against the pharmaceutical industry. Marvin was sold on the proposal. He returned to Maine to begin planning a Maine campaign for prescription drug price controls.

One of his first steps was to organize another prescription-drug-buying bus trip to Montréal. He made contact with labor unions, asking them to donate a bus and to help recruit 35 seniors. First on his list was Carl Leinonen, his successor as head of MSEA. The two decided that, while demanding Canadian prices for Mainers might not be legal, it was a simple concept that could be easily explained and that they could use to build political momentum on the prescription drug price issue. MSEA joined Marvin's campaign (Leinonen 2006).

To gain publicity for the trip, the MCSC sent faxes to the media, including *60 Minutes*. To their surprise, *60 Minutes* sent Mike Wallace and a camera crew to ride on the bus. On Sunday, 17 October, Marvin's campaign received a huge boost from the national media. In a broadcast seen on TVs across Maine and the country, *60 Minutes* aired a segment based on the taping of the bus trip. It featured an interview with Vi Quirion, detailing her plight in obtaining prescription drugs. It also interviewed Lena Sanford, a 73-year-old retiree. Part of the interview and Wallace's narration went as follows:

WALLACE: How much every month for drugs?
Ms. SANFORD: My drugs come to 13 . . . .
WALLACE: $ 1,365?
Ms. SANFORD: For what I'm paying here in the United States, it'd be one-third over in Canada.
WALLACE: Lena's insurance used to cover that $ 1,365, but as we said, like millions of other seniors across the country, her insurance plan recently stopped paying for her drugs. So she went to Canada, because it turns out the drugs she needs cost more than her total monthly income of $ 1,200 . . . .

The bus crossed over to Canada from Vermont, and once there, we

followed the seniors to a Montréal drugstore where many of them had their prescriptions filled for about half the price they paid in the US. Lena Sanford said that she saved more than $1,000.
Unidentified pharmacist (handing Maine residents their prescriptions): This in American dollars. What we have here is $9—$915.
Ms. SANFORD: Wow. That's good.
WALLACE: That's . . . .
Ms. SANFORD: That's great, and that's two months (Wallace 1999).

The *60 Minutes* episode was a political windfall for the MCSC. In wake of it, MCSC "got telephone calls and mail from all over," said Vi Quirion, who was by 2000 working for the group (Mishra 2000).

Senate Leadership Commitments to Supporting Price Controls

With his MSEA connections, Marvin followed up on the burst of interest and approached Pingree, who was still senate majority leader, and proposed that they combine to push a Maine prescription drug price control bill based on Pollina's model. At the time, Pingree did not expect the drug price control bill to be enacted in Maine; it seemed a goal too far. But she hoped that the threat of a price control bill would give her leverage on drugmakers in her ongoing battle with them to get better discounts for the Low-cost Drugs for the Elderly program and enable the program to better serve Mainers. Also, Pingree would "term out" of her legislative office in 2000 and, if she wanted to run for higher office, she could use an issue that would give her statewide visibility. She decided to put affordable prescription drugs high on the Democratic agenda for the upcoming session (Pingree 2000a).

Pingree and Marvin reached an understanding about how they would mesh their work for a price control bill. Pingree agreed to use her power as senate majority leader to build support for the bill. Marvin would use his power as a grassroots leader within the infrastructures of MCSC and MSEA. Marvin and Pingree looked to get MSEA to make support for their proposal a top priority and met with the group's leaders to enlist their commitment. Leinonen was looking for wedge issues that MSEA allies could use in the 2000 election. He didn't expect a proposal to improve prescription drug access to win in the legislature in 2000, but he thought he could help MSEA friends by giving them a popular measure for which they would likely vote and embarrass MSEA opponents by forcing their likely opposition into the public eye. So, he agreed to back Pingree on the issue. From then until the resolution of the price control debate, MSEA would supply substantial staff and financial resources for the campaign (Leinonen 2006).

With the legislative opening provided by Pingree and the resources made available by Marvin, the legislative campaign for a State of Maine statute containing prescription drug prices was under way. On 16 December, Pingree's aide, Allison Sweet-Lazos, attended Vermont Senate President Peter Shumlin's Montpelier meeting of northeastern legislators and staff concerned about prescription drug prices (Pingree 2000b). On behalf of Pingree, Sweet told the meeting that Senator Pingree wanted legislation that would regulate drug prices (Sweet 1999). Sweet came back with an updated draft of a prescription drug price control bill (Pingree 2000b).

Around the end of the year, Pingree made a list for herself showing how she could use her power as senate majority leader to support a bill that would contain prescription drug prices. Her list largely outlined events to come in the upcoming weeks and set the stage for the 2000 Maine legislative session:

Address the concerns of potential opponents like the state medical association, pharmacies, the state osteopathic association, the state hospital association, and the King administration;

Speak at community meetings at places such as senior centers and town halls;

Work to get guest columns in major papers like the *Portland Press Herald* and the *Boston Globe*;

Work with statehouse reporters (for example, by giving them human interest stories like individuals buying prescription drugs in Canada);

Hold capitol press conferences; and

Get legislators as co-sponsors for her bill (Pingree 2000e).

All of the tasks itemized she would find easier to do because of the power she was in legislative leadership. For example, potential opponents of a price control bill were likely to calculate how their opposition would affect their chances of prevailing on other legislative proposals on which the majority leader's power might decide the outcome. Some other legislators deciding on support of her prescription drug price proposal would consider how their support would affect their chances of getting the majority leader's valuable support for their proposals.

On 11 January, Pingree started calling potential opponents and potential co-sponsors. Her call list included Assembly Speaker Steven Rowe (D–Portland), Senate President Mark Lawrence (D–Kittery), and Rep. Joseph Bruno (R–Raymond), a rising house Republican leader with whom Marvin had already discussed the price control idea (Sweet 2000). Bruno's position was going to be important for Pingree. In addition to his standing in the Republican Party, he was both a licensed pharmacist and a businessman. He was president of Community Pharmacies, a statewide group of twelve independent pharmacies (Wolfe 2001).

To win local media support, Marvin and Pingree together visited the offices of all the dailies featuring coverage of Maine state politics and met with their editorial boards to discuss prescription drug access. As well, Pingree sat down with reporters of local papers with statehouse beats such as the *Lewiston Sun Journal*, *Bangor Daily News*, *Waterville Morning Sentinel*, and the *Kennebec Journal* (Pingree 2000b). Through Marvin, MSEA and the Maine American Federation of Labor-Congress of Industrial Organizations (AFL-CIO) staged several small, but successful, meetings with Pingree in support of action on prescription drug prices (Pingree 2000a). From there, MSEA organized and sponsored a subsequent series of town hall meetings on taking action against high prescription drug prices in January and February (Pingree 2000a). By holding meetings around the state, MSEA hoped to generate grassroots pressure on legislators to support a drug price control bill by Pingree. The meetings could generate local supportive press coverage and they could help convince participants to support a bill containing prescription drug prices. Also, they could gather contact information with which to reach participants when needed, and they could help spawn word-of-mouth support for drug price legislation. Marvin worked on getting administration and legislative leadership to join Pingree at the meetings. House Speaker Stephen Rowe was supportive. But, for the administration, Concannon wanted nothing to do with a prescription drug price control bill (Leinonen 2006). At this point, public pressure to do something about prescription drug prices did not yet appear that it might force the governor's hand. So, efforts to lower drug prices in Maine were going pretty much as they were going in Vermont: advocates for prescription drug access had tapped widespread public indignation, gained the support of a legislative leader in their effort to lower drug prices, and were not getting much help from the governor.

Leinonen

But, in January 2000, a key factor affecting the progress of price control legislation began to play out differently in Maine than it had in Vermont. While the Vermont State Employees Association was on the sidelines of the drug price fight, the MSEA began to put its resources behind Senator Pingree. Marvin had difficulty getting support from Senate President Mark Lawrence, so he got Leinonen involved. He found that some Democrats were worried that they could be blamed for provoking the pharmaceutical industry to retaliate against Maine for a price control bill by refusing to sell medicines to people in the state and that Republican opponents would use the retaliation against them in the 2000 elections. After a discussion with Leinonen making it clear to him that Pingree's bill would be a top priority for MSEA, Lawrence decided to support it and, although skeptical about the chances of a prescription drug price control bill, he agreed to attend some of the town hall meetings.

Once legislative leadership supported the meetings, it was easier to get rank-and-file legislators to attend the meetings and MSEA followed up, arranging for legislators' attendance (Leinonen 2006). The meetings were held in Grange halls and town halls around the state. In the case of a hearing at Presque Isle in far northern Maine, Leinonen got House Speaker Stephen Rowe into a car with him. They drove 350 miles through a snowstorm, spun out, and had to have the Department of Transportation pull the car out of the snow. But they reached the meeting (Leinonen 2006).

MSEA worked on public and media turnout for the town hall meetings. In their announcements, they noted that "all legislators were invited" (Leinonen 2006). These town hall meetings were attended by many seniors as well as members of seniors' support networks like their medical practitioners and family members (Pingree 2000a). At one public hearing, 200 people filled an auditorium. At the meeting, residents told the legislators stories of going without food or heat to pay for their drugs, or cutting back on their medications because they could not afford them (Kesich 2000b).

The meetings were jointly chaired by representatives of MSEA and MCSC. Legislators were there as guests. When local legislators didn't show, their absences were noted in some of the meetings. The public spoke first (Leinonen 2006). Seniors testifying at the meetings were often quite angry about drug prices (Pingree 2001a). Afterwards, often backed by Senate President Lawrence and House Speaker Rowe at the meetings, Pingree would use materials she had gotten from Vermont

Senate President Peter Shumlin to attack the industry's rationales for high prices (Pingree 2000a).

At the meetings in halls around the state, MSEA distributed leaflets saying "tell the president of the Maine Senate, Speaker of the House, and other top legislative leaders how the rising costs of prescription drugs are hurting you" (Maine State Employees Association 2000). Organizers at the meetings also distributed fact sheets with the phone number of the Office of Governor King (Pingree 2000b). Meeting organizers collected the names and phone numbers of those attending. The local press frequently attended and reported on seniors' statements at the meetings and on Pingree's points. The press often presented stories similar to those of Vi Quirion or Lena Sanford described above (Pingree 2001a). In all, there were ten town hall meetings across the state on drug prices, ending with a meeting on 8 March (Page 2000). Marvin and Pingree also got statements of support from both the Roman Catholic Diocese of Portland and the Maine Council of Churches. They convinced grassroots groups like the Dirigo Alliance and Maine People's Alliance to back the price control idea (Marvin 2000).

On 26 January, Pingree and Marvin held a press conference, announcing their plan for a bill to set up a fair drug price board to regulate prices (*Lewiston Sun Journal* 2000). Recalling 1998, Pingree said, "Three years ago we said to the pharmaceutical industry, 'How about you give us a bigger rebate?' They went ballistic and said 'no.' We've asked the drug manufacturers to play nice with us, and it's still not working" (Washuk 2000a). On 1 February, Pingree held another press conference, this time with Senate President Lawrence and MSEA. She cited Rep. Allen's 1998 study comparing Maine and Canadian drug prices. Carl Leinonen spoke and tied price controls to state employee and retiree co-pays, saying that they would save "$10 million overnight."

As momentum for Pingree's proposal was building, some started work to slow it down. Rep. Bruno said some drug companies might refuse to do business in Maine if her idea was adopted. If they carried out this threat, then it was suggested that Mainers might not be able to get essential medicines in-state. From the governor's office, Angus King moved to preempt a drug price bill by Pingree; he appointed a five-member blue ribbon commission to examine health care costs (Carrier 2000a). The commission could be an excellent excuse for legislative inaction in the 2000 session and effectively sidetrack Pingree's proposal.

Northeast Legislators

But Pingree pressed forward. On 8 February, she took a resolution that called on policymakers to "seek and demand fair prescription drug prices for all citizens" to the chambers of the house and senate; both houses adopted it.[4] On 11 February, Pingree could announce her progress to the second meeting of northeastern legislators concerned about prescription drug prices in the Massachusetts statehouse on Boston's Beacon Hill (Washuk 2000c).

In March, another key factor not present in Vermont came into play in the Maine battle for lower drug prices. Whereas state senate leaders in Vermont had to try working with a governor in their own party who had ties to the pharmaceutical industry, senate leaders in Maine did not. That month, the critical difference also began to play out in Pingree's favor. In Pingree's words, the meetings of New England legislators on drug prices made New England governors "nervous" (Pingree 2000b). Although governors usually set the policy agendas for states, New England legislative leaders were threatening to take the initiative on the prescription drug price issue. Thus, Vermont's Governor Dean was prompted to call the mid-February meeting of northern New England governors in Montpelier where they approved an invitation to the Quebec Premier Bouchard to discuss prescription drug prices. But that was all he had to do that month. Under pressure from both Pingree and Lawrence, Governor King had to do something more. In the wake of the Montpelier meeting, he directed his administration's point person on prescription drug prices, Kevin Concannon, to follow up on those tri-state discussions by developing some sort of Maine policy aimed at drug prices (Finnegan 2000).

The stars were aligning in favor of Pingree's effort to contain drug prices. Town hall meetings had produced large numbers of supporters who felt strongly about the issue. Her grassroots support was bolstered by the resources of MSEA. Among other things, it had already helped her to win the support of House Speaker Rowe. She was not particularly beholden to her governor, as he was not of her party, and could publicly challenge him to take strong action on drug prices.

LD 2599

On 3 March, Pingree introduced LD 2599, a prescription drug price control bill that would have penalties for drugmakers who didn't comply with state-mandated prices. Pingree's search for co-authors to build support for the bill had been extraordinarily successful. By the time it came to the joint Health and Human Services Committee hearing on 8 March, LD 2599 had 79 co-authors–including the leaders of both houses (Rowe 2000).[5] Commenting on the bill, House Speaker Rowe said, "LD 2599 is a thoughtful, carefully developed plan for limiting costs of drugs in Maine." Senate President Lawrence added, "it is up to each state to help their citizens . . . by establishing prescription drug prices" (Rowe 2000). Included among the co-authors was Rep. Glenys Lovett (R–Scarborough), lead house Republican on the committee.

Hearings on LD 2599 also showed that Pingree's efforts to neutralize potential opposition had been successful. The Maine Medical Association went on record as "neither for nor against" (MacLean 2000). The Maine Osteopath Association and a national drugstore chain, Rite Aid, were also neutral (Health and Human Services Committee 2000). Not even the Chamber of Commerce backed the industry. The chamber had decided it had other more pressing issues to address such as workers' compensation, taxation, economic development, and environmental regulation (Gore 2001). The only opposition to the bill came from the pharmaceutical industry itself. Representatives of the industry suggested that, the bill "could eliminate particular drugs from the market in Maine" (Kesich 2000c).

The King administration also took a neutral position; but it warned, like the industry, that "there are drugs with a single supplier that might be willing to pull out of this market to avoid setting a precedent. We might find ourselves in the position of only treating some diseases in this state." On the other hand, the administration noted that about 40 percent of people over 65 had six or more drug prescriptions, resulting in an average cost of $355 a month. As pressure from Pingree built, Concannon suggested to the governor that he may need his own proposal on prescription drug prices. That way, he could oppose price controls while appearing to be aggressive on the problem of high drug prices. So, the administration hired a private attorney to review the issue and began serious work on an alternative to LD 2599 (Finnegan 2000). A few days after the hearings, Governor King commented on the bill, "It's a creative idea. The question would be if it is workable. I start with a suspicion of price-fixing" (Kesich 2000b).

Pingree continued to work to build support for LD 2599. Through the campaign's grassroots, she distributed a targeted list of legislators, asking people to call them and urge support of LD 2599. Her flyer also included the governor's phone number in boldface (Pingree 2001b). On 15 March, a guest column by Pingree appeared in the state's main paper, the *Portland Press Herald* (Pingree 2000d). On 24 March, Pingree attended the Manhattan College meeting of northeastern legislators concerned about drug prices. There, she got encouragement from her Vermont counterparts, Senators Shumlin and Rivers (Pingree 2000b).

On 8 April, LD 2599 passed out of the Health and Human Services Committee. Three days later, it passed with veto-proof votes in both the senate (23–9) and the house (102–47). For its next hurdles, the bill needed to clear the joint Appropriations Committee and then, once more with Appropriations Committee amendments, both houses. At the time, the *New York Times* had been looking for a story on the politics of prescription drug prices. The 8 April Maine vote provided it with a news hook for the story and, on 12 April, Pingree and Marvin got a huge break from the *Times*. On its front page, it printed a story on the passage of LD 2599. In the wake of the *Times* story, Pingree's early work with the statehouse reporters of Maine's newspapers paid dividends. Many Maine papers began covering the bill on a daily basis as they would until the end of the legislative session. The coverage often put the bill in a good light with long stories that started on many of the local papers' front pages (Pingree 2001a).

In April, the difference it made to have SEIU's state employees association, the Maine State Employees Association, on the side of prescription drug access advocates became more evident. While the Vermont State Employees Association provided no noticeable support, MSEA threw its grassroots and political resources behind Senator Pingree. Marvin worked to unleash all the manifestations of grassroots pressure for lower drug prices that his organizational base could put before the governor and legislature. MSEA and MCSC organized a phone bank. From desks and phones provided by the groups, volunteers called supporters all over Maine. They used the lists that they had compiled through their 1999 petition drive and their 2000 public meetings on drug prices.

Tapping the indignation seniors were feeling over high prescription drug prices, these phone appeals worked. Members of the legislature then received numerous calls and letters supporting LD 2599 before every key vote thereafter. Seniors' determination could be seen as state retirees and state employees took to the halls of the legislature to make visits to their legislators' capitol offices. For the last three to four weeks of deliberation on LD 2599, ten to twenty grassroots supporters of the bill, conspicuously attired in MSEA-purple shirts and jackets, could regularly be seen in the capitol hallways or meeting rooms (Marvin 2001). Their pressure was noticed. "I know a lot of the elderly in my district and I know we need to do something," said Rep. Stavros Mendros (R–Lewiston) (Kesich 2000a).

Industry Response

Realizing how far the situation had gotten out of its control, PhRMA scrambled its tremendous political power to counterattack this rising threat to the industry's prices and profits. Three private jets flew lobbyists to the Augusta airport; twenty industry lobbyists attended a legislative work session (Cauchon 2000). These lobbyists were conspicuous in the Maine statehouse, sporting expensive suits (Pingree 2001c). Industry lobbyists worked overtime trying to peel away supporters and cut the bill's support to a level that it wouldn't have the two-thirds it would need to override a veto. "There's been a lot of arm-twisting," said Rep. Michael McAlevey (R–Waterboro), one of the Republicans who had supported the bill. Under industry pressure, Rep. Lovett said that week that she had withdrawn support for LD 2599. Instead, she submitted a bill with a $10 million program that would pay residents' prescription drug bills after they each paid the first $1,000 of their drug bills out-of-pocket. Using boilerplate PhRMA arguments, she said, "Our plan provides immediate relief now" (Kesich 2000c).

The industry also put its supporters into play. That week, a group of doctors, biotech backers, and senior citizen groups repeated industry claims that price controls might restrict access to drugs. They also said they threatened jobs in Maine. "If we put price controls on in Maine . . . that puts an onus on companies not to do business in Maine," said Clyde Dyar, economic development director of Fairfield, Maine (Goldberg 2000d). To dramatize the threat of cutting off drugs to Maine, drugmakers sent drug shipments to the Pennsylvania branch of Maine's major wholesale distributor of medications, marked the containers "Maine," and made the wholesaler ship them on to Maine (Pingree 2005). One prescription drug wholesaler in Maine threatened to move (Lazos 2000). The *Portland Press Herald* backed these objections, editorializing that "Maine is too small to go it alone" (Editorial Board 2000b).

LD 2599 opponents prepared more pressure for the end of the month. They planned a press conference featuring the industry and a number of astroturf lobbying groups, including the 60 Plus Association and the Seniors Coalition, both funded by Richard Viguerie, the Illinois-based Kidney Cancer Association, the Washington-based Alliance for Aging Research, and a member of the Biotechnology Association of Maine.[6] At that press conference, they would blast LD 2599, saying it would stifle research, stunt the state's fledgling biotech industry, and harm patients. The groups also bought an advertisement that was placed in the 27 April *Portland Press Herald* urging King to reject the bill (Sharp 2000).

In the midst of all the lobbying, LD 2599 cleared the Appropriations Committee and, on 14 April, the bill passed both houses the second time. But, in less than one week, PhRMA pressure had been effective in peeling off thirteen of the 8 April house supporters of the bill and the second house vote was 89-54. LD 2599 went to the governor without its veto-proof two-thirds' majority (Quinn 2000c).

Public Support to the Rescue

On 20 April, the local press gave price control advocates a big break. The *Maine Times*, an alternative weekly newspaper, published results of a statewide survey that showed that prescription drug costs were a critical problem for many people in Maine and, surprisingly, that there was overwhelming public support for price controls. [7] On the gravity of the prescription drug price problem, Table 4-1 shows the poll's results.

Table 4-1
Finding Cost of Prescription Drugs Is a Hardship

Annual Income	Percent of Maine Households
Under $10,000	42%
Between $10,000 and $20,000	38%
Between $20,000 and $30,000	35%
Between $30,000 and $40,000	23%

Source: Market Decisions 2000

The poll also underscored popular support for state policies containing prescription drug prices with a poll. When asked if the state should negotiate drug prices in cooperation with other New England states, 92 percent agreed. Did they favor the state's setting a maximum for drug prices through a state agency? An overwhelming 72 percent said "yes" (Market Decisions 2000). The poll showed that the ingredients for building public support for a policy to address a critical economic problem had come together in the case of LD 2599. To begin with, the problem it addressed, high prescription drug prices, was a critical hardship for many in Maine or their loved ones. Also, it showed that Mainers thought that the state government could do something about it.

April's developments demonstrated that Pingree and Marvin's campaign to corner the governor on the prescription drug issue was working. As Pingree put it, the *New York Times* article and the constant ringing of phones in the governor's office generated by the MSEA phone bank and by leaflets handed out at their town meetings "helped the governor to decide." The *Maine Times* poll further pressed him not to veto the bill. In the end, King decided that he didn't want to read a headline like "King kills drug bill, Seniors lose hope" (Pingree 2000b). It was time to bring out the alternative to LD 2599 that his administration was preparing.

On 28 April, Governor King announced that he would negotiate with Pingree. He said that he would veto LD 2599 as it was written, but that he was interested in fashioning some prescription drug price control effort with "teeth," that is, consequences for drugmakers who couldn't reach an agreement with the state on drug prices. As King was talking about taking state action against overcharging drugmakers, Pingree recalled the bill from the governor's desk, opening the King–Pingree negotiations.

King–Pingree Negotiations

With the legislative session set to end 11 May, talks began on 1 May. The first political issue that had to be addressed was the position of the state's pharmacies. The pharmaceutical industry had powerful leverage it could use on the national drugstore chains, as the chains had to negotiate the wholesale prices they paid with the drugmakers. If a national chain did not oppose Pingree's bill, it might see its wholesale prices sharply rising. So, some national chains were part of the group pressuring King to block the bill (Pingree 2000b).

On the other hand, drugmakers already charged the independents higher wholesale prices than the national chains. At the national level a few years earlier, these wholesale price differentials had led to a lawsuit of independent pharmacies against twenty-two drugmakers for price discrimination.[8] So, independents had less incentive to support drugmakers than the national chains did. Many independent pharmacies were marginal businesses and highly sensitive to wholesale prices drugmakers were charging them. In Maine, for example, high wholesale prices had left independent drugstores with an average net revenue of about $60,000 to $70,000 a year, leaving many owners with minimal profits (Pingree 2000b). If Pingree's bill were amended to increase what the state paid drugstores for their services through programs like Medicaid, independents might come out ahead if the bill were enacted.

Pingree and King acted on this opportunity to get the independent pharmacies on their side. The Maine independent pharmacies were represented by a lobbyist separate from the chains and were not as likely to side with them. Also, the pharmacies' Medicaid fees from the state, a significant part of pharmacy revenue, had not been increased since 1982 and they were long overdue for a raise (Pingree 2000b). The governor invited Rep. Bruno into the negotiations. This was a good opportunity for Bruno to address the Medicaid fee issue on behalf of the independent pharmacies. He accepted the governor's invitation and joined the negotiations.

Bruno and Pingree met with pharmacists and their lobbyists (both national chain and independents). Pingree told the pharmacists that she wanted to treat them as "benevolent players." She indicated that she would support increased Medicaid dispensing fees to show them her good faith (Pingree 2001a). With her promised support for increased dispensing fees, Pingree was successful at separating the pharmacies from the drug companies. They did not become opponents as they had in Vermont (Marvin 2001). So, the pharmacies were in the room where the negotiations took place. On the other hand, likely opponents to the bill and their allies were excluded from the talks, as they would be prone to impede them. So, representatives from the drugmakers were left out in the hallways (Pingree 2001a). Also not taking part in the talks were representatives from the Chamber of Commerce (Gore 2001).

In negotiations, Pingree made it plain that she would not let the governor off the hook: despite his stated suspicion of price caps, there would be no deal without them. Concannon also believed that the threat of price controls could be useful in negotiations with drug companies. However, as the negotiators were not sure they were ready for price controls, some interim stick was necessary (Marvin 2000). At this point, Concannon introduced the administration's alternative plan and took a major step away from Vermont's idea of containing drug prices with price controls. He proposed a policy of containing drug prices through a market mechanism. He took part of the method that Medicaid uses for getting lower drug prices. As described in Chapter 2, one of the ways that Medicaid programs get lower prices is by using its large group purchasing power. A program does so by setting up a preferred drug list (PDL), a list of drugs for which it will pay without requiring prior authorization (PA). Because obtaining PA requires additional documentation from prescribers, it discourages them from prescribing drugs needing PA and lowers the sales of those drugs.[9] In order the get on a PDL, drugmakers often offer Medicaid programs supplemental rebates or lower prices.

Concannon proposed using Maine's Medicaid purchasing power to get lower drug prices for Maine residents not on Medicaid. If a drugmaker would not give these residents lower prices, then Maine Medicaid would require PA for drugs purchased for people on Medicaid. He proposed using this step as an interim stick for getting lower drug prices for Mainers who were not on Medicaid (Pingree 2001b). He proposed that, if using Medicaid purchasing power didn't work, then the state would be empowered to impose price controls. At first, others in the room were unsure about his proposal (Dow 2005). Pingree didn't like PA, as attorneys representing people on Medicaid objected to it on the grounds that it restricted their clients' access to medicines; but she decided that, because industry was known to hate it, it could be useful in bargaining for lower prices (Pingree 2000b). Eventually, Concannon won everyone over to his proposal for first trying the threat of Medicaid PA for seeking prescription drugs discounts for non-Medicaid Mainers (Dow 2005).

With a nonregulatory "stick" selected, King and Pingree agreed that, if it didn't produce prices comparable to those of the Federal Supply Schedule or Canada, then Pingree's price controls would be implemented. Thus, they had developed a two-part plan to get drug discounts: the first would focus on using the threat of Medicaid prior authorization to negotiate discounts for non-Medicaid Mainers; the second would be price controls, if the prior authorization threat didn't work. The die of the pharmaceutical industry's policy defeat was cast. Negotiators then worked on the details of the compromise. They would call the program through which Maine residents could get lower drug prices "Maine Rx." Planners thought that they could get discounts about 30 percent below average wholesale price (AWP) for patented drugs (Finnegan 2000). They thought Maine Rx would be able to get these discounts across the board from manufacturers who would offer discounts to get on the PDL (Orbeton 2000).

The Maine Rx bill included a provision making "profiteering" grounds for suing drugmakers. Those suing could use the discovery process to find out how much manufacturers pay for production of drugs and what their profit margins are for each (Lazos 2000). Previously, this information had been very difficult for the state to obtain. With it, state negotiators could more precisely negotiate discounts. At the same time, they could also publicize information on drugmakers' profit margins, if they were inordinate, and keep the pressure on lawmakers to support Maine Rx (Pingree 2001b).

Enrollment of Mainers in the Maine Rx program would use state programs like Cub-care[10] and the facilities of physician offices, hospitals, pharmacies, and schools. There, Mainers could fill out enrollment forms for forwarding to state officials Then, enrolled Mainers could get discounts cards with which they could obtain medicines for the prices Maine Rx had negotiated for its enrollees. For independent pharmacies, participating in Maine Rx could give them a potential way to better compete with national chain stores (Orbeton 2000). Planners estimated that 325,000 Maine residents would be eligible.

Also for pharmacies, the Medicaid dispensing fee was raised from $3.35 to $6.35 per prescription. Pharmacies would be able to access this increase quickly as Maine employed an electronic reimbursement system for pharmacies (Finnegan 2000). In addition, for each prescription filled for Maine Rx, pharmacies would get an additional $3.00 (Holzman 2000). While both independent and national chain drugstores would get the Medicaid increase and the new Maine Rx fee, the bump in state payments would be more critical to the independents as they operated with slimmer margins.

Maine Rx

Pingree wanted the plan released when there would only be one day left in the legislature's session. That way, the industry would have little time to work the legislature's floor (Pingree 2000b). She had seen in April how quickly its lobbyists could change votes. Her proposed timing was adopted. On 10 May, King and Pingree announced their two-part plan. "This is not price-fixing," King said, "this is negotiation." Pingree expressed optimism that having the state use its Medicaid prior authorization authority to lower prescription drug prices would avoid the necessity of imposing maximums on prices. According to Pingree, the plan was designed to let the state, "use our power as a purchaser . . . to get best discounts." On price controls, she said, "We've tried to give it plenty of time so that hopefully we'll never get to that point" (Quinn 2000a).

With enactment virtually ensured, Rep. Thomas Murphy (R–Kennebunk), house minority leader, joined in support of the King–Pingree deal. He said he had previously objected because of constitutional issues such as the commerce clause and the cost of hiring state employees to implement the program. Rep. Lovett, lead house

Republican on the Health and Human Services Committee who had said she wanted quick relief from high drug prices, once again supported Pingree's bill (Murphy 2000). Both said that amendments to the bill arising from the negotiations had addressed their earlier concerns. Pulling all stops, John Marvin kept up the grassroots pressure supporting the bill, calling for a "veto day" demonstration at the statehouse to make sure it was not a veto day for LD 2599 and that the governor signed it (Consumers for Affordable Health Care 2000).

As momentum built for a legislative vote on 11 May, leaders continued to express support. Governor King touted the compromise, "if the companies don't come to the table and work with us in good faith, then there are, in fact, teeth." Speaker Rowe added, "I think we're finally standing up and saying we're not going to take it anymore." Earlier critics of the bill continued to come on board. According to Rep. Gerald Davis (R–Falmouth), who voted against the first drug bill, "to vote against this is to vote against motherhood" (Carrier 2000b). Recognizing that their constituents could hold them accountable if they did not support LD 2599, Republicans continued to embrace the bill. Sen. Jane Amaro (R–Cape Elizabeth), who had said an earlier version of the bill did not provide relief soon enough, said it was a "good beginning" (Washuk 2000b). "Sometimes in life you just need to stand up and wave around a 2-by-4 to get someone's attention," said House Minority Leader Murphy. John Benoit (R–Rangeley) explained, "I am voting in favor of it because my constituents' agenda reads that way" (Quinn 2000b). A *Portland Press Herald* editorial chimed in, "lawmakers should proudly vote in favor of the revamped bill and make Maine a leader in the effort to make prescription drugs affordable to all" (Editorial Board 2000a).

Fighting back, the industry ran full-page ads in Maine's largest daily papers. The ads employed some of the standard PhRMA scare tactics. For example, they claimed that bureaucrats could decide on what doctors could prescribe and that patients would be forced to take less-effective medicines (Higgins 2000). In the *Bangor Daily News*, a full-page ad featuring a Maine resident said, "she'll have to wait." The ad asserted that, if there were price controls, Maine residents would have to wait for new wonder drugs because price cuts would mean cuts in drug research funding, and asked readers to call on their state legislator to vote against LD 2599 (PhRMA 2000).

On 11 May, the senate passed LD 2599, 30-0. The house vote was 133-12 and Governor King signed the bill on the same day. "If the industry can consolidate and increase its market power, so can we," the governor said (Goldberg 2000c). The industry fulminated. Alan Holmer, president of PhRMA said, "Maine has become the most antibusiness state in the US" (Goldberg 2000c). Gabrielle Williams of PhRMA charged that "you have politicians deciding which drugs patients have" and that "it's like all they're concerned about is costs instead of quality" (Quinn 2000b). She called LD 2599 "the worst piece of legislation I've ever seen" (Galewitz 2000).

The elements necessary for beating the pharmaceutical industry that were missing in Vermont were present in Maine. While Vermont legislators pushing a policy to lower prescription drug prices could not aggressively push a governor of their own party, Senator Pingree was free to force her governor to support price controls. As Vermont legislators waited in vain for grassroots support for their efforts, the Maine State Employees Association came through for Pingree. Maine had not only voters outraged over the price of medicines and legislative leaders determined to do something about it; it had the political opening for beating PhRMA and resources to take advantage of that opening also.

PhRMA v. Concannon

The pharmaceutical industry has fought prescription drug policymaking in Maine ever since 2000, but Maine would long be in the ranks of states that generate new proposals to improve prescription drug access. After Concannon's June presentation at the scenic college campus in South Portland, the industry quickly went to federal district court and, on 26 October, won a preliminary injunction against implementing Maine Rx. The court found that Maine Rx was unconstitutional as it regulates out-of-state commerce and the US Constitution prohibits states from undertaking such regulation. Further, the court found that Maine Rx violated Medicaid law in that it would use Medicaid purchasing power in a way that would sacrifice the well-being of Medicaid beneficiaries for people not on Medicaid. It argued that applying prior authorization requirements on drugs for a Medicaid patient to save money for people not on Medicaid could deny the patient a necessary drug at no benefit to the Medicaid program that covered her. The state was not allowed to impose prior authorization requirements on Medicaid drugs in order to support the Maine Rx program (National Governors Association 2001). Maine appealed the district court ruling against the Maine Rx law to the US Court of Appeals for the First Circuit.

On 16 May 2001, the higher court found that Maine Rx did not interfere with regulatory conduct in other states and only regulates in-state activities. On the matter of the law's impact on Medicaid beneficiaries, the court found that Maine Rx's use of PA could be done in such a way that it would not deny them necessary medicines. Consequently, it reversed the district court ruling on the use of prior authorization and found that Maine Rx could use it as a stick in negotiating for Maine Rx with drugmakers (National Governors Association 2001; Weinstein 2001). But the Court of Appeals left the stay against Maine Rx in place until the US Supreme Court could consider the case if PhRMA appealed and PhRMA did so.[11]

While awaiting court action on the authority of Maine Rx to use Medicaid purchasing power to lower drug prices for Mainers not on Medicaid, Kevin Concannon's Department of Human Services set up a program to use that purchasing power to obtain lower drug prices for Mainers on Medicaid. The department instituted the use of prior authorization for its Medicaid program in 2001. In 2003, it began to negotiate supplemental rebates for Medicaid from drugmakers, exchanging waivers from the prior authorization program for the rebates. As a result, the per-user-per-year (PUPY) prescription drug cost inflation for its Medicaid program dropped sharply afterward and has remained at substantially lower levels ever since (Clair 2009).

The US Supreme Court took the Maine Rx case on 28 June 2002. There, Maine made a contribution to the prescription drug price issue as important as its development of the market-based approach to high prices. On 19 May 2003, Maine won at the US Supreme Court: Maine Rx was ruled constitutional and legal for states to use Medicaid leverage to lower prescription drug prices for people not on Medicaid. By a vote of 6-3, the court upheld the Court of Appeals and lifted the injunction on the use of prior authorization (California Healthline 2003). Maine had convinced the US Supreme Court that using Medicaid PA to make it easier for Mainers not on Medicaid to afford medicines could help the state's Medicaid program by keeping some people nearly eligible for Medicaid from becoming ill and poor enough to qualify for Medicaid. That way it would save the program money and leave more for its current beneficiaries (Castellblanch 2006). In their decision, the judges noted that Maine Rx would not necessarily undermine Medicaid, as it would help preserve the health of residents who lack insurance and keep them off the program. The dissenting opinions expressed concern about the possible burden that the PA requirement would place on Medicaid patients and providers; but, since Maine Rx hadn't started, there was no evidence to support those fears (Suarez 2003). Maine's victory in the US Supreme Court opened the door for all states to use Medicaid leverage to negotiate lower prescription drug prices for non-Medicaid residents.

The strongest prescription drug purchasing power that states possessed could now be used for broad numbers of residents.

Maine Rx Plus

On 13 June 2003, Maine enacted Maine Rx Plus to amend Maine Rx in conformity with the US Supreme Court decision and comments on the case. Specifically, the law allows the state to impose prior authorization in Medicaid "in order to encourage manufacturer . . . participation" in Maine Rx Plus. Taking into consideration court comments that the use of Medicaid PA must serve the interests of Medicaid, the legislature narrowed eligibility for discounts to those who would be more likely to need Medicaid if they got sick, and Maine Rx Plus was designed to cover 275,000 Mainers. On 13 January 2004, Maine was to launch the Maine Rx Plus program.

But the 2002 election meant changes for a number of the actors involved in Maine Rx. Angus King was succeeded as governor by John Baldacci (D), whose attitude toward the pharmaceutical industry was to turn out to be less combative. Kevin Concannon left shortly after Baldacci's election in 2002 and became Iowa's director of human services under Governor Tom Vilsack. Chellie Pingree also left the state; after unsuccessfully challenging Susan Collins (R) for the US Senate, she moved to Washington, DC., to be director of Common Cause.

Baldacci's administration decided that if PA authority were to be used on behalf of non-Medicaid populations, then they had to amend the state Medicaid plan to permit it, which required approval from the federal Center for Medicare and Medicaid Services (CMS). Steven Rowe, former house speaker and then state attorney general, didn't think Maine needed to amend its plan and go to CMS to use its PA authority on behalf of the Maine Rx Plus population. Rowe said that Maine's Supreme Court victory had "cleared the forest" of pharmaceutical maker legal challenges to using Medicaid PA for discount card programs (Castellblanch 2006). One explanation of Baldacci's reticence to take on the industry may be the heavy support Baldacci received from the Democratic Governors' Association. For the 2006 election when Baldacci ran for reelection, the DGA's #3 contributor was Pfizer; many other major drugmakers also contributed to the DGA (Center for Public Integrity 2006).

Under Baldacci, Maine did not exercise its hard-won right to use Medicaid purchasing power to lower prescription drug prices for people not on Medicaid. Instead, consistent with the governor's inclination, the person Baldacci put in charge of using Medicaid leverage to lower prescription drug prices has focused on such issues as the state's Medicaid budget problems instead of people who might become eligible for Medicaid if they couldn't afford medicines and got sick as a result.

Challenging Baldacci's setting aside of the hard-won right to use Medicaid leverage to lower drug prices would be difficult for the state legislature's contemporary Democratic leaders. Because they were in the same party, the leaders needed Baldacci both for campaign support and for support for their other pieces of legislation. As in Vermont, a one-party state government has made it easier to constrain legislative Democrats on issues like prescription drug prices.

Postscript

In 2008, Tom Allen gave up his US House seat to challenge Susan Collins for the US Senate and lost. Pingree returned to Maine, won Allen's congressional seat, and moved back to Washington. In 2009, Kevin Concannon also moved to Washington, DC. As his boss, Tom Vilsack, was appointed secretary of agriculture by President Obama, Concannon was appointed under secretary for food, nutrition, and consumer services. Joseph Bruno briefly was the chair of the Maine Republican Party.

As Chapter 5 shows, the work of Pingree, Marvin, Rowe, Concannon, Allen, and many others left the Maine legislature with a political culture that is particularly favorable for winning better access to medicines. As political developments and new ideas opened up opportunities for states to improve access in the next decade, Maine would be among the first states to take advantage.

Most importantly, Maine Rx elevated the battle for prescription drug access across the United States. Maine Rx has become an example for prescription drug access advocates from coast to coast (and Hawaii). Maine Rx showed that a state has the authority to use a market approach for lowering prescription drug prices for non-Medicaid populations. It inspired many other states to take up the idea of using Medicaid purchasing power to lower drug prices for the rest of the 2000s. As the next chapter also shows, it started a wave that pushed Congress to enact a sweeping reform that the industry hoped would stem the tide of demands for lower prices and got the federal government engaged in the issue. For the pharmaceutical industry, its worst-case scenario became the possibility that "as goes Maine, so goes the nation."

---

[1] To be eligible in 2000, single seniors needed an annual income less than $15,244; couples needed incomes below $20,461. The medicines it covered were for chronic diseases such as diabetes and heart disease (Pingree 2000c).

[2] MSEA officials had learned to use petitions in the 1991 workers' compensation battle as a technique for testing messages and sounding the opinions of members (Leinonen 2006).

[3] In other states, chapters of the National Council of Senior Citizens were more oriented toward lobbying on federal issues (Marvin 2000).

[4] Unlike a legislative bill, a resolution does not require a governor's signature to be successful.

[5] The Maine legislature uses joint committees of each house to hear bills rather than separate committees in each house.

[6] Drugs developed by the biotechnology industry were to generate its most explosive prices. Although they might not be affordable for large parts of the population, those who could afford them could be charged extremely high prices, even for medicines (Anand 2005). Some of these drugs could be blockbusters, if their prices were not controlled.

[7] The study was conducted by Market Decisions among 401 randomly chosen Maine residents. The sampling error associated with the survey was plus or minus 5%. The results were considered representative of Maine as a whole (Market Decisions 2000).

[8] The suit had resulted in a $408 million settlement. Although, divided amongst the plaintiffs ($5,000 per pharmacy, paid out over three years with no interest), the settlement did little to help them, it did show that independents were being charged higher wholesale prices (Rankin 1996).

[9] Concannon later observed that Medicaid prior authorization typically reduced sales by around 60 percent (Holzman 2000).

[10] Cub-care is Maine's federally subsidized health insurance program for children from low-income families who were not eligible for Medicaid.

[11] While he saw the US Court of Appeals for the First Circuit uphold the use of Medicaid purchasing power to lower the price of medicines for people not on Medicaid, John Marvin did not live to see the US Supreme Court's action. On 13 November 2001, he died. But, even if John Marvin's name fades with time, his work for government action on access to medicines will endure. In the end, advocates for the public interest can't ask for more.

5

PhRMA Tries Stopping State Action

In the wake of Maine Rx, the industry vigorously tried to head off state legislation on prescription drug access across the country. This chapter describes how PhRMA intensified its campaign to beat down the legislative action after 2000 and how state political leaders fought on anyway. It shows how PhRMA, then, used political power at the federal level to try preempting the states and how the industry maintained the extraordinary profits underpinning its political strength.[1] Finally, it shows how state legislators continued fighting even after PhRMA had won a congressional act meant to stop them. Events described below show that advocates for access to medicines can maintain traction in the political process even as a great economic power attempts to derail it.

PhRMA Political Spending in the Early 2000s

At the federal and state levels, the industry in the early 2000s went on a political spending spree that was second to that of no other industry. From 1998 to 2005, the pharmaceutical and health products industry spent more than $800 million for lobbying and campaign donations at the two levels, a Center for Public Integrity investigation found (Ismail 2005). At the national level, it would support 1,274 Washington lobbyists by 2005—more than two for every member of Congress (Drinkard 2005). At the level of the executive branch, the top federal recipient of pharmaceutical industry contributions in both 2000 and 2004 was George W. Bush (opensecrets.org 2004).

At the state level, PhRMA tried to choke the possibility of states following the Maine and Vermont challenges to its profits with an epic barrage of campaign contributions.

Table 5-1
Campaign Contributions to State Candidates

Election Cycle	1998	2000	2002
Dollars	$2,612,000	$4,366,000	$6,258,000

Source: Richards 2003

Pharmaceutical industry lobbying at the state level intensified concurrently; but the rise in industry lobbying at the state level cannot be easily measured because of the lack of uniform state disclosure requirements for expenditures (Ismail 2005). Still, given that lobbying got the lion's share of industry political money at the federal level, it is likely that contribution numbers only at the state level represent less than half of their political spending in the states.

Post-Maine Rx State and Local Legislation

Still, state legislators around the United States, spurred by events like those in Maine, continued raising hell for the industry. In New England, prescription drug access advocates tried new tactics as the Maine Rx lawsuit was pending. As mentioned in Chapter 3, in 2002, Vermont turned the focus on how industry detailers used gifts, fees, payments, subsidies, or other incentives to get physicians to prescribe their products. Senate President Shumlin introduced a bill that included provisions that would require pharmaceutical companies to disclose their gifts and cash payments of $25 value or more to doctors, hospitals, and other health care providers. If the reports showed excessive influence on physicians, then state legislators would be in a position to further crack down on detailers' use of gifts. The bill passed and was signed by Governor Dean, making it the first in the nation to address this issue (Peterson 2002).

The next year in Maine, a generation of legislative leaders succeeded Senator Pingree and Speaker Rowe. At their head was Senator Sharon Treat (D Hallowell), a native New Englander trained at Georgetown Law School who had specialized in environmental law. After Pingree had left the state senate, Treat had succeeded her as senate majority leader. Under Treat, advocates focused on the efforts of the pharmaceutical industry to undermine the ability of pharmacy benefit managers (PBMs) to lower drug prices. While PBMs advertised that they are getting lower prices for the health plans that hire them, it wasn't necessarily so. If they could make deals with drugmakers that promoted higher-priced drugs and the health plans could not see these deals, PBMs could raise their profits.

Not only were some PBMs making deals with drugmakers to put more expensive drugs on their formularies, they were taking advantage of the plans they represented in another way. In the process of billing their plans and paying pharmacies for the prescriptions, the PBMs made a "spread" or positive difference between what was billed to the plan and paid to the pharmacy. The PBMs got to keep the spreads. In extreme cases, one study found that there were spreads of over $200 on single prescriptions. Overall, the study found that the spreads averaged $2 to $4 per prescription (Garis et al. 2006). To maintain the confidence of their clients and to keep them from knowing about deals with drugmakers and excessive spreads, PBMs could make their arrangements with drugmakers and pharmacies hard for the plans they represented to see. So, rather than containing private group purchasers' pharmaceutical costs, some PBMs were using methods unknown to many of the plans they represent to drive them up.

In June 2003, Treat successfully promoted a bill, LD 554, that would increase the transparency of the arrangement PBMs make to the plans they represent. LD 554 required PBMs to provide greater transparency to their plans and established that PBMs had a fiduciary responsibility to them (Brierton 2004). PBMs challenged this law in federal court; but the suit was dismissed on 13 April 2005 (*Kaiser Daily Health Policy Report* 2005). After her 2003 effort, Treat was soon to become a national leader of state legislators challenging PhRMA. In 2004, she replaced Cheryl Rivers as the director of the National Legislative Association on Prescription Drug Prices.[2]

On the other side of the country, advocates for lower drug costs looked to an approach used in Oregon to try lowering health care costs. Under Governor John Kitzhaber (D) in the 1990s, Oregon's Medicaid program was distinguished among states by an attempt to focus Medicaid spending on effective treatments (Oregon Office of Medical Assistance Programs 2006). In the early nineties, his administration had ranked medical procedures by effectiveness and drawn a line in the rankings so that Oregon Medicaid would not pay for procedures below that line. The efforts drew strong criticism from many corners, including the charge of "rationing."

But Kitzhaber's effort continued, linking up with the research on evidence-based health care (EBHC), well known in much of the English-speaking medical research world. EBHC uses the highest standards of scientific inquiry to assess the effectiveness and safety of medical care practices. To this end, researchers free from health care industry control systematically identify and review the best available literature on a medical condition of concern and then, based on the literature, develop a consensus on the best medical care for that condition. For this work, researchers receive funds from a number of sources; in the United States, the Agency for Healthcare Research and Quality (AHRQ) has been supporting it since 1997. In practice, EBHC can be misused. For-profit insurers can use it to deny promising, if unproven, treatments. On the other hand, when put in the service of public health, it can be used to prudently allocate resources to medical care found to be most effective.

In 2001, Kitzhaber applied the concept of EBHC to prescription drugs, collaborating with researchers at Oregon Health and Science University (OHSU), the state's health and research university. At OHSU, an AHRQ–designated Evidence-based Practice Center began conducting comparative effectiveness research (CER) on several therapeutic drug classes for the Oregon Medicaid program. This research summarized the highest quality scientific research on drugs within therapeutic classes to identify which of them were the safest and most effective. Along with those in Oregon, Medicaid officials in Idaho and Washington State soon began drawing upon CER produced by the Evidence-based Practice Center in designing their drug formularies. In 2003, Kitzhaber, who left office that year, created the Center for Evidence-based Policy within OHSU to oversee the newly created Drug Effectiveness Review Project (DERP) that produces reports based on CER on many widely used drug classes (Neumann 2006). Despite harassment from the pharmaceutical industry, DERP has continued operations ever since.

Around the country, another approach that was tried for obtaining savings was taking advantage of the price differences shown in the comparisons between US and Canadian drugs. State and local government looked to foster importation of medicines from countries like Canada. In the Midwest, Kevin Concannon, then director of the State Human Services Department, considered paying Iowa pharmacies a $10 transaction fee to buy drugs from an approved Canadian wholesaler (Belluck 2003). Minnesota Governor Tim Pawlenty (R) directed his Department of Human Services to review the feasibility of buying prescription medicine from Canada (Minnesota Department of Human Services 2004). Illinois announced it was studying the purchase of Canadian medications for its state employees and retirees (Belluck 2003).

But the biggest early decade efforts to lower drug prices came in Ohio and Hawaii. In those two states, prescription drug access advocates worked to adopt the Maine Rx approach of using Medicaid purchasing power to lower drug prices for residents. In 2002, the Ohio AFL-CIO and senior citizen groups launched a signature-gathering campaign that obtained enough signatures to put on the state ballot an initiative that could have effectively organized the state's purchasing power to lower drug prices (Kaufman 2002). To beat down this effort, the industry was estimated to have spent $1 million in legal fees for a court challenge of the signatures. Further, the industry was prepared to spend $16 million to fight the initiative, if it did go to the ballot (Rivers 2003). But the measure never got that far: the labor and senior groups supporting it backed down. Instead, in 2003, they supported the enactment of a law establishing a pharmaceutical assistance program. However, the discounts it provided for medicines were rather small and 90 percent of them were subsidized by drugstores (Castellblanch 2005). It, therefore, did not come at much cost to drugmakers as the industry turned back the use of Medicaid purchasing power to lower prices.

In Hawaii in 2002, the state's most powerful union, the International Longshore and Warehouse Union, made adoption of the Maine Rx approach of using Medicaid purchasing power to lower drug prices for residents a top legislative priority (Voice of the ILWU 2002). Rep. Roy Takumi (D–Honolulu) authored HB 2834, a bill that would do that and it was enacted (Oshiro 2002). But implementation was delayed while the Maine Rx case worked its way through the US court system (Daranciang 2004). By the time the *Maine Rx* case was decided, Hawaii had a Republican governor, Linda Lingle. Lingle then decided that using purchasing power to lower drug prices was optional and refused to do so (Geller 2006). While the adoption of the Maine Rx approach of using Medicaid purchasing power only was enacted in Hawaii prior to 2006, political leaders in other states backed bills to accomplish the same goal. According to the Institute on Money in State Politics, in 2003, bills using the Maine Rx model were introduced in at least eighteen states.[3]

PhRMA's Turn to Congress

As serious state challenges to PhRMA proliferated, it worked hard to get the federal government to enact a law that would effectively preempt the state action on the costs of prescription drugs. Fortunately for the industry, it was well connected at the federal level, with both the House of Representatives and the White House in the hands of PhRMA-friendly Republicans. In 2001, during the 107th Congress, drugmaker lobbyists had begun pushing Republicans for a federal law that would suit the industry. While both parties were calling for prescription drug coverage for Medicare, Democrats wanted it offered by a public plan— an idea PhRMA opposed. A public plan could give the government strong purchasing power for lowering prices. The Republicans, on the other hand, wanted the coverage to be provided by private insurers (Pear 2002). If only private insurers were negotiating with drugmakers, PhRMA had no fear that there would be substantially lowered prices; so, the industry supported the Republican approach. The Republican House twice passed bills to provide private drug coverage for seniors, but both died in the Senate, which was in Democratic hands in 2001 and 2002.

To support the Republican bills, PhRMA initiated astroturf lobbying. In 2002, when House Speaker Dennis Hastert (R–IL) spoke on the capitol steps for the Republican proposal, a small group of United Seniors Association members sporting red, white, and blue clothing gathered to cheer his speech and the plan. But the group was more than just some folks posing on the capitol steps; it was another Richard Viguerie-backed group. During the 107th Congress (2001-2002), they ran a $9.6 million campaign focusing on Medicare prescription drug issues. In August 2001, USA's first set of TV ads on Medicare drug benefit issues began with a $3 million ad buy in nineteen congressional districts. In 2002, USA ran a $4.6 million TV ad campaign in May and June to coincide with Republican House leaders' push for legislative action on a Medicare drug bill. In early July 2002, it made a $2 million ad buy that thanked twenty-nine representatives for supporting the House GOP prescription drug bill. PhRMA admitted to funding much, if not all, of the $4.6 million ad buy in May and June through an "unrestricted educational grant" (Benore, et al. 2002).

With the help of PhRMA and groups like USA, Republicans got control of both houses of Congress in 2003. They proceeded to introduce a version of their earlier House bill, as part of the Medicare Modernization Act of 2003. The main provision of the act established a federal prescription drug program for Medicare that was called Part D and was to be run by private insurers.

The act would authorize hundreds of billions of federal dollars with which the federal government could have run the program and negotiated steep discounts in the prices Medicare paid for medicines, as it has for Medicaid, the Veteran's Administration, and federally qualified health centers. But the industry headed off public administration of Part D by showering Congress with campaign contributions and spending millions of dollars on highly paid lobbyists who swarmed Capitol Hill while the bill was being considered.

Infamously, they offered a $2 million a year lobbying job to a principal author of the bill, Rep. Billy Tauzin (R–LA), while he was moving the proposal through his committee.[4] At the same time, a drugmaker lobbying firm offered Thomas Scully, a lead executive branch official working on the bill, a lucrative health care job. Scully obtained a waiver from the ethics officer of the Bush administration's Department of Health and Human Services so that he could negotiate with potential employers while he helped write the Medicare law (Common Cause 2004).

To make sure that the private insurers that would administer Part D had no help from the federal government in obtaining discounts, the industry got Congress to insert a "nonintervention" clause in Part D. That clause forbad the federal government from using its purchasing power to negotiate lower prices for medicines on behalf of the private insurers running the program. Instead, drugs purchased under Part D would be paid for at the generally higher rates obtained by private insurers on their own. With the enactment of Part D, the industry gained this windfall as it tried to preempt state action on access to medicines.

Thus, Medicare's capacity to improve seniors' access to medicines was impaired by excess costs. The resulting limitations in Part D's coverage are best illustrated by its "doughnut hole," that is, a coverage gap between two amounts of an individual's annual drug costs. For example, in 2006, Part D plans generally failed to cover prescription drugs for a senior after her annual drug costs exceeded $2,251 and before they reached $5,100. After annual costs exceeded $5,100, her costs were, again, covered. Costs between $2,252 and $5,099 in this example fell into the doughnut hole and the senior had to pay them out-of-pocket, if she had adequate funds. It was estimated that 7 million people would fall into the hole during the first year (Cruz and Hickey 2006). The government was supposed to offer a subsidy to low-income beneficiaries to help pay for some of the costs not covered by Part D, but a survey of seniors in 2006 showed that, of the 4.7 million eligible for the assistance, 3.4 million were not getting it. Lack of awareness about the low-income subsidy, especially in communities of color, appears to explain this widespread failure to obtain it (Neuman, et al. 2007).

So, Part D still left many seniors and people with disabilities without prescription drugs. One indicator of people not getting needed medicines is the percentage not filling or delaying filling prescriptions. A survey of seniors found that Part D did little to change that percentage. While 23 percent of seniors without Part D coverage did not fill or delayed filling a prescription, 20 percent of seniors with Part D coverage also did not fill or delayed filling a prescription (Neuman et al. 2007).

While doing poorly at restraining drug prices and increasing access, Part D contained one more bonanza for the industry. It cut back one way that the US government program had contained drug costs: Medicaid prescription drug price discounts. Up until when Part D went into effect, people who were qualified for both Medicare and Medicaid (dual eligibles) had their medicines paid for by the government's Medicaid program, at the Medicaid price for drugs. Under Part D, the government pays private Part D plans to buy drugs for dual eligibles, but at the private plans' higher prices. So, the government's money for dual eligibles' drugs doesn't go as far as it did before Part D. Some estimate this change in prices to have increased industry profits by $2 billion or more in 2006 alone (Freudenheim 2006).

Overall, Part D has paid off magnificently for the industry. In addition to the windfall it received from moving dual eligibles to Part D, first-year pharmaceutical industry profits due to the "nonintervention" clause that forbad the federal government's use of Medicare's purchasing power were estimated to exceed $7 billion (Baker 2006). During the first year Part D was in effect, US prescription drug sales jumped an unusually high 8.3 percent (Agovino 2007).

Meanwhile, the industry's investment in the Bush campaigns seemed to pay off in other ways as the administration stepped up efforts to scare US residents out of buying lower-priced medicines from countries like Canada. The *Boston Globe* reported that the Department of Homeland Security seized some medicines seniors were legally importing by mail and sent them letters accompanied by a flyer featuring a snake coiled around a drug bottle. The notice stated that their medications had been seized because "virtually all" drugs imported by individuals into the United States are unapproved for consumption here or are dispensed without a valid prescription. Although the notice may be technically correct, as a practical matter the FDA had previously adopted a policy of not harassing individuals and families who import drugs for their own use and it declined to comment on the DHS action (Rowland 2006).

Another administration agency that PhRMA worked to block importation was the Office of the US Trade Representative (USTR), which shapes the country's trade agreements with other nations. Between 1998 and 2005, PhRMA filed fifty-nine lobbying reports on its attempts to influence the USTR, more than any other lobby or interest (Ismail 2005). Through influencing the USTR, PhRMA works to get provisions in "free trade" agreements (FTAs) that restrict importation of less expensive drugs.[5] One industry success was the US-Australia FTA, which prohibits importation of Australia's drugs into the United States at Australian prices (Democratic Policy Committee 2004). By loading up a bilateral trade agreement with such a provision, the industry can restrain how imports undermine their profits even if US domestic restrictions on importation are eventually eased.

Industry Building Its Economic Power

At the same time as they turned to the federal government to help fight off state challenges, drugmakers expanded old and developed new economic ways to keep their blockbusters profitable to help bankroll their political work. One way that the industry expanded an old method of building profits was attempting to increase its Medicaid revenues. Unfortunately, some of the ways they used to raise Medicaid dollars ran afoul of the law. From legal settlements that the government has reached with drugmakers in the late 2000s, we know that, in some cases, they were charged with withholding the rebates that they were required to pay Medicaid. There were also charges of promoting drugs to Medicaid physicians for uses not approved by the FDA and for conditions for which it was not medically accepted that they were indicated. One case in which drugmakers were accused of failure to provide Medicaid rebates was resolved in 2009, when AstraZeneca, a UK-based firm, and several other pharmaceutical businesses agreed to pay $124 million to settle charges of unpaid Medicaid rebates (Bloomberg News 2010). That same year, a case in which Pfizer was charged with aggressively promoting drugs to physicians paid by federal programs for uses not medically accepted or FDA-approved was concluded. The drugmaker agreed to pay $1 billion to settle charges of illegally promoting drugs like Bextra, a painkiller, making false representations about its safety and effectiveness and paying kickbacks to physicians to prescribe it (Stop Medicaid Fraud 2009).

One of new ways that the industry developed to keep blockbusters profitable was to address a major problem threatening their profits: the expiration of the patents on blockbusters. Patents on blockbusters, which can run up to twenty years, eventually expire. When they do, generic drugmakers, with the approval of the FDA, can begin marketing competing products to the drugs that had been the source of oligopolistic profits. So, drugmakers utilized a number of ways of impeding competition from generic drugmakers. One way that they could do so was by seeking to delay FDA approval of generic drugs. Branded drug manufacturers can delay approvals by filing "citizen petitions"[6] regarding their generic competitors and they have done so. The FDA has reported a significant increase in citizen petitions in the middle of the 2000s (Yi 2006).

A second way pharmaceutical companies can counter the generics' threat to their profits is to bring lawsuits against generic drug companies to deter them from entering their markets. Many branded drugmakers have taken this step as the European Commission, a collaboration of European governments addressing regulation, reported that there was a fourfold increase in patent litigation between 2000 and 2007.[7] The commission found that, although 91 percent of those cases were brought by pharmaceutical companies, most often invoking their primary patents, in those cases that went to final judgment, the generic companies won 62 percent of the time (Rosch 2009).

A third way branded drugmakers can slow competition from generic drugmakers is called "pay-for-delay." The way it works is that a branded drugmaker compensates a generic drug manufacturer to stay out of the market of its brand-name product by means of an "exclusion payment settlement." For example, in 2006, Bristol-Myers and Sanofi-Aventis, the brand manufacturers of Plavix, a blood thinner with $3.8 billion in annual US sales (about 20 percent of Bristol-Myers's sales), and Apotex, a generic drug company, struck a deal whereby Apotex will receive monetary compensation in return for deferring production of a generic version of Plavix. In return, Apotex was guaranteed a later date on which it could enter the huge market. Bristol-Myers and Sanofi-Aventis gained several years' protection against what they consider early market entry of that drug (Leibowitz 2006). The stock prices of both businesses rose upon the announcement of the agreement. A fourth approach to obstructing generic competition is developing an "authorized generic," essentially a brand-name drug with a different label either licensed or manufactured by the brand-name maker. Using this strategy, a branded drugmaker can initially underprice its generic rival and run it out of the market.

When branded drugmakers can't keep generic or even over-the-counter alternatives to blockbusters that have been found to be at least as safe and effective off the market, they can fight them with aggressive marketing. For example, the painkiller naproxen, found in over-the-counter drugs like Aleve, works at least as well for many as prescription nonsteroidal anti-inflammatory drugs (NSAIDs) (Peterson et al. 2010). So, the makers of NSAIDs like Celebrex spent heavily on direct-to-consumer advertising to keep Americans buying their products, despite the price. With these and other tactics, branded drugmakers kept their profits high and their political coffers ready to flood Congress and state legislatures with funds to support their political objectives.

PBMs also turned the economic threat posed by generic drugs in the early 2000s to their own advantage. Generics threatened PBMs as many of their clients were demanding that formularies push generic drugs, and one of their major sources of income was compensation from branded drugmakers for putting branded drugs into clients' formularies. But PBMs found ways to turn their clients' demands for generics into profits for themselves. One way PBMs did so was to report to their clients that a branded drug was a generic drug. That way, they did not have to pass through rebates to clients since PBM contracts almost always state that rebates will be passed through only on branded drugs. This practice also allowed them to overstate a health plan's generic drug utilization rate for marketing purposes.

PBMs could also make money by reporting that a generic drug was a branded drug. The PBM may call the dispensed drug branded because contracts can allow far higher charges on brands than generics. In 2008, it was reported that PBMs could charge around AWP minus 18 percent for brands whereas they would only charge around AWP minus 58 percent for generics (Learner 2008). By reporting generic drugs as branded, they could charge clients high prices for cheap drugs. So, by playing games with the classifications of branded and generic drugs, PBMs could gain and use some of the profits to fight state laws that would expose these practices to the plans they represent.

Advocates' Continued Fighting after Part D

In spite of Part D, state legislative leaders continued to focus voter frustration over access to medicines. Mid-decade, advocates turned the public's attention to the way that the industry intensively used health information data to push their products. Through the practice that Chapter 2 describes called data-mining, drugmakers used physician prescribing pattern statistics to pressure them to prescribe their most expensive medicines.

In 2006, state legislators began attempts to severely restrict data-mining with a law passed in New Hampshire, a state in between Maine and Vermont that had been moving from "red" to "blue" during the past two decades. The law, the Prescription Information Law, barred the collection of data on what drugs specific doctors prescribe. IMS Health and Verispan (now SDI Health), businesses that thrive on selling those statistics, sued the state Attorney General Kelly Ayotte (R) to block enforcement (Weintraub 2009).

On 30 April 2007, district Judge Paul Barbadoro overturned New Hampshire's law on the grounds that it violated IMS Health's First Amendment right to free speech (Electronic Privacy Information Center 2008). In 2007, as Barbadoro's decision was appealed, the Vermont and Maine legislatures followed New Hampshire's lead. Vermont passed legislation that provided strong privacy protections by limiting the use of personally identifiable prescription information for marketing purposes unless doctors and other health care providers explicitly agree to waive the protections. The law, S 115, included a provision that allowed physicians getting or renewing their licenses to opt in to having their prescribing patterns used for detailing. S 115 also makes PBMs provide more information to health plans on how they are charging them (Treat 2007). As they had in New Hampshire, IMS sued the State of Vermont. In Maine, Sharon Treat led the legislature in joining Vermont and New Hampshire in restricting the use of data-mining to track prescriptions written by prescribers by enacting LD 4. The new law allowed physicians to opt out of having their prescribing pattern data used for detailing.

IMS Health, which had already sued New Hampshire and Vermont for similar laws, then sued Maine. As part of its lawsuit, it gave one indication of how far it was prepared to go to harass prescription drug access advocates. Every person who testified in support of LD 4 was subpoenaed in connection with the lawsuit. Treat was subpoenaed and questioned not only on LD 4; Judge John Woodcock, a George W. Bush appointee, allowed the plaintiffs to grill her on the National Legislative Association on Prescription Drug Prices and how it operates (Woloson 2008). On 21 December 2007, the judge ruled against LD 4. In his decision on *IMS Health v. Rowe*, he concluded that the law, which was scheduled to take effect 1 January 2008, would prohibit "the transfer of truthful commercial information" and "violate the free speech guarantee of the First Amendment."

But, when the related *IMS Health Inc. v. Ayotte* got to the US Court of Appeals for the First Circuit in November 2008, the New Hampshire data-mining restrictions were upheld. The court ruled that data and speech are not the same. Data are just like any product, Circuit Judge Bruce M. Selya said, and states have the authority to legislate how companies sell their goods. "The plaintiffs . . . ask us in essence to rule that because their product is information instead of, say, beef jerky, any regulation constitutes a restriction of speech," wrote Selya in the November opinion. "We think that such an interpretation stretches the fabric of the First Amendment beyond any rational measure."

Another new policy developed by prescription drug access advocates mid-decade has sometimes been called academic detailing. While projects like Oregon's DERP were developing information on the safety and effectiveness of prescription drugs, many prescribers were not using it. It would take more than high-quality research to orient physicians toward prescribing more effective and safe medicines; it would take person-to-person outreach to physicians. To this end, the concept of academic detailing, as opposed to drugmaker detailing, was developed. Academic detailing programs are initiated and sponsored by health plans to provide information to physicians they pay in order to help them prescribe safer and more effective medicines. The programs are overseen by medical professionals, including specialists in educating physicians, and hire pharmacists, nurse practitioners, and physicians to present evidence-based materials about common prescribing choices. As evidence-based prescribing can lead to prescribing of less expensive medicines, these programs can result in significant savings to health plans.

In 2004, Vermont began an academic detailing program through the University of Vermont's Medical School sponsored by Blue Cross Blue Shield of Vermont/Vermont Health Plan. In October 2005, Pennsylvania hired Jerry Avorn of Harvard Medical School to direct an academic detailing program for its state pharmaceutical assistance program, the Pennsylvania Department of Aging Pharmaceutical Assistance Contract for the Elderly (PACE) program. In 2007, the New York State Medicaid Prescriber Education Program began academic detailing. In 2009, when the state comptroller found that Medicaid had paid $17.9 million over three years for AstraZeneca's Synagis, a drug used to treat a virus called RSV, when it had been prescribed out of RSV season, he recommended that the prescriber education program address the problem (Sossei et al. 2009). A follow-up report from his office found that the measures aimed at correcting problems with the prescribing of Synagis were working and recommended that the prescriber education program continue its work (Durocher 2011).

Despite industry efforts, each year since 2000 has seen hundreds of state bills aimed at improving prescription drug access introduced across the country. Generally, the industry's wealth has enabled it to contain assaults on its pricing of blockbusters in the political arena through mid-decade. But continued public anxiety over access to medicines and determination by state political leaders, almost all Democrats, meant that the wave of legislative proposals to increase access to medicines and threaten industry profits stayed high. Then, at mid-decade, the party politics of California would once again lead to the policy that the industry fears the most—the use of the purchasing power of a well-established government program to lower drug prices.

---

[1] In 2006, Kaiser Family Foundation reported that the big pharmaceutical businesses consistently had profits several times the median for Fortune 500 businesses (Kaiser Family Foundation 2005). For 2009, *Fortune* ranked the pharmaceutical industry as the second most profitable industry in America (out of 53). It was close behind the leading industry, oil, and far ahead of the industry in third, tobacco (CNNMoney 2011).

[2] As mentioned in Chapter 3, the NLARx was founded in 2001 and first headed by State Senator Cheryl Rivers of Vermont. It is a national policy group working for lower prices of and broader access to medicines.

[3] There were five southern states, seven in the Rockies and Midwest, and six in the Northeast (Richards 2003).

[4] In 2004, Tauzin took the PhRMA job.

[5] While these agreements are commonly thought to deregulate trade, they actually reregulate it. They now give states and businesses authority to enforce rules in other countries regarding tariffs, quotas, health and safety, and labor. In the United States, the executive branch is allowed to negotiate these agreements and go to Congress for approval afterward (Aaronson 2008). FTAs can be reciprocal in that they give parties in each country authority to regulate parties in the other.

[6] The petitions, which can be filed by any member of the public, are used to allege scientific and safety concerns about drugs being reviewed by the agency.

[7] As noted in Chapter 1, many major pharmaceutical businesses are European, although much of their profits come from the United States.

6

So Goes California

In September 2004, Kevin Concannon—then the director of Iowa's Department of Health Services—was again discussing prescription drug price policy, this time by telephone before the California State Senate Health Committee. He had been the architect of Maine Rx, the law that had initiated the Medicaid purchasing power approach to lowering drug prices, and he had been the lead defendant when the pharmaceutical industry sued to overturn the law in the case *PhRMA v. Concannon*. The health committee was wrapping up California legislative leadership's first year prioritizing efforts to lower the prices of medicines and was looking for policies to further pursue these efforts. Concannon discussed the possibility of using Medi-Cal's (Medicaid in California) purchasing power to obtain prescription drug rebates for Californians who couldn't afford their medicines. His testimony was broadcast over the speakers of the theater-size hearing room in the 1970's annex to the capitol building. Dominating the front of the room was a transplanted floor-to-ceiling WPA mural featuring both early Anglo and Latino settlers of California.[1]

Concannon's disembodied voice filled the air:

> a takeaway from our experience in Maine is that [for] the drug manufacturers, the item that they pay most attention to is market share. We know it actually doesn't cost them that much more to manufacture a particular pill or a tablet, but they worry about market share. And Medicaid, and I'm certain Medi-Cal even more so, has such significant ability to influence market share. That's where your marketing leverage comes.

For pharmaceuticals, market share is a drugmaker's percentage of sales within a therapeutic category in a region—for example, one's percentage of sales of cholesterol-lowering medicines in California. As Concannon emphasized, the ability to increase market share is the key to a drug buyer's ability to get lower prices. The more a buyer can raise market share for a drugmaker, the lower the prices it can get for itself and the people for whom it is buying medicines. And because Medicaid buys so many drugs in a state, it can significantly increase market share in many therapeutic classes of drugs. With the testimony of Concannon and others at that legislative hearing, California's discussion of prescription drug access policy caught up with those of the most advanced states. California's Democratic legislature was about to join states like Maine and Hawaii in taking on PhRMA.

California Overview

Unlike states like Maine or Vermont, California is the center for several key US industrial powers and political campaigning is big business. In Hollywood, California is the national base of television and movie production; in Silicon Valley, it is the national base of the computer equipment and services industry. California is third in the nation in oil production. Each of these industries puts millions, if not tens of millions, of dollars into buying state elections. While Maine and Vermont each saw state campaign spending in the millions in 2000, in California such spending was in the hundreds of millions (National Institute on Money in State Politics 2011). The pharmaceutical industry also is particularly well entrenched and politically active in California. California is by far the largest state in the United States in pharmaceutical research. It is #1 in the US in biotech academic research and in obtaining funding from the National Institutes of Health. California accounts for nearly twice the bioscience occupational employment than the next highest state, Texas. And, among the states, California businesses account for 38 percent of all bioscience venture capital invested during 2004 to 2009 (Battelle Technology Partnership Practice 2010). From 1997 to 2002, pharmaceutical industry campaign contributions in California were triple what they were in the state that got the second most industry campaign money, New Jersey. In that period, the state politician who got the most industry money anywhere in the country was California's governor, Gray Davis (Richards 2003).

In contrast to those of Maine or Vermont, California politics have several other features that increase the advantages of wealthy interests. It has several large urban areas where media are particularly expensive and a large number of voters live in those areas. Politicians and political interests who want media time in these areas must often raise huge, and sometimes record-breaking, sums to get out their messages and this need makes them especially dependent on large contributors. It is also harder to get grassroots stories free time via news programs in large urban media markets like California's than in smaller media markets like those in northern New England. So, it is considerably more difficult for stories from progressives to spread through the media.

The distance between voters and elected officials is often quite large in California. California's members of Congress must travel nearly three thousand miles to visit their home districts and are relatively unavailable to meet with progressive advocates. Even state politicians make policies in a northern state capital hundreds of miles away from most residents in southern California. So, it is considerably more difficult for progressives to get access to officeholders and press their cases. As a consequence, officeholders heavily rely on polls and focus groups to learn how the "grassroots" views the issues, another especially high expense for California politicians.

The political environment renders the role of groups like California's Public Interest Research Group (PIRG) affiliate to be significantly different from what it is in Vermont. Whereas in Vermont VPIRG could initiate a major confrontation with an international industry; in California a group looking to represent the interests of low- and middle- income residents such as a PIRG affiliate does not assume this kind of a role. Instead, such a group tends to make more modest proposals and let better-funded grassroots groups like unions provoke major clashes with big businesses.

It does help progressives (as it did in Maine and Vermont) that California has a relatively "blue" electorate. Further, the state's electorate is becoming increasingly Democratic as its Latino population in the south and Asian and Pacific Islander population in the north grow in proportion to the rest of those living in the state.[2] By 1998, the rising numbers of Latino and Asian voters had contributed to electing Democrat Gray Davis governor, ending nearly two decades of Republican hold on the office.

In addition to a growing "blue" electorate, California's progressives also have to have organizational support exponentially greater than that in Maine or Vermont. It has well-financed labor lobbies that can sometimes raise the money they need for statewide battles with big business. Two of its largest unions are affiliated with the country's two most politically active public sector unions, Service Employees International Union (SEIU) and American Federation of State, County, and Municipal Employees (AFSCME). These unions raise large sums for campaigns and can be very valuable to some Democratic officeholders.

Before the wave of legislation to lower drug prices swept across state legislatures in 2000, a staggering state deficit had pushed California to become a state innovator in the area of drug costs. In 1991, when Republicans held the governor's mansion, California was hit especially hard by the 1990-1991 recession. The administration of Governor "Pete" Wilson (R) took a wide range of measures attempting to balance the budget that year and one of them was aimed at obtaining lower prices for Medi-Cal drugs. The Department of Health Services (DHS) began invoicing drugmakers for supplemental rebates for prescription drugs in the first quarter of 1991. PhRMA's efforts to block state policy to lower prices were much weaker then than they were at the end of the decade and Wilson's idea encouraged the legislature to press on with the supplemental rebate concept. In 1992, the Democratic legislature made it part of the state budget. So, the 1992-1993 state budget authorized DHS to require prior authorization for all the drugs of manufacturers who refused to give Medi-Cal supplemental rebates. For the rest of the decade, the legislature continued that mandate on DHS (California Department of Health Care Services 2007). The program looked good on paper and was held up as a model by the National Conference of State Legislatures. Also, the Bureau of State Audits reported that it was a success.[3]

But, by the turn of the century, the California Senate Office of Research (SOR) wasn't so sure. It suspected that, sometimes, DHS was actually working with some drugmakers and using the program to promote some blockbusters ahead of less expensive generics (Agnos 2003). In connection with this concern, SOR developed doubts about the accuracy of DHS's calculations of the program's savings (Hansel 2003). In some cases, the agency may have counted rebates on high-priced blockbusters as savings when they could have more cheaply provided drugs by just using generics. Still, California had, at least, tried.

1999–2003

In 1999, as Cheryl Rivers and Chellie Pingree were elevating the issue of prescription drug access in the Vermont and Maine legislatures, some California legislators sensed a growing urgency over the issue of drug access and tried to implement a series of measures to ameliorate the problem. The first was newly elected State Senator Jackie Speier (D– San Mateo) who was appointed chair of the Insurance Committee.[4] That year, Speier knew that some could lose their Medicare managed-care plans with drug coverage.[5] She knew that seniors without drug coverage were paying higher prices for drugs than insurers covering younger people and that some pharmacists were being "gored" by the same insurers (Speier 2007).

But Speier was not only from a state in which biotech was a huge employer; her own district was heavy with biotech businesses. So, it would be politically more difficult for her to press for lower prescription drug prices than prescription drug access advocates in Maine and Vermont. Further, unlike Maine and Vermont, California did not have a State Pharmaceutical Assistance Program (SPAP) on which to build a discount program. Had California had such a program, it could have simply tried to change its eligibility standards to cover more residents or increase its discounts to save residents more money. Further, Speier had to deal with a governor, Gray Davis, who was close to the industry (McKinnell 2002; Ismail 2006); drugmakers could count on him to oppose a policy like Vermont's proposal to regulate drug prices (Speier 2007).[6]

So, Speier hit upon an idea that she thought could get seniors discounts at no cost to the state or drugmakers—discounts for seniors that would be borne by the pharmacies. She authored SB 393, which required Medi-Cal pharmacies to sell prescription drugs to seniors at the average wholesale price (AWP) minus 17 percent (plus a $7.25 dispensing fee). Because it would not lower the prices drugmakers could charge, it generated no opposition from PhRMA. Both the capitol's senior lobby and the state retailers association got behind the bill, many Republican legislators voted for it, and it was enacted. In a modest way, Speier had gotten California on the road to legislating prescription drug access for non-Medicaid residents.

Afterwards, the pharmacy association commended Senator Speier for the bill, hoping that it would help their members beat competition from mail-order pharmacies. The governor also used the act to his political advantage; he bragged about it before senior groups and referred to it in his own publicity (Speier 2007). Unfortunately, the program was not well publicized and few seniors received the promised discounts (Barry et al. 2002). Substantially improving prescription drug access may have been as popular in California as in Maine; but the political and policy challenges to doing it were much greater.

In the spring of 2000, as State Senate President Shumlin in Vermont and State Senate Majority Leader Pingree in Maine were promoting the use of Medicaid purchasing power to lower drug prices, Byron Sher (D–Palo Alto), a state senator from the Silicon Valley district next to Speier's, tried a different tack than Speier for lowering drug prices. Sher was a Stanford University law professor who had specialized in consumer protections before coming to the state senate in 1996. Once in office, he was consistently ranked as one of the state's top ten legislators for intelligence and integrity by the nonpartisan *California Journal*. Through legislators in other states, he heard of a 1999 Massachusetts law, H 4900, authored by State Senator Mark Montigny. H 4900 established a state-appointed pharmacy benefit manager to bargain with drug companies and pharmacies for price reductions on prescription drugs for state employees, Medicaid recipients, and state aid relief clients.[7]

At the time, the major labor-backed California organization of seniors was the Congress of California Seniors (CCS). It was California's counterpart of Maine's Maine Council of Senior Citizens and, like the MCSC, was the statewide nexus of union retiree organizations. Looking to get California to join Maine and other states pushing for improved access to prescription drugs, Bill Powers of the CCS drafted a proposal to promote a study of joint purchasing of medicines by the state's Medicaid program, its state employee health program, and other groups. CCS got Sher to introduce the proposal as SB 1880. If implemented, the bill would have allowed the use of Medicaid purchasing power to lower the prices drugmakers charged for non-Medicaid groups. By raising the specter of Medicaid purchasing power, the bill posed a much greater threat to the pharmaceutical industry than SB 393 had. SB 1880 passed both houses, but was vetoed by Governor Davis. In excusing his veto, Davis wrote that California should wait and see what other states did on prescription drug access. There wasn't much Sher could do about Davis's veto. Sher would need the governor's backing for other pieces of legislation.

Speier again picked up the issue in 2001 and took another tack that would not antagonize PhRMA. Given Medi-Cal's reputation for negotiating supplemental rebates, it appeared to Speier that another state program to do so for people not on Medi-Cal could have an impact (Speier 2007). The industry had been supportive of discount programs that did not use Medicaid leverage to help non-Medicaid people. So, Speier authored SB 696, a bill that would create a prescription drug purchasing pool that would not use Medi-Cal leverage but attempt to lower what drugmakers charged Medicare beneficiaries. The bill was backed by the Congress of California Seniors. As there was no one actually in the proposed purchasing pool and it didn't, therefore, have any evident purchasing power, it was given a pass by the pharmaceutical industry and enacted as the Golden Bear SPAP.

In 2002, State Senator Sher resumed his effort to reduce drug costs to the state by promoting bulk purchasing. Backed by the California PIRG (CALPIRG), he introduced SB 1315, a bill that would make the

Department of General Services responsible for negotiating with drugmakers for those in the state prison systems and its departments of mental health and developmental disabilities. PhRMA was not concerned enough about the negotiating power of DGS representing these state providers of health care to oppose the bill and it was enacted. As PhRMA may have anticipated, the Department of General Services had little experience with negotiating drug discounts and, under Davis, was very slow to implement it (Health and Human Services Committee 2003).

Yet another approach to lowering drug costs was a plan put forth by Nell Soto, a Democrat from Los Angeles. When the term limits law adopted in 1990 had forced the legislature's old guard from office, she and many other Latinos quickly moved up the political ladder. Soto was a strong ally of organized labor. For a policy idea that would lower drug costs, she had her office check with the Senate Office of Research where they learned of Oregon Health and Science University (OHSU)'s reviews of drug safety and effectiveness. As discussed in Chapter 5, these reviews used comparative effectiveness research summarizing the highest quality scientific research on drugs to indicate which drugs within a therapeutic class were more likely to be safe and effective. Soto introduced SB 1727, a bill that would have asked the University of California to undertake a similar program in California. The likelihood that such a program would identify alternatives to some blockbusters in generics that would be at least as safe and effective alarmed the pharmaceutical industry. If less expensive alternatives to blockbusters that would be at least as safe and effective were identified, then access would improve but profits would suffer. While the bill passed the senate, PhRMA prepared to head it off in the assembly Health Committee.

At the time, the chair of that committee was Dario Frommer (D–Los Angeles). Like Speier, Frommer was a California native who had earned his law degree in the University of California system and quickly moved into politics. Frommer had begun working with Gray Davis when Davis was state controller and stayed with him all the way to the governor's office where he oversaw Davis's appointments to state boards and commissions. In 2000, Frommer was elected to the state assembly where containing health care costs was one of his main concerns.

But, when Soto's proposal to have the University of California review drug safety and effectiveness reached his committee, Frommer said he was skeptical that it would work. When his committee had its hearing on the proposal, both Republicans and Democrats used PhRMA arguments to attack the bill. It was argued that only physicians should decide which drugs are best and that the academic reviews could interfere with that prerogative and so forth. After a bitter round of these kinds of remarks, it was clear that the bill would fail in the committee. So, Soto didn't even press for a vote on her proposal and the bill died.

Still, her proposal got Frommer thinking about containing prescription drug costs as a part of the solution for the high costs of health care. Frommer could reasonably hope to rise higher in legislative leadership before term limits would force him to leave the assembly in 2006. So, though SB 1727 failed, it brought the issue of prescription drug costs to the attention of someone who could soon be in legislative leadership and in a position to act on it assertively.

At the turn of the twenty-first century, the tremendous power of PhRMA in California was manifest as a few senators and grassroots organizations with modest resources had worked to capitalize on the problems caused by rising high prescription drug costs. Any serious threats to the industry profits like SB 1880 or SB 1727 were easily shot down. As the 2002 gubernatorial election approached, the industry had allowed only a few policies that posed no evident threat to blockbusters to be enacted and the industry appeared completely in control of the state's prescription drug policy. Its chances of maintaining its dominance seemed good. No powerful group was interested in challenging PhRMA, legislative leadership was not working on the prescription drug access issue, and the industry had a governor who could keep the state from enacting major legislation it opposed. Nevertheless, 2003 was a year in which those things would change and, by the end of it, what had seemed like a nearly hopeless situation for advocates for prescription drug access would no longer be so.

The first factor that would begin to change was the certainty that Gray Davis would be a long-term obstacle to PhRMA-opposed legislation. As accessible as Davis was to California business lobbyists, there was still concern that he would show some deference to public employee unions and support taxes on occasion that could help fund their members' work. So, he antagonized some well-financed Republican constituencies. To secure himself election in 2002, Gray Davis had worked to undermine a moderate Republican who could have defeated him and promoted the nomination of a right-wing Republican whom he would likely beat (Bradley 2002). This move met with success and a general election matchup between a right-wing Republican and Davis that resulted in his reelection in November 2002.

However, as 2003 unfolded, the governor's hold on his office was surprisingly reduced. Although he had just been reelected governor, developments that were already under way were soon to undermine his electoral strategy of being more acceptable to voters than right-wing

Republicans. The first of these developments was the early 2000s dot-com bust and economic downturn. High-tech, which led the state's economy during the boom of the late 1990s, suffered the brunt of the ensuing recession. The unemployment rate in the Bay Area jumped from 2.6 percent to 6.1 percent between March 2001 and November 2002. Then, combined with losses due to rising unemployment, tax revenues from stock options and capital gains plunged. So, California faced a fiscal crisis of unprecedented magnitude. In January 2003, the state's legislative analyst estimated the gap at $26.1 billion, while the governor, using a different set of assumptions, pegged the shortfall at $34.6 billion. Although Davis would largely seek to balance the budget with cuts to government programs like health and education, as a Democrat he did include some tax increases in his proposal—most notably, a vehicle license fee that hit owners of large cars like Hummers hard (California Budget Project 2003).

Responding, Ted Costa, a self-styled "anti-tax activist" started to gather the requisite signatures to file a petition to recall Davis. Behind card tables in front of supermarkets, stores, movie theaters and other places where registered voters were likely to be walking all over California, paid signature gatherers began collecting names. In support of the petition, gatherers complained that Davis was spending too much while, at the same time, petition circulators blamed him for cuts to local government (Mathews 2003).

Others from Costa's faction of the Republican Party followed suit. In May, Congressman Darrell Issa (R), who was planning to run for governor in 2006, formed a committee to back the recall petition, Rescue California, supported by $1.7 million from his personal car alarm fortune. Funded by Issa, Rescue California petition gatherers paid $1 a signature and collected hundreds of thousands of names of California voters who felt no strong sense of loyalty to Davis. For more financial support, when Rescue California mailed out a fundraising appeal, it sold space in its solicitation materials to Republicans planning to run in the 2004 party primaries (Blumenthal 2003).[8]

As the recall effort was gaining energy, the possibility of legislative leadership paying attention to the prescription drug issue began to stir as Dario Frommer, an assembly member on track to legislative leadership, became directly involved. While the Davis administration had shown no inclination toward helping ordinary Californians to save money on prescription drugs, the budget crisis had increased its interest in reducing the state's costs for medicine. In the immediate wake of the *PhRMA v. Concannon* decision, Frommer was requested by the administration's Medi-Cal administrator, Stan Rosenstein, to propose the use of Medi-

Cal purchasing power to help the Department of General Services (DGS) implement SB 1315. Frommer had an unrelated bill, AB 1739, waiting for action in the Senate Health Committee, and he amended Rosenstein's idea to fit into it. But the committee chair, Deborah Ortiz, opposed the idea. In her committee's analysis, it was argued that DGS should have more time to implement SB 1315. Also, the analysis raised a PhRMA argument that had just been rejected by the US Supreme Court: that the use of Medicaid purchasing power for non-Medicaid populations would, somehow, hurt people on Medicaid (Health and Human Services Committee 2003). SB 1793 went down to defeat (Thomason 2007).

At the same time, I had then been back in California for about a year. I had returned to my home state the previous year to join the faculty at San Francisco State and I had been looking for a niche in the state capitol as an advocate for a progressive health policy. I still had a few connections in the state capitol as, in the early 1990s, I had been the health policy lobbyist for one for the state's largest unions, SEIU.

California Works, the research arm of the state's central union political organization, the California Labor Federation, called together a few union leaders who were particularly concerned about high drug costs and wanted to find market solutions to this problem. If they did not, these high costs could weaken the ability of the unions' health plans to provide benefits to members and a decline in benefits could expose the unions' leaders to challenges in union elections. I was invited to participate. The same senate Office of Research staff who had provided Senator Soto with the concept for SB 1727 had told me how some pharmacy benefit managers put their own interests ahead of their clients' when establishing drug formularies. So, I suggested to the unionists that they should check to see how much their PBMs were using evidence-based health care to develop less expensive formularies. As some of the staff at the meeting provided advice to their state capitol lobbyists on health policy, I also presented them with the idea of Maine Rx, based on my work on prescription drug access in New England.

By mid-summer, the recall campaign had a full head of steam and Davis's need for allies among labor and consumer advocates was rising. On 23 July, the secretary of state reported that the recall petition had qualified for the ballot (Institute of Governmental Studies Library 2004). The election was set for 7 October. The recall ballot would have two parts. The first would ask if Davis should be recalled. The second would ask, if Davis were recalled, who should then be governor. If Davis were recalled, one would not need a majority vote on the second part of the ballot to become governor, only a plurality.

As summer ended, Davis's hold on the governor's office was in serious trouble. The Republican Party had recognized the recall situation as a special opportunity for it to get its candidate into the governor's mansion. While it was difficult for electable candidates to win statewide Republican primaries, they wouldn't have to run a candidate in a Republican primary to get his name on the second part of the ballot. In August, Republicans prevailed on a Republican member of the nationally powerful Kennedy clan, the movie star Arnold Schwarzenegger, to enter the race. Schwarzenegger, a pro-choice, pro-gun control, and pro-gay rights Republican who had laid the groundwork for a run in the 2006 gubernatorial election, linked up with former Governor Pete Wilson's "brain trust" (Blumenthal 2003).[9] They represented the less radical wing of the Republican Party that was having trouble winning party primaries. Schwarzenegger announced that he was running for governor to a national TV audience on the set of the *Tonight Show* with Jay Leno. Davis's lesser-of-two-evils strategy was outflanked.

The California Chamber of Commerce threw its support to Schwarzenegger's candidacy. In anticipation that he could carry out its agenda, the chamber also promoted a cap on state spending, a measure that could slash business taxes and result in massive layoffs for public employees—slashing the revenue for the Republicans' bête noire and most stalwart political opposition, the public employee unions (Rojas 2005). The linking of the chamber's agenda for public employees and Schwarzenegger would ultimately come to involve the pharmaceutical industry, as the industry would become a strong supporter of the governor's agenda, including his attack on public employee unions.

As the Davis situation was coming to a head, the California Labor Federation began looking at state legislation for 2004. The federation could coordinate the political power of two of the largest public employee unions in California, SEIU and AFSCME. It also worked closely with other service unions like the United Food and Commercial Workers (UFCW) and the teamsters (IBT). When it had its major constituents focused on one issue, it could on bring decisive pressure on the legislature.

One idea the labor federation considered was to address the problem of high prescription drug costs. Among other concerns, union officials were beginning to wonder about the PBMs they had hired and to ask if they didn't need to get political on drug costs. In September, the labor federation held a meeting of about thirty union representatives in its offices across the street from the state capitol and announced that prescription drug cost containment was on its legislative agenda for

2004. I was invited and, for suggested legislation, I presented the group with the options of emulating Maine Rx and using comparative effectiveness research on drugs to lower costs. With that meeting, prescription drug access advocacy became a serious issue for California labor organizations that also had substantial resources to back it.

The recall election took place on 7 October and the electorate delivered the coup de grâce to Davis's governorship. Of those voting, 55 percent chose to recall him. On the second part of the ballot, Schwarzenegger got a plurality, 49 percent of the votes, and was chosen as the new governor of California. The leading Democratic candidate on the ballot got 32 percent of the vote and the right-wing Republican 14 percent.

So, as 2003 was ending, the door for strong prescription drug access legislation was opening. There was then a powerful political force, the California Labor Federation, keenly interested in prescription drug policy. Dario Frommer, a rising star in the legislature, had come on board as a player on the issue. Finally, legislative leadership no longer had to kowtow to a governor strongly linked to the pharmaceutical industry. The stage was getting set for prescription drug legislation to come front and center in the legislature.

An additional helpful factor, legislative staff conversant on the latest policy options, came into play shortly afterward. Two days after Davis's recall, at the invitation of the University of California's California Program on Access to Care, I convened a session in the attorney general's office a few blocks from the capitol to discuss California prescription drug policy options for the 2004 legislative session. Most of the state capitol staffers who would work on the issue were present. I arranged for the executive director of the National Legislative Association on Prescription Drug Prices, Cheryl Rivers, to be the featured speaker. She provided an up-to-date view of state efforts across the country to increase access to prescription drugs. She discussed the Maine Rx model and comparative effectiveness research on drugs. She spent a substantial amount of time on the regulation of pharmacy benefit managers (PBMs). She confirmed that states' promotion of importing lower-priced drugs was snowballing (Rivers 2003).

The labor federation, with its potential to add an ingredient critical for success in California policymaking, powerful allies, convened a meeting in November on prescription drug policy. In attendance were representatives of senior and consumer groups. Also present was a lobbyist from the California Medical Association (CMA). We discussed Maine Rx, drug effectiveness research, and importation. We also raised the issues of pharmaceutical industry marketing practices. We learned then that assembly member Frommer was looking to take a lead on the prescription drug access issue.

At the same time, a new group arose that could provide the emerging coalition with a creditable grassroots—another essential ingredient for challenging PhRMA. The AFL-CIO was reorganizing its retiree organization, changing its name from the National Council of Senior Citizens to the Alliance of Retired Americans. In conjunction with that move, the state labor federation helped fund a state chapter of the AFL-CIO's new senior group; the California chapter was called the California Alliance of Retired Americans (CARA). Some of the leaders of CCS then moved over to CARA. A favorable situation for the pursuit of tough legislation on prescription drug access was developing. Legislative staff was getting educated on this complex policy area. Legislative leadership was getting ready to make drug access a big issue in 2004. A group that could put a human face on the issue for legislators, CARA, was in place.

In December, the prescription drug access group convened by the labor federation formalized as the OURx Coalition with the goal of promoting legislation in 2004 to improve access to medicines. It included the labor federation, CARA, CALPIRG, and Consumers Union, the publisher of *Consumers Reports*. Also present was a group I was representing at the time, San Francisco's Senior Action Network (SAN), a local senior group that was to be CARA's most active affiliate. A decisive addition was Health Access, the state's SEIU-backed health care advocacy coalition. With a group strongly backed by one of the two most politically powerful unions in the state, the chances of keeping the interest of legislative leadership greatly increased. For our 2004 legislative agenda, the coalition had enough staff to work on bills supporting use of comparative effectiveness research on prescription drugs and the regulation of PBMs. Although the Maine Rx approach was considered, no one in the legislature was willing to author such a bill, and OURx did not advocate that approach at that time.

2004: Legislative Leadership Taking the Stage

Along with assembly leadership, state senate leaders decided to tackle the prescription drug issue in 2004. As Democrats were looking for prescription drug access policy options to promote, the practice of importing medicines from Canada had gained considerable political support around the United States. Following the bus rides to Canada by advocates for prescription drug access described in Chapters 3 and 4, governments had begun institutionalizing these importation efforts.

Springfield, Massachusetts had started importing drugs for city programs; the Democratic governor of Illinois was also moving forward on helping state residents get Canadian drugs, as was the Republican governor of Minnesota.[10]

So, senate leadership combined the idea of importation with some of the bulk-purchasing policies that the legislature had already approved. John Burton introduced SB 1144, a bill that would authorize the Department of General Services to import prescription drugs as part of its effort to lower the state's drug costs. State Senator Don Perata (D–Oakland), who would become senate president when Burton's term ran out, introduced SB 1333, which would authorize Medi-Cal to import medicines.

Also getting on the Canadian bandwagon was Senate Health Committee chair Deborah Ortiz. Ortiz, a Sacramento native, had earned a BA from the University of California at Davis and graduated from the McGeorge School of Law. From there, she served as a staff member for Richard Polanco (D–Los Angeles), when Latinos in power were few. Elected to the Sacramento City Council in 1993, Ortiz went from that position to an assembly seat in 1996, and the state senate in 1998, where she rose to chair of the Senate Health Committee. In 2004, Ortiz introduced SB 1149, which would have required the state to establish a website to publish information on Canadian prescription drug vendors who violated safe shipment, handling, and processing standards.

State Senator Sher joined in too, introducing SB 1765, a bill that would codify the voluntary standards promulgated by the industry limiting drugmakers' gifts to physicians and require reporting on compliance with these standards. The bill was sponsored by CALPIRG, meaning it would provide support for the bill through such tasks as providing research and making contact with legislators on its behalf, along with the office of the bill's author, Senator Sher. Although the bill's standards would be voluntary, leaving drugmakers' gift-giving to physicians unregulated, its passage could be a first step in more tightly restricting drugmakers' influence over prescribers.

On the assembly side of the legislature, Dario Frommer, now assembly majority leader, second highest-ranking position in the assembly, introduced his own set of bills in February, calling his package, the Affordable Prescription Drug Act of 2004. Impressed by work in Minnesota, Illinois, and Wisconsin on importing prescription drugs, he authored AB 1957 to set up a state website to help Californians identify Canadian prescription drug vendors through which they could buy medicines (Thomason 2007). The Frommer package of bills also included AB 1958 (Frommer), which would have encouraged the health plans of the California Public Employees' Retirement System (PERS) to allow non-PERS beneficiaries to access medicines through their purchasing pool. Another bill, AB 1959 (Chu), would improve implementation of SB 1315, which had established a prescription drug purchasing pool of some state programs, excluding Medi-Cal. Also in the package was AB 1960 (Pavley), sponsored by the labor federation, which would make PBMs more accountable to their clients with such measures as requiring them to use more transparent processes for developing formularies. Introduced shortly after Frommer's package, AB 2326 (Corbett) would require the state to provide residents a website with evidence-based information on the safety and effectiveness of popular medicines.[11]

At the beginning of March, Senator Ortiz amended her Canadian prescription drug website bill to take the same approach as Majority Leader Frommer's. Whereas she had initially proposed a website that would identify Canadian sites where it wouldn't be safe for Californians to purchase drugs, she then proposed to identify sites where it would be safe for them to do so. Ortiz's shift to model her website on an existing assembly bill raised the longstanding issue of interhouse rivalry. Some assembly members believed that state senators felt entitled to take their policy ideas and then get credit for them. Frommer called Ortiz and hotly protested her amendments to SB 1149. By the end of the conversation, Frommer and Ortiz were far along a course of interhouse rivalry that would shape the politics of prescription drug access for the next two years. Over that period, Ortiz would routinely use her power as chair of the Senate Health Committee to block Frommer's prescription drug bills; Frommer would use his power as assembly majority leader to block Ortiz's prescription drug bills.

As new prescription drug policies were being proposed, Governor Schwarzenegger terminated an old one. On 23 March, his administration killed State Senator Speier's Golden Bear program enacted in 2001, concluding that it had "exhausted the potential for implementation." Since the program had no enrollees, both the Davis and Schwarzenegger administrations had no basis for convincing drugmakers that it could increase market share and, thus, justify discounts.

Meanwhile, the OURx Coalition continued to develop support for the Frommer package (AB 1957–importation, AB 1958–wider access to PERS medicines, AB 1959–better implementation of the law setting up a state agency pool for buying drugs, and AB 1960–PBM regulation) and AB 2326—promoting use of comparative effectiveness research. On 7 April, we organized a legislative briefing to discuss the need for these bills. The next week, CARA and SAN organized vanloads of seniors to come to the capitol, attend hearings on the assembly bills, and visits legislators' capitol offices on behalf of the OURx bills. Throughout May and June, OURx Coalition members continued to work to move their bills through the legislative process, keeping tabs on legislators' positions and applying pressure on those "on the fence." When assembly member Leland Yee (D–San Francisco) said that he had questions about some of the bills, SAN sent a large contingent of constituents to a San Francisco pancake-and-maple-syrup breakfast he was hosting armed with their own questions about his lack of support for the OURx legislative package. His ambivalence over the bills suddenly disappeared. In June, SAN also staged a demonstration in San Francisco supportive of the pending legislation. The chances Democratic legislators would stick with party leadership on their prescription drug policy initiatives were increasing.

The Rise of Tension between the Governor and Legislative Leadership

The Republicans and the interests who bankrolled them expected their new governor to bring the legislature to heel so that their agenda of lower taxes and reduced government spending on education, health, and social programs could be implemented. As part of that agenda, they wanted to undermine the power of the interest groups backing progressive programs like the powerful teacher and other large public employee unions. In his effort to employ the governor's office to further this agenda, Schwarzenegger used his first budget proposal to take on those unions. In particular, he wanted to cut spending and penalize school teachers—a base of Democratic support—through reductions in the education budget. In July, the governor also directly attacked the legislative leadership "girlie men" and urged voters to "terminate" them at the polls in November if they didn't pass his proposed cuts (Nicholas 2004). But the Democrats largely prevailed in that year's budget fight (Gledhill et al. 2004). This loss sent the governor on to other plans to get more control over the legislature. As he came to intensify his focus on going after legislative leadership and the public employee unions that supported it, the governor drew his administration and its backer, the pharmaceutical industry, closer to an all-out battle involving access to prescription drugs. By August, Schwarzenegger announced his support for twelve new Republican challengers for legislative seats in an effort to move toward Republican majorities in both houses. Most of the challengers were in key races identified by Republican legislative leadership. Some were in districts where a once reliably Democratic electorate had voted for Schwarzenegger (Hinch 2004).

Meanwhile, PhRMA and major drugmakers strongly opposed AB 1957 and AB 2326. They argued that importation was illegal and dangerous; on AB 2326, they claimed that promoting use of drug effectiveness research would improperly intrude on physicians' practice in prescribing medicines. PBMs claimed that AB 1960 would make it harder for them to get discounts. Nevertheless, Democratic leadership moved these bills and AB 1958 (wider access to PERS medicines) through the assembly and senate. Near the end of session, the two most high-profile bills, SB 1149 (Ortiz) and AB 1957 (Frommer), the bills to establish a website on Canadian prescription drugs, were stalled by the rising feud between Senate Health Committee chair Ortiz and Assembly Majority Leader Frommer. Ortiz held AB 1957 in her committee; Frommer saw that SB 1149 didn't get out of the assembly.

While the Canadian bills were thus pending, PhRMA had regular and ongoing contact with the Schwarzenegger administration. Under pressure from the industry, the governor decided he would, at least, veto the Canadian website bills, if they reached his desk. When word of the planned vetoes leaked out, there was no longer any political advantage for Frommer or Ortiz in getting credit for Canadian website bills. So, each then released the other's bill and both went to the governor.

As the bill-signing deadline approached, the OURx Coalition put pressure on the governor to sign the bills. The AIDS Health care Foundation had joined the coalition and contributed an experienced media consultant, Jim Farrell, who had served as campaign manager for the late Senator Paul Wellstone (D–MN), to improve the coalition's visibility. CARA and SAN collected 40,000 signed postcards to the governor from seniors, urging him to sign all the bills. On 8 September, CARA and SAN sent vanloads of seniors to the capitol to demonstrate and to present the postcards to the governor's office. At its first annual convention in mid-September, a two-day affair at a Sacramento hotel, CARA brought in state legislators to meet with delegates and discuss legislation, including pending prescription drug bills.

On 29 September, the governor vetoed all but one of the OURx bills to reach his desk, including the importation bills, the PBM accountability bill, and the PERS bulk- purchasing bill. It couldn't be said that he had vetoed every prescription drug price and access bill put on his desk, as he signed one, SB 1765 (Sher), the CALPIRG bill that codified the industry's own standards on gifts to physicians and that was without an enforcement mechanism.

The issue of access was gaining such traction that to ignore it was risky, even for the governor. So, to avoid the political risk of seeming indifferent, Schwarzenegger decided to do something on prescription drug policy. He had Kim Belshé, his health and human services secretary, begin promoting the kind of legislation the industry supports when threatened: a voluntary drug discount plan (Chorneau 2005). Insisting that providing affordable prescription drugs was a top priority for his administration, the governor subsequently announced that he planned to propose legislation in January that would establish a discount program—called California Rx—based on the voluntary plan promoted by Belshé. In response, Senator Ortiz called the proposed program "heavily reliant on the goodness of prescription drug companies" and said she would introduce her own bill in 2005 (Ainsworth 2004).

Senator Ortiz called a hearing on Schwarzenegger's California Rx proposal. That was the September, 2004 hearing described at the beginning of this chapter at which Kevin Concannon, Iowa's Director of Health Services, spoke via speaker-phone in the theater-size room. Before the hearing, Ortiz's staff had gotten in touch with me to help plan it and it was I who suggested Concannon as a speaker. At the hearing, I argued that, to get the deepest drug discounts for Californians, the state's best tool was the power it could get using its Medicaid leverage and that the US Supreme Court had upheld the states' authority to use that tool. Based on his experience in Maine, Concannon concurred. Dan Carson of the Legislative Analyst's Office further emphasized the need to use Medicaid's purchasing power: "if you don't have the hammer through something like the connection to Medicaid–there is [sic] strong disincentives for the industry to agree to lower prices" (Carson 2004).

In the wake of this hearing, the policy of using Medi-Cal purchasing power to lower drug prices for ordinary Californians had the interest of legislative leadership. It would be available for use in 2005, as the battle between Schwarzenegger and the legislative leadership intensified.

Only two weeks after Schwarzenegger's vetoes of the drug access bills, PhRMA got behind his effort to impose much of the Republican agenda on the legislature. It raised nearly $360,000 for distribution largely to Republican candidates backed by the governor. Records show that drug companies gave nearly $300,000 to the PhRMA political action committee during a one-week period in October. The PAC then distributed $249,500 to Republican candidates through a series of intermediaries, including four county Republican central committees, the California Chamber of Commerce, and two other business-oriented PACs. It also gave $49,500 to the California Business and Affordable Housing Council and another $75,000 went to the chamber's Jobs PAC for the same purpose (Chorneau 2005). Despite considerable backing from business, the November 2004 elections went badly for Schwarzenegger and his supporters. None of the candidates he backed to take seats away from the presumably vulnerable Democrats won.[12]

2005

On 5 January, in his State of the State speech, the governor called on the legislature to pass another proposed package of constitutional amendments that targeted Democrats and their constituencies such as public employee unions in time for ratification by voters in an early summer special election. If legislators did not act according to his timetable, he said he intended to mobilize for a fall special election on his proposals without their cooperation (Cal-Tax Staff 2005). As the special election threat loomed, preparation for the 2005 round of prescription drug legislation got under way.

Senator Ortiz and Majority Leader Frommer both drew from Kevin Concannon's recommendations and proposed the Maine Rx model (see Chapter 4), using Medicaid prior authorization authority as a tool to obtain drug rebates for Californians who couldn't afford their medicines. For 2005, Ortiz introduced it as SB 19 and Frommer introduced it as AB 75. Following the testimony at Ortiz's September hearing on drug access, both bills borrowed from Frommer's package and the OURx Coalition introduced AB 75 with a press conference in the speaker's antique press room in the old capitol building. We wanted to use a hammer to illustrate our point that something like Medi-Cal purchasing power was needed to get serious discounts. One of the better-connected people in our group succeeded in getting one inside the metal detectors at all the capitol doorways. So, the hammer was sitting on the speaker's podium as the press conference started. I picked up the hammer and waived it as I made my points about the need for Medi-Cal leverage to obtain substantially lower prices. Each speaker then used it as a prop when he or she spoke. On behalf of AB 75, Senator Speier joined us, held up the hammer, and told the media that she had learned the hard way that, without a hammer like Medi-Cal purchasing power, the state couldn't seriously lower prescription drug prices for residents.[13]

Concerned how the politics of prescription drug access might play out, Schwarzenegger proposed that Senator Ortiz gut SB 19 and insert his California Rx proposal into it. The offer was a golden opportunity for Ortiz to be the author of a prescription drug access bill that could get signed. She agreed. It seemed she had the option of improving the governor's proposal as it moved through her committee, giving the proposed prescription drug program some sort of leverage with which to negotiate serious discounts for ordinary Californians. One idea was to threaten to raise the taxes the state charges drugmakers, if they would not give her proposed prescription drug program large enough discounts. Frommer, meanwhile, stuck with the Medi-Cal purchasing power approach to winning prescription drug discounts.

The Legislative Analyst's Office took a different tack on shaping a policy that could result in the use of Medi-Cal purchasing power to obtain lower drug prices for residents not on Medi-Cal. Dan Carson of the LAO issued a report criticizing the governor's voluntary discount proposal, noting that a similar effort had failed in Iowa. He suggested a two-step process that would combine the governor's and Frommer's approaches: the first step would be a voluntary plan to obtain discounts for Californians, and, if that didn't work, the second step would be the use of Medi-Cal leverage. Although nobody was listening for such a compromise at the time, this suggestion had the capacity to be important, if legislators and the governor ever came around to negotiating a compromise.

In response to the governor's threat to use a special election to attack Democrats and their supporters, the public employee unions, led by the California Teachers Association and California SEIU, decided to look for ballot measures they could use to counterattack the governor's backers, thereby forcing them to divert some of their political campaign funds away from supporting Schwarzenegger's ballot initiatives. Among the leading interest groups to get their attention was the pharmaceutical industry. A ballot initiative to negotiate lower drug prices for Californians could offer the unions a way to strike back at one of the governor's key supporters. If it was nearly certain that the governor would veto AB 75, propose a much weaker alternative, and chance voter disapproval, then the only way SEIU, CTA, and allied public employee unions could threaten Schwarzenegger's ally, PhRMA, was through an initiative put directly to the voters. SEIU got together with the other California public employee unions and they considered putting an initiative on the state ballot to support prescription drug access. If they did so, access advocates would have the full support of organizations with the capacity to seriously challenge PhRMA.[14]

The first model the unions considered was to use the purchasing power of state employees to negotiate lower prices for Californians. However, this idea was problematic for both political and policy reasons. State employee programs spend much less on medicines than the Medi-Cal program and, therefore, have less leverage. Also, it was not clear that state employee unions would support using their drug plan to help people who were not state employees. When public employee unions invited my participation in a discussion of the best approaches to lowering drug prices, I again suggested the Maine Rx model that I had been touting the previous year. Jim Farrell, now working for the assembly Democrats' top campaign consultant, Gail Kaufman, agreed. He asked SEIU to draft an initiative based on the Maine Rx model.

Its first draft had several problems. First, it required that all drugs produced by drugmakers who wouldn't give the proposed discount program the Medi-Cal "best price" be dropped from the Medi-Cal formulary. This stipulation could mean Medi-Cal would deny essential medicines to beneficiaries. Second, it required that the federal government provide a waiver for the program, making the initiative next to useless until at least 2009, since the Bush administration would never grant a waiver to a program opposed by drugmakers and Bush's successor was unknown at the time. Redrafting the initiative to fix these problems would shorten the time available to gather signatures and raise the costs of doing so.

As it was, another session for state capitol staff and lobbyists for California prescription drug policy options had been organized. The new executive director of the National Legislative Association on Prescription Drug Prices, Sharon Treat, was the featured speaker. To gain a better understanding of the problems with the first draft, I suggested that Farrell join me at an early breakfast meeting with Treat prior to the session for capitol staff and lobbyists. To my surprise, Farrell joined us at our table. Treat strongly recommended fixing the problems of the first draft. After he left the meeting, Farrell arranged for a second draft that used Medi-Cal purchasing power to get prescription drug discounts for ordinary residents. What might go before the voters could, at least, be workable.

Following through on his threat to force a special election that would target Democrats and their public employee union constituents, Schwarzenegger held a news conference on 1 March to announce that he was beginning to gather signatures for ballot initiatives he would give his full support unless lawmakers gave him the reform package he had requested. One initiative would make tenured school teachers more liable to dismissal, attacking the members and, effectively, the leadership of the California Teachers Association (CTA). Another would redraw the lines of legislators' districts, lowering the election chances of some Democrats. He then jumped into a Humvee tagged "Reform 1" to begin his "signature drive," and headed to a restaurant where he was met by protesting public workers (California Teachers Association 2005).

That month, the public employee unions I had been working with, including SEIU and CTA, formed the Alliance for a Better California (Brenner 2006). By forming ABC, the leading public employee union officials coordinated their resources to meet Schwarzenegger's ballot threat. After considering the chances of getting it on the ballot, ABC agreed to collect signatures for a ballot initiative based on the Maine Rx model, calling it the "cheaper prescription drugs" initiative. The Schwarzenegger backer they had targeted was the pharmaceutical industry. A ballot initiative to use Medi-Cal purchasing power to lower prices might force the industry to divert substantial funds away from that threat. Paid signature gatherers began collecting signatures at sites where voters gathered.

In response, PhRMA flexed its muscles. It committed $10 million dollars to a ballot initiave for a voluntary drug discount program and to fight the governor's political opponents. In addition, the industry committed to an initiative to cut contingency fees for the trial lawyers, a key Democratic constituency, and said it might back another initiative that would require public employee unions to get annual written permission before using any member's dues for political purposes, seriously undermining their financial resources and hence political power (Furillo and Delsohn 2005). Public employee unions got the message: they would be threatened by the industry's full financial power without the ability to match it. ABC agreed to sharply limit funding the Maine-model ballot initiative if they had collected enough signatures to put the measure on the ballot. If the Maine-model measure qualified for the ballot, it would provide almost no funds to campaign for its support among voters.

By April, the California Labor Federation had identified SB 19 as part of the governor's anti-union, anti-Democrat campaign. It threw its full weight behind opposition to the bill when it was considered by its first committee, the Senate Health Committee. As planned, Ortiz asked the governor's staff if she could amend the bill to put some teeth in it. But the administration refused, figuring that the purely voluntary version of the bill should go to the assembly and, if strengthening amendments were needed to get it through that house, they would take the necessary action at that time. However, the administration miscalculated. Without any amendments to strengthen the bill, the bill couldn't even get enough votes to get out of its first committee. With the exception of Ortiz, the California Labor Federation persuaded all the committee Democrats to vote against it and the bill was killed. Legislative consideration of the voluntary plan had ended.

Meanwhile, signature gathering for ABC's prescription drug initiative went better than organizers had expected. Doing something about high prescription drug prices was an effective hook for stopping voters and signing ABC's petitions gave them a way to express their worries about it. On 10 May, the signatures were submitted to the secretary of state. That Friday, the pharmaceutical industry lawyers filed a lawsuit–seeking to block the counting and verification of signatures for the initiative on the grounds that the initiative gave inappropriate power to the private groups, the California Chamber of Commerce and the labor federation, when it named them as partners in setting up public purchasing programs for small employers. In fact, the petition only allowed advisory roles for the chamber and federation, in setting up a state Department of Health Services purchasing pool to assist small businesses and union health plans in getting lower drug prices. The case was so weak that when the PhRMA lawyer started his presentation in front of Superior Court Judge Thomas Cecil, he said, "I realize I have a mountain to climb." The judge responded, "That's putting it mildly." PhRMA lost in both superior court and appeals court (Wright 2005).

In June, the governor called the special election he had been promising; he called it for 8 November. Qualifying for that ballot was ABC's cheaper prescription drugs initiative (Proposition 79) and the voluntary drug discount program initiative financed by the pharmaceutical industry (Proposition 78).[15] Four additional propositions were aimed at tempering the influence of the Democratic Party and its supporters. Two struck directly at the ABC's members. Proposition 74 would extend the probationary period for school teachers from two years to five, making it easier to fire teachers who would, otherwise, have been tenured. This, in turn, could discourage teachers from financially supporting their union's political agenda. Proposition 75 was the initiative PhRMA had threatened to back to require public employee unions to get annual written permission to use members' dues for political purposes (Brenner 2006). Proposition 76 would impose a spending cap on the state budget, imperiling public programs, their beneficiaries, and their staffs. Such staff cuts could undermine political funds for the unions. Proposition 77 would require mid-decade redistricting of legislative districts, which could break up many of the "safe" districts Democrats enjoyed at the time.[16] In a case of politics making for strange bedfellows, Chellie Pingree, author of Maine Rx and then director of Common Cause, made appearances throughout 2005 on behalf of Proposition 77. She argued that the proposition takes the power to draw legislative and congressional districts out of the hands of partisan legislators in Sacramento and puts the issue before the voters.

"This proposal is not perfect, none ever is. But this is an important first step, and I urge the people of California to vote yes on Prop. 77" (Common Cause 2005).

That month, Frommer's bill promoting Maine's Medicaid leverage approach to prescription drug discounts cleared the assembly and was referred to the senate Health Committee chaired by Frommer's rival, Deborah Ortiz. In July, Billy Tauzin, CEO of PhRMA, flew out to the state capitol for a private meeting called by Assembly Speaker Fabian Nuñez (D–Los Angeles).[17] Tauzin had played a central role as chair of the US House Committee on Energy and Commerce in ensuring that the 2003 Medicare Modernization Act (MMA) would be highly favorable to PhRMA. [18] At the meeting, also attended by Frommer and Ortiz, questions about a possible compromise on the issue of lowering the cost of prescription drugs were raised. Reports were that the meeting lasted about four hours and ended with little agreement (Myers 2005). Back in her committee, Ortiz held up Frommer's bill and denied him a chance to get the credit for a major program to lower drug prices in 2005. He decided to let it sit in the senate Health Committee with the option of bringing it up in 2006.

Still, a proposal to create a prescription drug purchasing pool that used Medi-Cal purchasing power for residents was on the November ballot in the form of Proposition 79. The pharmaceutical industry spent at least $80 million to oppose Proposition 79, a national record for spending by any industry on a single state ballot initiative campaign. The PhRMA TV campaign against Proposition 79 commenced in mid-August, weeks before such campaigns usually begin (Wildermuth 2005). The ads employed hot-button words such as "bureaucracy" and "government", claiming "Proposition 79 creates a costly new bureaucracy" and "Prop. 79 creates a big new government program." The industry relentlessly broadcast an ad featuring a bald-headed, older white male actor dressed as a low-level white-collar government worker wielding an oversized rubber stamp that he used to deny medicines to people. Meanwhile, PhRMA asserted that physicians supported Proposition 78 when, in fact, the California Medical Association hadn't taken a position (Hiltzik 2005).

As the election drew near, Proposition 79 advocates heard that PhRMA was targeting African-American and Latino political activists and voters and passed this information on to the *San Francisco Chronicle* political reporter, Phil Matier, who verified the rumor. Two days later, he reported in his column that former Democratic Assembly Speaker Willie Brown had been paid at least $450,000 to recruit African-American and Latino politicians to oppose Proposition 79

(Matier and Ross 2005). Through Brown's effort, the leadership of such groups as the NAACP and the Mexican American Political Association were also enlisted to fight Proposition 79. As a final touch in the effort to turn African-Americans against Proposition 79, African-American women around the state found pieces in their mailboxes titled "The Black Woman's Guide to California Politics." The flier urged voters to support Proposition 78 and featured photos of leading African-American politicians including US Rep. Barbara Lee, (D–CA), Rep. Juanita Millender-McDonald (D–CA), Rep. Maxine Waters (D–CA), Rep. Diane Watson (D–CA), Assemblywoman Karen Bass (D–Los Angeles), Los Angeles County Supervisor Yvonne Brathwaite Burke, and former Assembly Speaker Herb Wesson. The problem was that they were all opposed to Proposition 78 (Levey 2005). A number of African-American officeholders repudiated the campaign. Rep. Waters said some of the African-American politicians who took this money had "dishonored the NAACP" (Lawrence 2005), and Rep. Lee's district office reported that the Congresswoman was "really distressed — we have never had so many confused, distressed, angry phone calls." All and all, the industry spent $1.4 million on this part of its campaign against Proposition 79.

Proposition 79 supporters spent much of their time working on wording arguments for Proposition 79 and against Proposition 78 that would appear in the voters' handbook circulated by the state.[19] We did not have the resources to do much outreach to labor organization leaders, not even developing a rationale for their support. We aired nearly no television ads. The California AARP, which had supported the voluntary approach in SB 19, was at least persuaded to oppose Proposition 78.

Still, some of the policy work that went into developing support for Proposition 79 was helpful. It forced its advocates to understand how prescription drug discounts were actually obtained. Many health access supporters had not been strong on the concepts. But because they had to talk regularly to the press about discounts, they sharpened their policy skills considerably. As it was to turn out, these skills would be of considerable use in 2006.

By September, support for both Propositions 78 and 79 was declining. According to the Field Poll, Proposition 78, the industry's initiative, had 57 percent of the voters' support in June; Proposition 79 had 48 percent.[20] As PhRMA's political TV ads blared, support for both 78 and 79 fell to about 40 percent. Most likely the barrage of ads increased many voters' uncertainties about any policy claiming to increase prescription drug access.

California's unions responded to Schwarzenegger's Propositions 74–77 by pooling an unprecedented amount of money, spending more than $100 million to oppose them. The California Teachers Association provided more than $53 million, while SEIU put in more than $20 million (Brenner 2006). As Proposition 79 was fading, polls showed that these union investments were paying off. The governor's measures to impose a spending cap on the state budget and redistrict legislative districts in mid-decade were failing to gain public support. Under a barrage from ABC, the early lead of Proposition 74, making it easier to fire teachers, evaporated. So did the lead of Proposition 75, which would require public employee unions to get annual written permission before using any member's dues for political purposes.

At the end of September 2005, Schwarzenegger began to give signs that he would reposition himself more into the center of the political spectrum. With the date for his reelection little more than a year away, his administration looked to deescalate its battle with Democrats and their backers. His spouse, Maria Shriver, hired Daniel Zingale, Grey Davis's former chief of staff. With Zingale that close to Schwarzenegger, he had by his side someone who could help him productively negotiate compromises with the Democratic legislative leadership in 2006.

In the end, both Propositions 78 and 79 lost. Supporters of Proposition 79 had lacked the financial resources to tell voters their story through the mass media and develop support for it. The industry used TV ads, misleading mailers, and payment to some leaders in the African-American and Latino communities to raise voter doubts about a state program to lower drug prices; but Proposition 78's original 9 percent lead had over 79 actually shrank. In the end, Proposition 78 got 42 percent of the vote, Proposition 79 just 39 percent.

Although the industry's $80 million attack on Proposition 79 worked, the campaign had elevated the use of Medi-Cal purchasing power to lower drug prices for residents to a key point of contention between organized labor and the governor. On top of that, under the campaign spending barrage from ABC, all four of the governor's major initiatives were defeated. According to the Field Poll, voter approval of Schwarzenegger had dropped below 40 percent—a dangerous level for an incumbent facing reelection.

In the wake of the Proposition 79 effort, the use of Medi-Cal purchasing power to help many to obtain lower drug prices was no longer a marginal idea in California politics. Many of the capitol's health policymakers had gotten to understand it. One of the most powerful unions in the state, SEIU, had become deeply involved in its promotion. Majority Leader Frommer's bill, AB 75, which would authorize the use of Medi-Cal purchasing power for Californians, was still alive in the senate Health Committee. Advocates could move their support from ABC, which was closing down with the election, to the OURx Coalition, which was still active in the legislature. Although tensions between Frommer and committee chair Ortiz might block AB 75, advocates for the policy had the opportunity and resources they needed to move their policy forward.

2006

With the next gubernatorial election getting closer and Schwarzenegger badly defeated at the polls for the second time, his chances for reelection were starting to look like those of a Republican running as a right-winger in a general California election. So, he began a move to the center. In November 2005, he hired Susan Kennedy, a top aide to former Governor Gray Davis, as his new chief of staff. According to Kennedy, "It was pretty immediate in terms of what we had to do," namely, quickly end countless battles with special interest groups around the capitol. As Schwarzenegger's campaign manager Steve Schmidt put it, they had to end the war with the "coalition of the pissed off," that is, the teachers, law enforcement, firefighters, nurses, and other "stakeholders" angry about the governor's attacks on them (Salladay 2007). In January 2006, his administration got in touch with Jude Walsh, who had become the Maine official who had taken the role of Kevin Concannon in dealing with drugmakers. The governor's staff wanted to learn more about Maine Rx. The governor would have to take a few positions to show himself as a centrist and, in the wake of the Proposition 78/ 79 campaigns, promoting access to prescription drugs may have seemed as good as any. That same month, he wrote Congress, supporting the importation of Canadian drugs. Although his support was highly conditional, it was a step away from his earlier adamant opposition to importation.

Policy developments at the federal level gave Schwarzenegger another opportunity to revamp his position on access to prescription drugs. In January, Medicare Part D, designed to pay part of the prescription drug costs of people on Medicare, went into effect, creating massive problems. Most critical were those associated with moving people eligible for both Medicare and Medicaid (dual eligibles) from Medi-Cal to private Part D drug plans. Of the approximately one million dual eligibles in California, hundreds of thousands had trouble with the transition. Drugstores around the state saw scenes of dual eligibles coming in, expecting to pick up prescriptions as before, only to learn that they could not get their medicines. Some of the private Part D drug plans into which they had been enrolled by the government didn't cover their particular medicines or didn't have contracts with the drugstores that they had been using. Pharmacists across the state reported nightmare situations as they broke this distressing and sometimes life-threatening news to frail elders (Colliver 2006).

In a few days, the governor and legislature leadership enacted AB 132, a bill that appropriated $150 million to cover the drug costs of dual eligibles in these situations so that they could take home their medicines. The parties moved so expeditiously that the committee hearing for the authorizing bill took place in a matter of minutes in an anteroom to the assembly chamber. When AB 132 expired weeks later, the governor and legislature quickly acted to extend the emergency program through May and then again into 2007. Although these Part D problems occurred across the country, California became a leader in addressing them. Meanwhile, Frommer's AB 75 was still pending before the senate Health Committee, but Ortiz was still holding up the bill. And the April deadline for the bill to either move out of her committee or die there was approaching.

With Frommer's bill likely to die in Ortiz's committee, Beth Capell, representing SEIU, went to the very top of legislature leadership, Assembly Speaker Nuñez and Senate President Perata, and asked them to author another bill like AB 75. Capell was a southern Californian with a PhD in political science from the University of California at Berkeley. After working as legislative staff, she moved on to lobby for the California Nurses Association from 1986 to the early 1990s. In the mid-1990s, she moved on to the California Council of SEIU. At the time, legislative term limits and a growing fund for political expenditures were enhancing SEIU's power in the state legislature. By the end of the decade, Capell had joined her experience with SEIU's rising power to lead health policy discussions among California's labor and consumer lobbyists.

A bill like AB 75, but authored by Perata, would get through the senate Health Committee, as he had a great deal of leverage over Ortiz, including the ability to remove her as chair of the committee. With the co-authorship of Speaker Nuñez, the bill would have the backing of the most powerful person in that house and the best chance of making it to the governor's desk. Furthermore, Capell proposed that the bill adopt the compromise suggested by Dan Carson of the Legislative Analyst's Office–trying a voluntary approach to obtain discounts for Californians first and using Medi-Cal leverage if that approach didn't work. Given that the labor-based ABC had backed a Medi-Cal "hammer" in Proposition 79 and that organized labor was among Nuñez's and Perata's major backers, they saw Capell's proposal as a top priority. Thus, they agreed and authored a pair of bills promoting the LAO compromise, AB 2911 (Nuñez) and SB 1702 (Perata).

In March, Billy Tauzin came to California to meet with Fabian Nuñez, looking to see if he could get him to drop his support of using Medi-Cal purchasing power for Californians. Tauzin suggested that he was willing to discuss a voluntary approach to lowering costs first and using some sort of leverage if that was not effective. But he wouldn't support using Medi-Cal leverage and couldn't offer any convincing specifics on what his leverage would be. Under pressure from groups like SEIU, Nuñez remained firm and the talks produced no compromise.

The administration, meanwhile, brought in Stan Rosenstein, its policy authority on Medi-Cal, including use of Medi-Cal leverage to obtain prescription drug discounts. Rosenstein had been with the state Department of Health Services since Jerry Brown (D) was governor in the eighties and had run Medi-Cal for ten years. But, despite his experience with Medi-Cal's prescription drug supplemental rebate program, he initially argued that Medi-Cal leverage wouldn't work to obtain discounts for people not on Medi-Cal.

Legislative staff was concerned about Rosenstein's assertion and, in April, an OURx Coalition technical group of which I was a member met with the staff in an old western- style conference room in the old capitol building to discuss how to proceed with AB 2911 and SB 1702. As a result of the Proposition 79 campaign, the OURx contingent was well versed in why we needed a "hammer" and we forcefully argued that there was no alternative to using Medi-Cal purchasing power for people not on Medi-Cal and that using it could lower drug prices. SB 1702, Senator Perata's bill carrying the LAO compromise, stuck with the use of Medi-Cal purchasing power and came up for a vote before the senate Health Committee. With Perata backing the bill, Ortiz voted for it and her committee passed the bill.

In June, as SB 1702 and AB 2911 were moving through the legislature, the course of California politics once again had a critical impact on drug access legislation. In the Democratic primary for governor, the labor-backed Phil Angelides defeated the more pro-business Steve Westley to win the party nomination to oppose Schwarzenegger in November. In 2005, Angelides had opposed Proposition 78 and could move to the governor's left on prescription drug issues (Political Campaigns 2005). With his voter approval numbers still low, Schwarzenegger had to continue to move toward the center to cut off the Angelides threat. As part of his effort to deescalate his feuds with Democratic supporters, he began to take issues that were the base of Angelides's election strategy out from under him (Garcia 2006). There were a number of issues on which he could act to preempt Angelides from using them in the election campaign. Among them was prescription drug access for people not on Medi-Cal. Until this point, there was still no agreement between the governor and legislative leadership on SB 1702. Under pressure from organized labor, the Democrats wouldn't give in over getting a serious "hammer" like Medi-Cal purchasing power with which to negotiate discounts, and PhRMA wouldn't agree to any form of state leverage known to be effective.

Making a Deal

By July, Schwarzenegger's aides recruited from the Davis administration had begun a move to make a deal for the governor that he could use to soften opposition from groups like SEIU. Schwarzenegger's team was willing to look at the compromise proposed by the LAO as long as the governor didn't have to use something like the Medi-Cal "hammer" while he was in office. The Schwarzenegger administration called Nuñez to indicate this willingness. Nuñez's staff went to Beth Capell and asked if SEIU would be willing to negotiate on the LAO proposal; it was. The administration assigned Daniel Zingale, Maria Shriver's chief of staff, and Herb Shultz, a former colleague of Zingale in Governor Davis's Department of Managed Health Care, to staff-level talks.

To get such a deal into legislative form, staff members would have to meet to work out details and language. They met in the ornate conference room adjacent to the speaker's office in the old capitol building. In addition to Zingale and Shultz, the administration was represented by Stan Rosenstein. Legislative leadership was represented by staff; Capell and Casey Young of AARP led the OURx contingent. Young had extensive industrial relations experience and a long record of work in the state capitol. Unlike his predecessor at California AARP, he was quite interested in using Medi-Cal leverage to get lower prescription drug prices. Unlike Governor King in Maine, California political leaders were not about to leave PhRMA out of the room; in California, they had too much power to be treated that way. So, PhRMA was in the room, represented by Jan Faiks, PhRMA vice president.

Where they could have more privacy, principals such as Nuñez and Perata met in less frequent higher-level talks that would produce directions for staff talks, when needed. For those meetings, PhRMA also sent out its top gun, Billy Tauzin. Tauzin met with Frommer and other leaders of the legislative and executive branches regularly. He used every resource at his disposal from PhRMA's clout to his Cajun charm. But, owing to the positions of PhRMA's constituents, he was unable to introduce any effective alternative to the use of Medi-Cal purchasing power in case the voluntary approach failed (Thomason 2007).

Once staff talks got under way, it became clear that two issues related to the voluntary approach were blocking a deal. They were (1) what the industry called "a firewall" and (2) the reference price from which discounts would be calculated. The firewall concerned the prescription drug purchasing office within the Department of Health Services (DHS) that had negotiated discounts for Medi-Cal. The industry suggested that, if the state were to negotiate discounts for people not on Medi-Cal, those working in the DHS office negotiating for Medi-Cal and those negotiating discounts for people not on Medi-Cal had to be barred from communicating with one another. Counting on our gullibility, the industry negotiators suggested the firewall was somehow a legal requirement. I got in touch with Sharon Treat, who had considerable experience dealing with the industry. She told me that there was no legal need for a firewall and that it was merely a tactic to weaken the hand of those who would be negotiating discounts for people not on Medi-Cal.

Reliable reference prices—that is, the prices from which discounts would be calculated—would be critical to winning meaningful discounts. If one were to negotiate a discount from an inflated price, one could end up with no real discount at all. For each reference price, the industry wanted what it called a "lowest best price" as the reference price. But, in an industry where there were many prices for some drugs and some of them were secret, there would be no reliable way of knowing the lowest best price for many drugs. In many cases, negotiators would have to take the industry's word for it. So, using "lowest best price" wouldn't be of much help.

On this issue, I got Steve Schondelmeyer, a nationally known expert on the subject at the the University of Minnesota, on the phone with Capell and Young. Schondelmeyer suggested that we use the average manufacturer price (AMP) as the reference price. It is verifiable in that it is easily available. It is reliable in that is based on actual sales data. While it is six to twelve months out of date and also not listed for some branded drugs, it would be a good start. Capell and Young then demanded that the reference prices had to be "verifiable and reliable." To back them up, Dean Tipps, executive director of Capell's client, the California Council of SEIU, went to the higher level of talks. He called

Nuñez and reiterated the point that the reference price needed to be verifiable and reliable.

Beyond these issues related to the voluntary phase of seeking discounts, PhRMA's negotiator still refused to budge on the "hammer." She wouldn't agree to any purchasing power leverage that might work, even if it were only used in the second stage of a state-run prescription drug discount program. She wanted the OURx negotiators to make more concessions in negotiations.

On 17 July, Capell decided that she had had it with PhRMA's intransigence over the use of Medi-Cal purchasing power in case the voluntary approach didn't work. That night, she labored over an e-mail to Perata's staff member handling the negotiations, stating that the OURx Coalition was finished compromising. She let him know that SEIU would either get enforceable discounts or that it would use all its power to keep legislative leadership from reaching an agreement and leave Schwarzenegger without a prescription drug access policy for which he could take credit.

The next day, Perata handed Capell's note to Tauzin in a meeting of the principals. The lingering polarization of the governor and legislature created an opening for prescription drug access advocates. The election was close and Schwarzenegger wanted to claim a victory on prescription drug access. Democratic leadership was in a position to reward its union backers by pushing the LAO proposal, Medi-Cal "hammer" and all, on the governor at the expense of PhRMA. Events had gotten out of PhRMA's control. The governor and legislature agreed that the LAO proposal would be the basis of a deal; Nuñez was particularly close to the governor and his bill, AB 2911, became the one that would embody the deal.

To make sure that the emerging deal could actually work and to ensure that I would recommend a version of AB 2911 amended per the negotiations to leaders of the capitol's lobby for seniors, CARA and SAN, Capell asked me and Richard Thomason, the Frommer staffer who had overseen his prescription drug legislation and had recently gone to work for an SEIU affiliate, to meet with Stan Rosenstein and discuss the details of an amended AB 2911.

As Rosenstein had overseen the state office responsible for negotiating Medi-Cal's prescription drug supplemental rebates and the state auditor had found its work to be effective, I was interested in hearing him out. Also, he had worked for both Republican and Democratic administrations and struck me as someone who might be able to effectively use Medi-Cal purchasing power to obtain discounts for people not on Medi-Cal. Capell, Thomason, and I went to meet him at the new Department of Health Services building bordering the capitol grounds. Rosenstein brought Kevin Gorospe to our meeting on 20 July, where both assured us that they would be working on the voluntary phase of implementing an amended AB 2911. I had interviewed Gorospe years earlier on the supplemental rebate program and found him to be knowledgeable in negotiating discounts. Their presence also made it clear that the state would be negotiating the discounts in-house, increasing public accountability for their work.

Rosenstein agreed to use the average manufacturer price (AMP) as a reference price for calculating discounts. He proposed that he also be allowed to use the "lowest commercial price." He claimed that he would demand documentation from a drugmaker to back up a claim about the "lowest commercial price." He said that the state auditor and state controller could check his success. Rosenstein and Gorospe assured us that we could continue to meet to discuss implementation, after SB 2911 was enacted. We could all check his prices against those from the AMP.

As negotiations over the compromise bill concluded, it was clear that the OURx Coalition didn't get all it wanted. The Medi-Cal purchasing power "hammer" for obtaining drug discounts for people not on Medi-Cal could not be used until 1 August 2010. Given his own interests, there would be no time in the next four years that Schwarzenegger would agree to an earlier date. We simply couldn't do any better on that point. Also, while AB 2911 had defined Californians eligible for the new drug discounts as all those in households with incomes at or below 350 percent of the federal poverty level, the administration wanted the cutoff at 300 percent of the FPL.[21] Those of us in the meeting representing the OURx Coalition didn't see why that should be the deal-breaker.

Still, we won on our basic demand on using the Medi-Cal "hammer" to lower drug prices. In that context, and believing that Rosenstein and Gorospe were long-term state employees who had carried out drug discount policy under both Democrats and Republicans and their assurances on accountability, I agreed that we should take the framework of their deal. So did Thomason. A couple of days after the 20 July meeting, the OURx Coalition held a conference call involving all of its constituents regarding our response to the pending compromise. It was announced that Thomason and I supported the framework of the deal. Capell explained that legislative leadership had demanded final language from the administration. So, it was urgent that the OURx Coalition come to a decision. Some lobbyists expressed concern about giving Schwarzenegger this election campaign boost, noting that a deal would give Angelides one less issue to use against Schwarzenegger.

Others advocated going forward with the pending compromise. The group decided that it wouldn't tout the pending deal but would authorize Health Access, our coalition's best-known advocate for health care consumers, to say something positive about it.

One last-minute "detail" was a proposed $10 discount card enrollment fee proposed by the administration. This fee could seriously limit enrollment of low-income people. Even if we had our "hammer," the program wouldn't succeed without heavy enrollment. When many objected to the $10 fee, it was finally amended. First, it was eliminated for all Californians enrolled by nonprofits such as senior advocacy groups. Second, although it was required for all Californians enrolled by for-profits like drugstores, it was understood that they might well "waive" the fee for customers and pay it themselves in order to attract business.

PhRMA continued to strongly object to AB 2911 and pressed rank-and-file Democratic legislators to vote against it. But the administration and its backers had gotten too far down the road of making a deal to turn back. Schwarzenegger was about to get a deal with Democrats and they were about to hand their public sector union backers a major win. Schwarzenegger's representatives formally agreed to authorization of a Medi-Cal purchasing power "hammer" to win discounts for people not on Medi-Cal in 2010, an AMP reference price, and Rosenstein's office handling negotiations with drugmakers. On 21 August, the final version, which the OURx Coalition had approved, came before the senate Appropriations Committee in the form of an amended AB 2911 (Nuñez). With organized labor's backing, the bill got all the Democratic votes on the committee, including that of Senator Ortiz. On 29 August, AB 2911 came before the senate Health Committee. Ortiz acknowledged that Senate President Perata could well be listening to her from his office and that she had best vote for the bill. Calling her "aye" a "courtesy vote," she voted for AB 2911. Nevertheless, Senator Ortiz asserted that using Medi-Cal leverage to gain discounts for people not on Medi-Cal imperiled Medi-Cal recipients' access to medicine and that the bill's proponents didn't care about people on Medi-Cal.

The bill went to the senate floor where PhRMA continued to battle for votes; but, with intense labor pressure on Democratic legislators, Perata held all their votes against PhRMA's opposition. The next day, the bill came back to the assembly where Nuñez, also relying on continuing pressure from labor lobbyists to overcome PhRMA's resistance, delivered all but two Democratic members and sent the bill to the governor. Labor lobbyists did little to pressure Republican legislators; so nobody in the governor's party deserted PhRMA to vote for AB 2911.

With the gubernatorial election pending, the governor decided to stage a signing ceremony in the rotunda of the old capitol building. Whether or not to attend the ceremony generated considerable debate within the OURx Coalition. Should we go and take credit for a victory? Should we stay away and deny the governor our faces as a backdrop for a photo on his campaign website? Most of the union members of our coalition stayed away. On 29 September, I attended. We had stuck to our guns on the "hammer," the reference price, and the "firewall," and had handed the pharmaceutical industry a serious defeat. AB 2911 was about to become the California Discount Prescription Drug Program.

The capitol rotunda is dominated by a monument of Christopher Columbus receiving funds from Queen Isabella for his planned trip to the Indies.[22] It was originally put there as a nineteenth-century advertisement for California as the Promised Land. To advertise to voters his action on access to medicines, Schwarzenegger's staff had a table set up alongside of the monument for the televised signing of AB 2911. Schwarzenegger and Nuñez took their places at the table, bathed in the lights of local TV stations. Also present was a representative from Rite Aid, the part of the health care industry that was ready to make lemonade out of what some chains might see as a lemon. I also saw a few local AARP members in the capitol for the first time. From outside of the bright lights, Dario Frommer looked in uncertainly at the speaker. When he caught Nuñez' eye, the speaker waived him into the picture and the governor put his name to AB 2911 with Nuñez and Frommer at his side.

The national press did not treat the enactment of AB 2911 as a major event, even though it portended great costs to the pharmaceutical industry. Several months after the bill was signed, the *Boston Globe* noted it had "quietly passed this fall." In observing that the California Discount Prescription Drug Program was the "looming concern" of the pharmaceutical industry, the article quoted several industry leaders describing the bill as establishing "price controls" (Henderson 2006). In November, Schwarzenegger was reelected; his margin of victory was 16 percentage points (55 percent to 39 percent). His strategy of "letting Arnold be Arnold," rather than point man for the Chamber of Commerce's war with public employee unions, had succeeded (Salladay 2007). Frommer and Ortiz were both termed out. Frommer went to work for Mayer Brown, one of the country's most prestigious and profitable law firms. Ortiz became a consultant for the California Endowment, a conversion foundation that Blue Cross of California was required to set up when its executives sold it to investors to run as a for-profit medical insurance business.[23]

Implementation Delayed

Initially, the governor indicated he was serious about implementing the California Discount Prescription Drug Program (CDPDP). His proposed budget for fiscal year 2007-2008 allocated $8.3 million to the program. He proposed funding fifteen positions to operate it. Some money was also allocated for physicians to help enroll patients (Douglas 2007). In a meeting with state administration officials in March 2007, OURx representatives learned that the Department of Health Services was actively planning to ramp up the CDPDP. It had started the bidding process for an administrator to handle tasks like program enrollment. February 2008 was the target start date (Douglas et al. 2007). Subsequently, the department selected First Health as its administrator and manufacturers were signing contracts with the state to provide Californians with drug price discounts (Douglas 2007).

Then, in mid-2007, another economic downturn began to take a heavy toll on the California state budget. This time, the crisis had begun with the subprime bust. In 2006, many homeowners, particularly in what is known as the Inland Empire, had found that their variable-rate mortgage payments were increasing beyond their ability to pay.[24] Some defaulted on their mortgages and their houses went on the market, becoming part of a trend that began driving housing demand and prices down. Housing construction slowed, throwing many construction and real estate workers into unemployment. These developments led to sharp unexpected drops in state revenue throughout 2007 (California Legislative Analyst's Office 2007).

So, the governor and legislature had to keep revising upward the deficit the state was facing and they weren't able to agree to a budget for 2007-2008 until 21 August, two months into that budget year. As part of the agreement, Schwarzenegger promised to use his line-item veto authority to reduce spending by approximately $700 million (California Budget Project 2007). While the brunt of these cuts came down on the Medi-Cal program, the governor took the opportunity to eliminate the $8.3 million he had allocated for the CDPDP from the state budget (Gilman 2007). Manufacturers stopped signing contracts. First Health stopped its administrative work. In addition to these problems, there was another. Although the OURx Coalition had made sure that there was no specific requirement in AB 2911 that the state ask the federal government for a waiver to use the Medi-Cal "hammer," the administration claimed in September that approval from the federal Center for Medicare & Medicaid Services would be needed (Douglas 2007). [25]

In 2008, the Schwarzenegger administration again proposed to fund the California Discount Prescription Drug Program. OURx Coalition representatives again met with Rosenstein and were assured of the administration's good faith. However, by 2008, events triggered by the subprime crisis hit California particularly hard and had economic activity in the whole state plunging toward that year's Great Recession. Housing starts in California fell from 2007 levels and unemployment had gone from a moderately high 5.3 percent in October, 2007 and was heading toward a catastrophic 9 percent at the end of 2008.[26] State revenues fell sharply and the state found itself facing a massive budget crisis (California Legislative Analyst's Office 2008). Under the Democrats, the senate Budget Committee eliminated the funding for CDPDP. When the budget got to the assembly side, Capell and OURx Coalition advocates vigorously objected to the cut and the funding amounting to $11.7 million was restored. Even in California, a culture supporting access to medicines has taken root among health policy progressives working in the capitol. But, when he signed the state budget for 2008-2009, the governor once again eliminated all funding for the CDPDP (California Budget Project 2008). The next year, when signing the state budget for 2009-2010, Schwarzenegger wrote that he would delay implementation of the CDPDP until 1 July 2010, one month before AB 2911 authorizes the state to use Medi-Cal purchasing power to lower drug prices for Californians not on Medi-Cal (California Budget Project 2009). As Schwarzenegger's term in office ended January 2011, he effectively passed implementation of the CDPDP to use Medi-Cal purchasing power to the next governor.

In the meantime, the CDPDP didn't serve as Maine Rx had to trigger a wave of state legislation that would use Medicaid purchasing power for non-Medicaid residents, as it wasn't well publicized outside of California and the problems associated with rollout of Part D drew a lot of state prescription drug policymakers' attention. To boot, as Table 6-1 shows, the industry maintained the steep level of political spending at the state level it had initiated at the beginning of the decade in order to reduce the chances of such legislation.

Table 6-1
Campaign Contributions at State Level

Year	2004	2006	2008
Dollars	$7,446,838	$10,046,939	$11,538,298

Source: Bauer 2009

So, as of this writing (December 2011), it remains to be seen if the enactment of the CDPDP will have a direct impact on Californians' drug access. Jerry Brown is once again governor and he is empowered to take steps to improve access for residents not on Medi-Cal, using Medi-Cal purchasing power. Whether or not he does, fighting for AB 2911 when it seemed like the industry had all the cards paid off in other ways. The fight helped keep California advocates for seniors together and ready for times when they could effectively address injustices hurting their constituencies. A chance for advocates for prescription drug access to act along these lines quickly came at the federal level with the election of the 110th Congress (2007-2008).

In the same year that AB 2911 was enacted, Democrats won majorities in both the US House and Senate and put themselves in a position to start federal action against high drug prices for the first time since 1992. Shortly after the Democrats took office, leaders of the OURx campaign went to Washington and met with the top health policy staff of House Speaker Nancy Pelosi (D–CA) and Rep. Pete Stark (D–CA). In the meetings, the Californians expressed anger over how Part D had done little to improve access to medicines and demanded that Congress do something about the problem. In this group, House leadership saw an example of the kind of grassroots support that it would need in order to fix the high expense and poor coverage of the Medicare Modernization Act. Just as at the state level, righteous indignation over the lack of access to medicines would be fuel for political action.

In the first one hundred hours of the 110th Congress, the new House majority passed a series of bills. Included among them was one that took the same tack as California in dealing with the pharmaceutical industry, namely, it authorized the use of government purchasing power to lower the price of medicines. The legislation did this by repealing the "nonintervention" clause of the Medicare Modernization Act (MMA) that had prohibited such use of purchasing power on behalf of the

Medicare program. While the bill was later killed by a Senate filibuster, it helped frame the prescription drug policy debate for the 111th Congress. Then the Democrats would not only control the Congress, but they would have the White House and a filibuster-proof Senate as well.[27]

In 2007, the veterans of the AB 2911 fight were better prepared to battle PhRMA and other health care industry interests than they were before the battle had started. OURx not only pressed for implementation of the CDPDP, but also urged a range of other policies improving Californians' access to medicines. Although, eventually, the coalition broke up, some of its organizations still use the infrastructures that they built during the OURx campaign to advocate for their constituencies in the state capitol.

Overall, the battle over AB 2911 shows that, even in a state where a business lobby like PhRMA is very powerful, a strong and fully involved union, an issue that deeply concerns voters, and legislative leadership in a position to take on a governor can combine to produce a major legislative defeat for a powerful industry. It also shows that, in winning such a victory, campaigns could build momentum that would empower subsequent efforts to improve health access.

---

[1] Although they arrived in California at the same time as the Anglos, Asian and African-American settlers were absent from the mural.

[2] While, in 2009, 41 percent of California "whites" registering in either the Republican or Democratic Party were Democrats, 55 percent of Asian-Americans choosing between the parties were Democrats and 74 percent of Latinos making the choice were Democrats (Just the Facts 2009).

[3] In 2005, it was estimated that the administrators negotiating supplemental rebates for Medi-Cal saved about half a billion dollars a year through its use of Medi-Cal purchasing power (California Bureau of State Audits 2005).

[4] Speier had been a tireless political and policy activist since growing up in the Bay Area and earned both her college and law degrees from the University of California system. Her career started her serving as an aide to Bay Area Congressman Leo Ryan (D–San Mateo). In 1978, both Speier and the Congressman had gone to Jonestown, a supposedly utopian community in Guyana, South America, headed by the Reverend Jim Jones, to investigate constituent complaints that relatives were being held captive. They discovered that some residents were, in fact, being held against their will and the congressional delegation was gunned down in an ensuing massacre. Ryan died where they were shot; Speier was hit five times and left for dead, but was found alive when rescuers arrived. Ten years later, she was elected to the state assembly where she distinguished herself for her expertise in health policy.

[5] As described in Chapter 2, in response to rate cuts to Medicare managed-care plans in the Balanced Budget Act of 1997, plans began withdrawing drug coverage for seniors.

[6] Davis's connection to the large drugmakers Pfizer and Merck indicates the closeness of the relationship. Three years later, in 2002, when Pfizer opened a new plant in California, Davis said it is "the kind of employer we want to nurture and develop." Pfizer CEO Hank McKinnell reciprocated, "Under the leadership of Governor Davis, it is clear that the bioscience industry has a welcome home here in California" (California Manufacturing & Technology Association 2002). Merck also showed its appreciation of Davis and his policies by making him the top gubernatorial recipient of its campaign contributions (Barber 2007).

[7] Montigny was one of the members of Vermont Senate President Shumlin's group of New England legislators concerned about drug prices. But H 4900 provided that the state should contract out the bargaining and Massachusetts never did so.

[8] As money came in, Rescue California was able to hire Frank Luntz, pollster to such right-wing Republicans as former US House Speaker Newt Gingrich. Based on focus-group research conducted in Orange and Sacramento counties, Luntz outlined seventeen ways to "kill Davis softly." "It is important to trash the governor," Luntz wrote, but he added, "Issues are less important than attributes and character traits in your recall effort." Luntz pointed out that the majority of Californians "are unfamiliar with the recall process—and this uncertainty means voters can be easily swayed in either direction." (Blumenthal 2003).

[9] Included in that group were former Wilson lieutenants Bob White, Patricia Clarey, and Martin Wilson. Schwarzenegger took his finance and tax advisers from the Hoover Institution, where Wilson was a fellow (LeDuff 2003).

[10] In 2004, the option of states helping residents to import Canadian medicines was relatively new and, although it was subsequently found that few seniors would avail themselves of it, initially it seemed a promising solution.

[11] Based on her advocacy for access to prescription drugs and other issues of concern to consumers, Ellen Corbett (D–San Leandro) has subsequently won numerous awards from California's consumer advocate organizations.

[12] Schwarzenegger also lost a ballot measure to have the voters change the state's system of primary voting; this change was calculated to produce more Democratic legislators friendly to him.

[13] Speier's remarks proved to be her swan song on using state purchasing power to lower prescription drug prices. Until she termed out in 2006, she focused on other issues. In 2008, the seat in the US House of Representatives once held by Leo Ryan came open and Jackie Speier was elected to it.

[14] To put an initiative on the ballot, backers must take a number of steps. After they have drafted it, they have to submit it to the attorney general to get back a title and summary, a process that can take up to fifteen days. The attorney general can also require the draft to be reviewed by the Department of Finance and the Joint Legislative Budget Committee, a process that can take up to another twenty-five days. When the attorney general returns it with a title and summary, they can begin collecting the needed signatures. They had to collect those signatures quickly enough to allow at least 131 days before the next statewide election—in this case, a fall election (Initiative & Referendum Institute 2002). So, in this case, they could expect to have about four months.

For these kinds of measures, about one million signatures are needed (Repeal Prop 8 in 2010 2010).

[15] Even though the signatures for Proposition 79 were turned in first, the Republican secretary of state gave the industry's initiative a lower number. Lower proposition numbers improve the chances of measures passing because voters become increasingly more likely to vote "no" as they go down the ballot.

[16] PhRMA's threatened initiative to cut contingency fees for the trial lawyers did not materialize.

[17] Nuñez had gotten into the political profession as a union advocate in Los Angeles, was elected to the assembly in 2002, and took the speaker's post in 2003, only a year later.

[18] As discussed in Chapter 5, although the MMA was the largest financial commitment made by the US government toward establishing a health program and should have resulted in strong government pressure to lower drug prices, it was purposely restricted in its capacity to decrease prices and, thus, became a huge windfall for the pharmaceutical industry.

[19] I was one of the signatories for the "no on 78" argument.

[20] The Field (California) Poll has operated continuously since 1947 as an independent, nonpartisan, media-sponsored public opinion news service and has issued over 2,000 different reports. The Field Poll appears regularly in national and state media.

[21] In 2007, 300 percent of the federal poverty level for an individual would have been about $30,000 a year; for a family of three, a little more than $50,000 a year.

[22] When the statue was removed from the rotunda for capitol restoration in the 1970s, Latino groups objected to its return, on the grounds that Columbus ushered in an era of genocide and colonialism for the Native Peoples of the Western Hemisphere. But, when the restoration was finished, Latinos were still on the political margins and the statue was returned to confront tourists to this day.

[23] Since federal law requires that proceeds from the sale of assets of tax-exempt entities like the nonprofit Blue Cross be directed towards charitable purposes, one result of these conversions has been the creation of a number of new foundations, commonly referred to as "conversion foundations." When Blue Cross executives converted it into a for-profit business, they created the endowment to receive the proceeds of the sale.

[24] In California, Inland Empire refers to the counties immediately east of southern California's urban coastal counties.

[25] See Chapter 4 for discussion of the *PhRMA v. Concannon* decision.

[26] By January 2009, it would be 13.2 percent.

[27] The work of the 111th Congress on the Medicare prescription drug program is discussed in Chapter 7.

7

Politically Organizing for Access to Medicines

David stunned Goliath in Maine and PhRMA was again beaten in California. In Maine in 2000, the pharmaceutical industry with its many highly compensated lobbyists and consultants, its political allies, and media campaign was not able to stop the enactment of a law authorizing use of its Medicaid purchasing power to lower drug prices. In California in 2005-2006, the record-breaking sum that the industry spent to influence an initiative vote on drug prices and its financial support of the governor were also inadequate to stop that state from taking the same action. Although Goliath had his day in beating those promoting the use of Medicaid purchasing power in Vermont, prescription drug access advocates in Maine and California showed us ways to beat him. These victories contain lessons for people working to advocate for prescription drug access that may also be useful for those promoting progressive policies more generally. This chapter discusses some of those lessons and concludes by noting some of their implications for current US policymaking, particularly health policy.

Hearing Voters' Righteous Indignation

In both cases in which PhRMA was beaten, popular support of policies containing prescription drug prices undergirded the victories of advocates for prescription drug access. In Maine, by the time the legislation to restrain drug prices was on Governor King's desk, public opinion as reflected in a state poll (Market Decisions 2000) had helped force him to negotiate with Senate Majority Leader Chellie Pingree. In California, as Governor Schwarzenegger considered his chances of reelection, he decided a capitol rotunda signing ceremony of a bill authorizing the use of Medicaid purchasing power for lowering drug prices could help him.

In these cases, righteous indignation was the foundation of the residents' support for political action. Righteous indignation meant holding the pharmaceutical industry responsible for high prescription drug prices and poor access to medicines. These high prices caused widespread indignation because the way they impeded access to needed medicine posed a critical hardship for many voters. As described in Chapter 2, medicine has become increasingly essential to health care. Prescription drug costs have risen much faster than the incomes of most senior citizens—the age group by far the most likely to use medicines (National Center for Health Statistics 2009)—forcing many to forego essential medicines or other necessities. When they gave up medicines, they were risking their health, if not their lives. This indignation was righteous in that many seniors saw that the industry was using its great power to set the prices high. The industry's economic and political advantages were continually on display as it promoted its products and policy agenda. These shows of force helped complete a picture that showed the high prices and limited access to be the result of price-gouging.[1]

In all three states, progressives heard the strong voter indignation stirring over rising drug prices. In Vermont, Anthony Pollina heard it when he discussed the exorbitant prices of medicines with residents at a senior center. State Senator Cheryl Rivers looked at the House report on prescription drug prices released by Congressman Bernie Sanders, documenting the economic injustice of US drug prices, and saw the potential anger. From Maine, senior leader John Marvin heard rising indignation in Pollina's meeting at the Vermont senior center and at meetings in Maine. In California, the leaders of the Alliance for a Better California saw in the rapid collection of signatures to put drug price restraints on the ballot that there was deep voter concern over the price of medicines.

Allying with Powerful Progressive Organizations

Yet, righteous indignation was not enough to force progressive policy change by itself. In Vermont, there was righteous anger and progressives tried to harness it, but their efforts failed in 2000. A second lesson that prescription drug advocates can take from these case studies is that progressives needed to ally with organizations powerful enough to get a political party's leadership to strongly support a challenge to PhRMA. In Maine, it was Marvin's winning the support of the Maine State Employees Association (MSEA) that pushed Pingree and her legislative allies to try and win a battle over prescription drug prices with the governor. In California, progressives won the support of the California Council of Service Employees International Union (SEIU) by giving it the policy of using Medicaid purchasing power to lower drug prices for non-Medicaid residents for a ballot initiative against its adversary, PhRMA.[2] With SEIU pushing legislative leadership, it was able to force Schwarzenegger to agree to authorize the use of Medicaid purchasing power to lower drug prices.

Both the California Council and MSEA were affiliated with a powerful national union, SEIU. Unions with national affiliations are particularly useful in supporting progressive efforts because the national unions can provide organizing assistance and have the financial power that ensures direct access to top policymakers. Since the US political system is heavily influenced by political campaign contributors who then get the ears of politicians, it is quite difficult for progressives to sway legislators' votes without an ability to connect with them during the policymaking process.

In contrast, Vermont drug access advocates lacked the backing of a group with the political capacity of the California Council of SEIU or MSEA. Vermont's state employees union was not affiliated with a national union a sign of a state with a weak union tradition,. A look at private-sector unionization rates in 1983 (before Reaganism had taken its toll on US unions) shows how weak Vermont's union tradition was. In that year, Census Bureau data show that, while unions represented 16.5 percent of private-sector workers nationally, only 6.7 percent of Vermont's private-sector workers were unionized, ranking it 48th in the nation. In contrast, 17.7 percent of California's and 14.2 percent of Maine's private-sector workforces were unionized (US Census Bureau 2008). By the 1990s, they both had strong public-sector unions. In the twenty-first century, Vermont is still paying the price for a weak union movement in the twentieth century.

In Maine and California, the interests of union leadership and the grassroots aligned because the leadership of the unions was effectively threatened by the practices of the pharmaceutical industry that was angering voters, even if for different reasons than were voters. In California, for example, the pharmaceutical industry was threatening the public union officials who were considering support of what was to be Proposition 79. If Schwarzenegger's 2005 PhRMA-backed agenda had been realized, the state's top public employee union officials would have suffered a serious loss of power. If drugmakers continued to raise prices, many California voters would continue to lack essential medicines. So, in PhRMA, union officials and many voters had a common opponent.

Politically Isolating the Pharmaceutical Industry

A final lesson that can be taken from these case studies is that, in addition to the support of strong progressive organizations in Maine and California, prescription drug access advocates also politically isolated the pharmaceutical industry. At the end of the legislative battles over prescription drug prices in Maine and California, the pharmaceutical industry's intransigence had become problematic for its respective gubernatorial administrations and its other backers. The window of opportunity was open for making progressive policy regarding access to needed medicines.

In Maine, Governor King came to a point where sticking with PhRMA could weaken public support for his administration enough so that it might impair its ability to carry out other parts of its agenda. So, advocates for access to medicines had PhRMA in a position where it was effectively pitted against all the other interests looking to King. Then, PhRMA's power was not enough to overcome legislative leadership's push for lower prices for medicines. In California, Governor Schwarzenegger and his backers needed the "coalition of the pissed off" to be mollified in order to ensure victory over Angelides. As the powerful public employee unions effectively pressed legislative leadership to stay firm on prescription drug prices, PhRMA's intransigence made breaking with it his best option. At that point, legislation to use Medicaid purchasing power to obtain lower drug prices for Californians not on Medicaid was headed to enactment.

In summary, these three case studies show that the keys to success for advocates for prescription drug access were (1) hearing voters' righteous indignation over the high price of essential medicines, (2) allying with progressive organizations with the power to push a party's leadership to fully support a progressive policy, and (3) politically isolating the pharmaceutical industry.

"Framing" after Righteous Indignation

Versions of the second and third of these suggested lessons—allying with powerful organizations and making policy when the window of opportunity is open—have long been discussed in the literature of what academics call resource mobilization theory (McAdam et al. 1996).[3] But many academics using this theory have given the first of the larger lessons—progressives must build on widespread righteous indignation engendered by critical hardships—considerably less attention (Jasper 2004). Rather than offering hypotheses along this line, the academic theoretical literature often puts forward "framing," that is, building popular support by fashioning "shared understandings of the world and of themselves that legitimate and motivate collective action" as the key to winning popular support (McAdam et al. 1996). In mid-decade, many Democratic Party leaders used this idea to develop an approach for winning votes and called the tactic "messaging" (Green 2005).

But evidence from the case studies suggests that reliance on the concept of framing or messaging misses the point of why voters were angry. Seniors may have widely agreed that the prices of certain medicines were too high; but without the underlying threat to their health posed by the high prices, such framing would not have been very compelling. There was strong public support for lower prescription drug prices because drugmakers' drive for profits was creating critical hardships that led to widespread indignation. When outrage was expressed at town meetings, it was before politicians thought of the issue and it was not particularly reliant on the message-crafting of health access advocates.[4] The framing view would put power in the hands of professionals—such as the academics who espouse it—who are supposed to give voice to the inchoate masses. But it would fail to explain popular behavior in this book's case studies.

This is not to say that groups mobilizing voters feeling righteous anger don't need to choose apt and concise descriptions of the source of their anger. The capacity to frame such problems to facilitate popular mobilization is one of the organizational resources that they need for success. But this book's case studies suggest that progressives must build on righteous indignation, not well-crafted messages. They need messages that articulate widely felt economic disparities and point out viable solutions for voters.

Inferences beyond Fighting for Medicines

Access to prescription drugs is one in a set of progressive policies that support what is called in the US a middle-class standard of living, which includes, among other things, access to medical care, decent housing, affordable education, limited work weeks, and jobs that help make such things possible. If many US voters believe that they have a right to this standard of living and that the government should restrain those business practices that work against them, then the keys to success of movements for access to prescription drugs may apply more generally to movements supporting policies to protect the components of the so-called middle-class standard of living.

If this is so, then, to take on powerful businesses, advocates for progressive policies need to recognize righteous indignation that has been caused by business practices that are creating critical hardships for many. With this indignation, they may have the basis for promoting progressive policies.[5] What may be considered a critical hardship in the US could be the loss of many elements of the middle-class standard of living. As is discussed below, there are a number of problems that could prompt popular outrage. Moreover, if righteous indignation can support more fair policies, then progressives do not have to merely wait for hardships to bring voters to the brink of outrage over widespread injustice. They can employ political-economic analysis to anticipate those problems that could generate that anger and then have viable policies to address them in reserve.

From among the many policies that could, at least in theory, address causes of righteous indignation in the grassroots, progressive should focus on those for which there are political opportunities. In the United States, as it suffers through the great recession of the early twenty-first century, there are policy areas beyond access to medicines that might meet this criterion. Policies that would protect access to medical care, home ownership, higher education, and jobs may all be viable. For jobs, progressives may find success working to develop policies that reverse the government drift toward laissez-faire policy that lets jobs move to other countries and act in favor of old-fashioned industrial policy, policy that is proactive in creating jobs in the United States. Progressives could find allies and opportunities supporting a government lifeline to critical US industries on the verge of going under on the condition that the industry keeps the jobs at home. If there is financial pain to be borne, as a condition of such lifelines, progressives could work to ensure the share that workers bear is not onerous, distributing costs more equitably among industry stakeholders.

Secondly, it could be more generally the case that, to defeat powerful businesses, progressives should gain the backing of organizations with sufficient resources to push a political party's leadership to fully support a progressive policy. Organizations with campaign finance resources can provide progressives with effective channels to policymakers. Without such backing, support for progressive policies can be broad, but shallow, and vulnerable to major setbacks even when faced with relatively minor organizational challenges.

Progressives can advance their agenda by rebuilding the organizations that give them the power to take advantage of an opportunity when, for example, forces like the Democratic Party hierarchy are seriously considering a policy promoting economic justice. Labor unions especially are important in this regard. They have resources and operate with infrastructures that sometimes make it possible for the rank-and-file to push their leaders to take on industries that are responsible for economic injustices. But, of course, they are not what they once were. From the Taft–Hartley Act of 1947 to President George W. Bush's appointments to the National Labor Relations Board, anti-union forces have steadily weakened their ability to support the kind of popular uprisings they backed in the 1930s. While the residual strength of unions was still enough to help spark the civil rights movement in the 1960s,[6] their overall decline since the war has come with a huge price for the public's well-being, especially after Reagan became president. Across America, inequality has been growing since he made union-busting a federal policy, and it has become tougher and tougher for ordinary citizens to take on big business.[7] Efforts to help strengthen unions would, ultimately, benefit progressives in general.

Finally, it could be more generally the case that, for progressives to win such progressive policy initiatives, they should look for situations where the businesses creating the widespread hardship at issue can be politically isolated. Sometimes, an industry's overconfidence threatens to weaken the power of politicians whom other powerful interests rely upon. Then, it is one industry against many and the isolated industry can lose, even if it has great political power.

Besides identifying the kinds of issues that can be used for organizing, the Vermont, Maine, and California cases presented here also suggest that political opportunities for taking on the powerful businesses that lie behind economic injustices are more likely to be found first in smaller political arenas. In a small population state like Maine, a handful of advocates for increased access to prescription drugs was able to visit personally all the editors of the papers covering the statehouse. Small-state politicians like Chellie Pingree can also have more personal contact with the ordinary citizens and better understand their problems. In a large state like California, campaigns need large amounts of money for expenses like television ads in large media markets. Legislative and organizational leaders have less personal contact with voters and are slower to sense their anger. It is more difficult to get access to legislative leadership in larger states. Although a Public Interest Research Group affiliate in Vermont could work directly with legislative leadership, a PIRG affiliate in California could mainly work with lower-level legislators and must set policy goals to accommodate that limitation. Further, more successful policies developed in smaller jurisdictions can shape those in larger ones. The battle for access to prescription drugs in Maine influenced policies proposed in California where a "do it yourself" effort like John Marvin's is much less possible.

In summary, if this book's cases are a guide, then the chances of enacting a policy that promotes access to the economic components of what is called the US middle-class standard of living that are threatened by industry practices rise to the extent progressives are: (1) hearing righteous indignation over critical hardships generated by profit-seeking practices, (2) allying with a progressive organization powerful enough to push a political party's leadership to support that progressive policy, and (3) politically isolating industries causing widespread hardships.

Implications for US Health Policy

In the foreseeable future, US health policy will face a century-long buildup of the consequences of policies that have heavily relied on the private sector, raising costs and making access problematic for millions as it has for pharmaceuticals. As in access to medicines, access to health care in general will be inexorably restrained by private-sector profiting and excessive costs. These costs and the resulting inadequate care will continue to generate righteous indignation toward those profiting from our health care system. Without powerful allies and political opportunities, it will be challenging for advocates for health care access to do much about containing costs and seeing that more Americans get needed care.

But, history has shown us that opportunities for health care cost containment do arise. In the mid-1960s, Medicare started paying for hospital care and, by the early 1980s, it capped what it would pay for a given treatment, thus sharply reducing hospital costs and sustaining the viability of the program. Medicare also began paying for specialists' services in the mid-1960s. Physicians understood that this policy change threatened their incomes and vigorously resisted government action on physician costs. But, by the early 1990s, Medicare revised its fee schedule for specialists, intending to impose price restraint on that group to further extend Medicare's capacity to finance care. Although hospitals and physicians managed to hold off Medicare payment restraints for many years, eventually they are in place going forward. Furthermore, the US government already restrains prescription drug prices in its older programs, including Medicaid, the Veterans' Administration, and the 340(b) program, giving them the resources to better fund access to medicines.

Similar sequences of government spending on health care leading to price controls and public program viability have occurred in the states. In California in the 1980s, the administration of Governor Jerry Brown (D) used Medi-Cal purchasing power to lower the price of hospital care and maintain coverage. In the same decade in Oregon, the administration of Governor Victor Atiyeh (R) used its Medicaid program to successfully take on the costs of the nursing home industry by instituting a widespread home care program that extends the capacity of the state's Medicaid program to finance care (Kane et al. 1996).

At the national level, the 2009 inauguration of Barack Obama as president weakened Republican advocacy for PhRMA and created new opportunities to promote access to medicines. With its strong links to businesses like Goldman Sachs (opensecrets.org 2010), the Obama administration saw lowering US government debt, including reducing Medicare cost inflation, as a priority (Weisenthal 2009). Since comparative effectiveness research (CER) could lower Medicare costs as described in Chapter 5, the administration used its 2009 economic stimulus package to give it a boost. The package allocated $1.1 billion for promoting CER. With the funds allocated in 2009, the federal Agency for Health care Research and Quality has looked to fund state projects to provide physicians with information from CER to make decisions about health care, including prescribing medicines. This project could be to the advantage of the state advocacy groups for lower drug costs that are discussed in this book and give them a chance to better institutionalize their efforts.

In 2010, when President Obama's Affordable Care Act (ACA) was enacted, the act addressed the problem of the "doughnut hole" in Medicare coverage for prescription drugs, the coverage gap between two amounts of an individual's annual drug costs established in the Medicare Modernization Act. Under the ACA, the federal government is paying an increasing share of drug costs that fall into the doughnut hole and, by 2020, it will pay 75 percent of the costs of the drug purchases that fall into that coverage gap.

This change will give the federal government a much larger stake in Medicare prescription drug costs and a very strong incentive to contain them. Partly in anticipation of increased federal interest in containing drug prices, the ACA contains a provision that could undo the "nonintervention" clause of the Medicare Modernization Act of 2003 that had forbidden the government from using its purchasing power to negotiate lower prices for medicines. That provision establishes an Independent Payment Advisory Board (IPAB) to recommend policies to cut Medicare costs, including negotiating lower prescription drug prices.

The board's recommendations will become law unless Congress passes a bill making alternative cuts (Arnold 2010). While cheering other parts of the ACA, PhRMA's statement on it acknowledged its potential subjugation to the board: "we continue to have concerns about a number of issues including the overly broad powers of a non-elected IPAB, which could enact sweeping Medicare changes without action by Congress and would not be subject to judicial or administrative review" (PhRMA 2010).

To boot, the ACA established the Patient-Centered Outcomes Research Institute (PCORI), a new agency for comparative effectiveness studies of drugs and devices—and arms it with a $500 million annual budget. With the new funds, the institute may well study interventions such as use of prescription drugs and medical devices. That funding institutionalizes the efforts of AHRQ to promote comparative effectiveness research on medicines. The act also included a provision based on a series of state laws started by Vermont's State Senate President Peter Shumlin in 2002. It took his idea that drugmakers should report their gifts to physicians so that policymakers could see how this influence was being exercised and made it federal law that drug, device, and biotech companies report gifts, compensation, or other things with a value of more than $10 given to medical professionals and institutions (Arnold 2010).

When considering a timeline for major victories on high prescription drug prices in the United States, I learned a lesson in the mid-1990s, when I was teaching a public health advocacy course for Johns Hopkins in Washington, DC, that might be helpful. I decided to structure the course around a series of guest lectures given by people from Capitol Hill who had experience winning battles for health access and economic justice. Our guest speakers discussed campaigns for such goals as gun control, safer autos, playground safety, fire-safe cigarettes, improved nursing home quality, recall of unsafe medicines, restriction of alcohol advertising, and labor law enforcement. But our guests were too busy to concisely formulate the "lessons learned" for the students. So, the class decided that after each guest speaker left, we would spend time drawing such lessons from the stories we had heard. In my view, the biggest overall lesson we learned was that it took at least twenty years for each of our guests to gain a definitive win in their public health battles. Over the years, they each had to move the ball downfield as well as they could. Some years, they made progress; some years, their opponents were too powerful and they had to be patient.

By the twenty-year yardstick, the fight for access to prescription drugs is about halfway as of this writing. Use of government purchasing power to reduce prices is being explored at the national and state levels; policy to counter aggressive marketing to physicians by the pharmaceutical industry has advanced. Whether or not we will have celebrated major victories over PhRMA ten years from this writing remains to be seen. But, if progressives don't try, there is no chance there will be one.

Even when progress is slow or appears blocked, it is worthwhile in itself to nurture a culture of concern for the underdog and press the capacity of our political system to do something about it. In and of itself, this culture is valuable in maintaining the capacity of progressives to win when conditions are more favorable. To the extent that this culture is present, progressives can be inspired to continue battling for the underdog. To the extent our political system is pressed to give voice to all its constituents, progressives can push those who are rich and powerful to make concessions to those who are not.

The chance for promoting justice can arise at surprising times. What appears to be a blocked situation can open as unlikely events come into play. In California, events led some union leaders to see a challenge to PhRMA as in their interest, the governor needed to shift to the center to hold off a Democratic challenge to his office, and the time suddenly arrived to address the grievances of those who couldn't afford medicines. At the national level, PhRMA was so sure that President Obama's health insurance reform proposal was dead in January 2010 that it fired its lobbyist, Billy Tauzin. But President Obama resisted the advice of top aides to abandon large-scale health care reform and, two months later, he was signing the Affordable Care Act, the biggest national health insurance act since the 1965 act establishing Medicare and, possibly, ever.

When the next surprise comes, it may well first be signaled in much the same way as the movement for access to essential medicines was at the town meeting in New Britain, Connecticut, in 2000. As the legislative panel that had come to hear what citizens thought of drug prices, we saw the elderly woman who could walk one day in three come up to the mike with her brown paper bag full of pill bottles. Sitting on the panel was a state representative who would be in legislative leadership the next year.[8] Behind us were organizers from Connecticut affiliates of powerful unions like SEIU and the United Auto Workers. The ingredients to make change were there. As the woman looked up from the mike and began to speak, we saw the righteous anger that was the spark we needed. The time had come for fighting Goliath.

¹ The understanding that the industry was responsible for high prices in these cases is why I call the indignation righteous. Righteous indignation, in this sense, can only be aimed at those with the economic and political power needed to create widespread hardship. So, it is not at all the same as the anger that drives movements aimed at others with little power, for example, racist anger.

² SEIU is a big spender in state politics; in the 2007-2008 election cycle, it spent over $10 million (York 2009).

³ One way that this book differs from resource mobilization theory (RMT) is that it does not attempt to explain a broad set of movements as does RMT. RMT attempts to explain more movements than just those for progressive policies. Although RMT theorists discuss struggles for progressive policies, they also discuss the dynamics of the Hare Krishna group (Rochford 1997). They discuss movements for civil rights and, at the same time, they discuss movements for genocide (McAdam et al. 2001). For the purposes of this book, such breadth is not needed. Indeed, trying to combine such movements in one model may lead to a fundamental theoretical shortcoming. In attempting to theorize about both progressive and nonprogressive movements, RMT must skirt the question of why people join them (Eckstein 2004).

⁴ A theoretical approach that better explains how this anger becomes political can be found in the "bounded rationality" model of Herbert Simon (Simon 1987). Simon argues that people's rationality in making political choices is bounded by what they know of their options and what they know of the chances of realizing their choices. So, while many in the grassroots may know when they face critical hardships, they may not support a policy solution owing to their limited understanding of what options exist or of the likelihood of realizing those options.

The data from Maine suggest that, when many people do see a political option, they are more likely to support it. In that case, voters could see that the government might act to restrain price inflation on drugs. They could see the efforts of political organizations that were pushing for this restraint.

⁵ A writer who noted that, for a progressive proposal to win popular support among seniors, it had to address a critical hardship that many of them were facing was Richard Himelfarb (Himelfarb 1995). In his book, *Catastrophic Politics*, he writes that the 1988 federal program expanding Medicare benefits for seniors went down to defeat because there was "no deeply felt need for the program among beneficiaries."

Jacob Hacker sees the need for policies that address critical hardships in discussing the twenty-first century unraveling of the safety net (Hacker 2006).

⁶ For example, the director of the August 1963 March on Washington, at which Martin Luther King, Jr., made his immortal "I have a dream" speech was A. Philip Randolph, president emeritus of the Brotherhood of Sleeping Car Porters. The idea of a march on Washington was first developed by the labor leader Randolph in 1941.

⁷ From 1979 to 2006, the richest 1 percent of households more than doubled their share of the country's total taxable income, rising from about 10 percent to nearly 23 [ercent, for an average income of about $1.3 million per household within this group. About 91 percent of all income growth in the country went to the top 10 percent by income, leaving just over 9 percent to be

parceled out among the remaining 90 percent. Young workers now start out behind their peers from previous generations: Young men with only a high school education earned $2.55 less per hour in 2007 (after inflation adjustment) than their predecessors did in 1973 (down from $14.34 to $11.79). Real hourly pay for young women fell $1.05 per hour (from $10.50 to $9.45) over the same period (Mishel et al. 2010).

[8] James Amann (D–Milford)

Appendix:
Useful Websites on
Health Care Policy and Politics

Campaign finance

CampaignMoney.com
http://campaignmoney.com/

Center for Responsive Politics
http://www.opensecrets.org/

National Institute on Money in State Politics
http://www.followthemoney.org/

State Policy

National Conference of State Legislatures
http://www.ncsl.org/

National Governors Association
http://www.nga.org/cms/home.html

Stateline
http://www.stateline.org/live/

Health Policy

California Healthline
http://www.californiahealthline.org/

Center for Evidence-Based Policy
http://www.ohsu.edu/xd/research/centers-institutes/evidence-based-policy-center/

Kaiser Family Foundation
http://www.kff.org/

National Health Policy Forum
http://www.nhpf.org/

Pharmaceutical Policy

Drug Benefit News
http://aishealth.com/marketplace/drug-benefit-news

DrugChannels
http://www.drugchannels.net/

Drug Store News
http://www.drugstorenews.com/

Drug Topics
http://drugtopics.modernmedicine.com/

FiercePharma
http://www.fiercepharma.com/

PRIME Institute
http://www.pharmacy.umn.edu/centers/prime/

Bibliography

Aaronson, S. A. (2008). "Primer on Trade Agreements", George Washington University, Washington, DC.

Achman, L., and Gold, M. (2002). "Medicare+Choice 1999-2001: An Analysis of Managed Care Plan Withdrawals and Trends in Benefits and Premiums." *Report No. 497*, Commonwealth Fund, New York, NY.

AFL-CIO. (2007). "Facts About America's Broken Health Care System", AFL-CIO, Washington, DC.

Agnos, S. (2003). "Interview on Prescription Drug Policy Options", California Senate Office of Research.

Agovino, T. (2007). "Prescription Drug Sales Rise 8.3 Percent." *Newsday*, New York, NY.

Ainsworth, B. (2004). "Veto kills effort to open door to Canadian drugs." *San Diego Union-Tribune*, San Diego, CA.

Alazraki, M. (2009). "Pfizer Wins Dismissal of 23 Prempro Lawsuits." *Daily Finance*.

Allen, T. (2008). "Interview on Prescription Drug Fairness for Seniors Act of 1998." Tom Allen for US Senate Campaign.

America Votes 2004. (2004). "Howard Dean." *CNN.com*, Atlanta, GA.

Anand, G. (2005). "As biotech drug prices rise, US hunts for solution." *Wall Street Journal*, New York, NY.

Angell, M. (2004). *The Truth about the Drug Companies: How They Deceive Us and What to Do About It.*, Random House, New York, NY

Anrig, G. (2007). "Who Strangled the FDA?" *American Prospect*, Washington, DC.

Arnold, M. (2010). "In the Long Run, Reforms Mean Less Risk, Lower Rewards for Pharmas." *Medical Marketing and Media*, New York, NY.

Associated Press. (1991). "Workers Protesting Budget Delays Rally in Pennsylvania and Maine." *New York Times*, New York, NY, 10.

Baker, D. (2006). "The Origins of the Doughnut Hole: Excess Profits on Prescription Drugs", Center for Economic and Policy Research, Washington, DC.

Barber, D. R. (2007). "Names in the News: Merck & Co", National Institute on Money in State Politics, Helena, MT.

Barry, L., Grant, D., and Livingston, B. (2002). "A Prescription for Cheaper Drugs for Seniors", Senior Action Network, San Francisco, CA.

Battelle Technology Partnership Practice. (2010). "Battelle/BIO State Bioscience Initiatives 2010", Biotechnology Industry Organization, Washington, DC.

Bauer, A. (2009). "Take $2 Million...and Call Me in the Session", National Institute on Money in State Politics, Helena, MT.

Bello, J. (1999). "PhRMA Statement", Vermont Senate Study Committee, Montpelier, VT.

Belluck, P. (2003). "Boldly Crossing the Line for Cheaper Drugs." *New York Times*, New York, NY.

Benore, A., Knott, A., and Quesada, E. (2002). "United Seniors Association: Hired Guns for PhRMA and Other Corporate Interests", Public Citizen, Washington, DC.

Bever, F. (2000a). "Adjournment snagged by prescription drug legislation." *Rutland Herald*, Rutland, VT.

Bever, F. (2000b). "Drug bill dies in final hours of legislature." *Rutland Herald*, Rutland, VT.

Bever, F. (2000c). "Panel deletes price regulation from drug bill." *Rutland Herald*, Rutland, VT.

Bleifuss, J. (2005). "Sanders Steps Up." *In These Times*.

Bloomberg News. (2010). "Mylan to Pay $65 Million Over Drug Prices." *New York Times*, New York, NY.

Blumenthal, M. (2003). "California Confidential." *American Prospect*.

Bonauto, M. (2000). "The Vermont Ruling: A Status Update." *Report No. 2*, Partners Task Force for Gay & Lesbian Couples, Seattle, WA.

Bradley, W. (2002). "Making the Right Enemy." *New York Times*, New York, NY.

Brenner, M. (2006). "California Nurses Lead the Fight against Arnold." *Labor Notes*.

Brierton, J. (2004). "Regulation of Pharmacy Benefit Managers." *Report No. 2004-R-0071*, Conneciticut Office of Legislative Research, Hartford, CT.

Brownlee, S. (2003). "Health, Hope and Hype." *Washington Post*, Washington, DC.

Burton, B., and Rowell, A. (2003). "From Patient Activism to Astroturf Marketing." *PR Watch*, 10(1).

California Budget Project. (2003). "The Social and Economic Context of the Governor's Proposed 2003-04 Budget", Sacramento, CA.

California Budget Project. (2007). "Governor Signs 2007-08 Budget", Sacramento, CA.

California Budget Project. (2008). "Governor Signs 2008-09 Budget", Sacramento, CA.

California Budget Project. (2009). "Governor Signs Budget Revisions", Sacramento, CA.

California Bureau of State Audits. (2005). "Pharmaceuticals: State Departments That Purchase Prescription Drugs CAn Further Refine Their Cost Savings Strategies." *Report No. 2004-033*, California State Auditor, Sacramento, CA.

California Department of Health Care Services. (2007). "Dispute Resolution Frequently Asked Questions", Sacramento, CA.

California Healthline. (2003). "Supreme Court Lifts Injunction Against Maine Rx", California Health Care Foundation, Oakland, CA.

California Healthline. (2004). "FDA Study Estimates More Than 27,000 Heart Attacks Linked to Vioxx", California Health Care Foundation, Oakland, CA.

California Legislative Analyst's Office. (2007). "The Subprime Mortgage Situation", Assembly Banking and Finance Committee, Sacramento, CA.

California Legislative Analyst's Office. (2008). "California's Fiscal Outlook", Sacramento, CA.

California Manufacturing and Technology Association. (2002). "Pfizer Inc. Opens Major Life Science Research Campus", Sacramento, CA.

California Teachers Association. (2005). "Coalition Battles as Legislature Hears Gov's Bills." *Legislative Update*, Sacramento, CA.

Cal-Tax Staff. (2005). "Ballot Box Tax Threats Surface as Schwarzenegger Battles Public Employee Union Over Government Overhaul." *Cal-Tax Digest*, Sacramento, CA.

CampaignMoney.com. (2010). "Jan Backus for US Senate Committee", Public Campaign Action Fund, Washington, DC.

CareerOneStop. (2010). "State Profile: Largest Employers", Minnesota State Colleges and Universities, St. Paul, MN.

Carreon, L., Linehan, K., Pérez, M., and Spellman, T. (2000). "State Pharmacy Programs." *Report No. GAO/HEHS-00-162*, United States General Accounting Office, Washington, DC.

Carrier, P. (2000a). "Bill Would Set Prescription Price Controls." *Morning Sentinel*, Waterville, ME, A1.

Carrier, P. (2000b). "King's Approval Assures Drug Bill." *Portland Press Herald*, Portland, ME.

Carroll, N. V. (2007). "Pharmaceutical Patient Assistance Programs: Don't Look a Gift Horse in the Mouth or There's No Such Thing as a Free Lunch." *Journal of Managed Care Pharmacy*, 13(7), 614-616.

Carson, D. "Schwarzenegger Prescription Drug Discount Proposal." California Legislative Analyst's Office, Sacramento, CA.

Castellblanch, R. (2005). "Comparison of Maine Rx Plus and Ohio Best Rx", Senior Action Network, San Francisco, CA.

Castellblanch, R. (2006). "California's Policy Options for Improving Access to Prescription Drugs", California Program on Access to Care, University of California, Berkeley, CA.

Cauchi, R., and Hanson, K. (2006). "2002 Prescription Drug Discount, Bulk Purchasing, and Price-Related Legislation", National Conference of State Legislatures.

Cauchi, R., and Victoroff, A. (2006). "Pharmaceutical Bulk Purchasing: Multi-state and Inter-agency Plans, 2006", National Conference of State Legislatures, Denver, CO.

Cauchon, D. (2000). "State Legislators Take the Lead on Drug Prices." *USA Today*, McLean, VA, 7A.

Center for Public Integrity. (2006). "Democratic Governors' Association", Washington, DC.

Center for Public Integrity. (2009). "Drug Industry Influence Timeline", Washington, DC.

Center for Responsive Politics. (2009). "Pharmaceuticals/ Health Products: Long-Term Contribution Trends", Washington, DC.

Centers for Medicare & Medicaid Services. (2009a). "Medicaid Drug Rebate Program", US Department of Health and Human Services, Baltimore, MD.

Centers for Medicare & Medicaid Services. (2009b). "National Health Expenditures", US Department of Health and Human Services, Baltimore, MD.

Chen, M. (2007). "Drugmakers Hurry Sales, Delay Safety Studies." *NewStandard*, Syracuse, NY.

Chorneau, T. (2005). "Drug companies' PAC gives big after Schwarzenegger's vetoes." Associated Press, New York, NY.

Church, Z. (2004). "Vermont Congressmen Lead Fight For Drug Imports." *Bennington Banner*, Bennington, VT.

Clair, J. A. (2009). "Response to the Professional Services Request for Proposals." *Proposal No. (RFP) MED-10-001*, Goold Health Systems, Augusta, ME.

CNNMoney. (2009). "Top industries: Most profitable 2005." Cable News Network, Atlanta, GA.

CNNMoney. (2011). "Top industries: Most profitable 2009." Cable News Network, Atlanta, GA.

Colliver, V. (2006). "Druggists overwhelmed." *San Francisco Chronicle*, San Francisco, CA.

Committee on Government Reform and Oversight. (1998). "Minority Staff Report: Prescription Drug Pricing in Vermont", US House of Representatives, Washington, DC.

Committee on Government Reform Minority Office. (2005). "Decline in FDA Enforcement Efforts", US House of Representatives, Washington, DC.

Common Cause. (2004). "Democracy on Drugs", Washington, DC.

Common Cause. (2005). "State and National Reform Groups Endorse Prop. 77", Washington, DC.

Connecticut Citizen Action Group. (2010). "CCAG History", Hartford, CT.

Consumers for Affordable Health Care. (2000). "One Last Chance", Augusta, ME.

Cosgrove, M. (2000). "Jaunts Across the Border Best Rx for High Drug Prices?" *Stateline.org*, Pew Research Center, Washington, DC.

CPTech. (1999). "Frequently Asked Questions About H.R. 626", Consumer Project on Technology, Washington, DC.

Crosse, M. (2006). "Improvements Needed in FDA's Oversight of Direct-to-Consumer Advertising." *Report No. GAO-07-54*, US Government Accountability Office, Washington, DC.

Crotty, P. (2009). "Novartis Wage and Hour Litigation Order." *Case No. 06-MD-1794 (PAC)*, US District Court, Southern District of New York, New York, NY.

Cruz, J., and Hickey, R. (2006). "Falling into the Doughnut Hole", Institute for America's Future, Washington, DC.

Cummins, K. (1991). "NRA Losing Influence On Legislators." *Sun Sentinel*, Fort Lauderdale, FL.

Cutrona, S. L., Woolhandler, S., Lasser, K. E., Bor, D. H., McCormick, D., and Himmelstein, D. U. (2008). "Characteristics of Recipients of Free Prescription Drug Samples: A Nationally Representative Analysis." *American Journal of Public Health*, 98(2), 284-289.

Daemmrich, A. (2004). *Pharmacopolitics: Drug Regulation in the United States and Germany*, University of North Carolina Press, Chapel Hill, NC.

Daemmrich, A. (2009). "Where is the Pharmacy to the World?" *Working Paper 09-118*, Harvard Business School, Boston, MA.

Daranciang, N. (2004). "Lingle signs prescription drug bill." *Honolulu Star-Bulletin*, Honolulu, HI.

Davis, R. (2000). "Interview on S. 300", Vermont Consumers' Campaign for Health.

Davis, R. (2000b). "March 2000 Status of Vermont Campaign to Lower Prescription Drug Prices." *Prescription Access Litigation Project Meeting*, Boston, MA.

Davis, R. (2000c). "Press Release: Rockingham Town Meeting", Vermont Consumers' Campaign for Health, Brattleboro, VT.

Dawson, P. T. (1994). "Decision and Order, Maine State Employees Association v. State of Maine." *Case No. 92-19*, Maine Labor Relations Board, Augusta, ME.

Democratic Policy Committee. (2004). "United States - Australia Free Trade Agreement Implementation Act", US Senate, Washington, DC.

Donohue, J. M., Cevasco, M., and Rosenthal, M. (2007). "A Decade of Direct-to-Consumer Advertising." *New England Journal of Medicine*, 357(7), 673-681.

Douglas, T. (2007). "California Discount Prescription Drug Program." *California Program on Access to Care in the Capitol Briefing*, San Francisco, CA.

Douglas, T., Williams, P., Rosenstein, S., and Gorospe, K. (2007). "March 2007 Update on California Discount Prescription Drug Program." California Department of Health Care Services.

Dow, C. (2005). "Interview on Development of Maine's Medicaid Prior Authorization Policy." Maine Attorney General's Office.

Drinkard, J. (2005). "Drugmakers go furthest to sway Congress." *USA Today*, McLean, VA.

Durocher, E. J. (2011). "Letter to New York State Commissioner of Health." *Report No. 2010-F-46*, New York Office of Comptroller, Albany, NY.

Eckstein, H. (2004). "Theoretical Approaches to Explaining Collective Violence." *Political Psychology*, J. T. Jost and J. Sidanius, eds., Psychology Press, New York, NY.

Economist. (2005). "The Drug Industry: An Overdose of Bad News", 72-74.

Editorial Board. (2000a). "Pingree-King accord will lower drug prices." *Portland Press Herald*, Portland, ME.

Editorial Board. (2000b). "State's drug pricing bill needs regional power." *Portland Press Herald*, Portland, ME.

Electronic Privacy Information Center. (2008). "IMS Health Inc. v. Ayotte", Washington, DC.

Elgie, R. (2002). "How the Patented Medicine Prices Review Board Contributes to Controlling Drug Prices in Canada." *Patented Medicine Prices Review Board Symposium*, Toronto, Canada.

Elliott, E. (2000). "Letter to Timothy Westmoreland, Health Care Financing Administration Medicaid Director", Vermont Agency of Human Services, Waterbury, VT.

Ellis, R. (1999). "Constitutionality of S. 88, "An Act Relating to the Vermont Prescription Drug Pricing and Consumer Protection Program"", Office of the Attorney General, Montpelier, VT.

Equal Time. (2005). "Biography of Anthony Pollina." WDEV, Waterbury, VT.

Evans, D., Smith, M., and Willen, L. (2005). "Drug Industry Human Testing Masks Death, Injury, Compliant FDA." Bloomberg News.

Families USA. (2001). "Case Study: Maine", Washington, DC.

Farrell, J. (2003). "Dean's No Wellstone." *Nation*.

Fein, A. J. (2010). "Drug Forecasts: Oops!...They Missed It Again." *DrugChannels*.

Finnegan, F. (2000). "Interview on Public Law 786.", Maine Department of Human Services.

Flynn, S. (2007). "The Constitutional Battle Over State Regulation of Data Mining", Community Catalyst, Boston, MA.

Freudenheim, M. (2006). "A Windfall From Shifts to Medicare." *New York Times*, New York, NY.

Freyne, P. (2000). "Money's the Best Medicine." *Seven Days*, Burlington, VT.

Frothingham, N. (2000). "Vermont Panel Foreshadows Outcome of Gay Rights Debate." Stateline.org, Pew Research Center, Washington, DC.

Furillo, A., and Delsohn, G. (2005). "Drug companies approve $10 million for California ballot fight." *Sacramento Bee*, Sacramento, CA.

Galewitz, P. (2000). "Maine Negotiates Drug Prices." Associated Press, New York, NY.

Garcia, E. (2006). "Strategy works against Angelides." *San Jose Mercury News*, San Jose, CA.

Garis, R., Clark, B., and Siracuse, M. (2006). "Is the Pharmacy Benefit Manager Truly Transparent? Trust but Verify." *US Pharmacy Review*, 1-4 Reference Section.

Geller, L. (2006). "State Circumventing Prescription Drug Law." *Honolulu Advertiser*, Honolulu, HI.

Gillespie, G. (2009). "Price Regulation of Patented Medicines in Canada." *First Pan-American Seminar on the Economic Regulation of Pharmaceuticals*, Brasília, Brazil.

Gilman, J. (2007). "Update on California California Discount Prescription Drug Program." *California Program on Access to Care in the Capitol Briefing*, San Francisco, CA.

Gledhill, L., Hubbell, J. M., and Berthelsen, C. (2004). "State budget issues resolved." *San Francisco Chronicle*, San Francisco, CA.

Goldberg, C. (1999). "New England Lawmakers Consider Drug Strategies." *New York Times*, New York, NY, A20.

Goldberg, C. (2000a). "Governor of Vermont Signs Gay-Union Law." New York Times, New York, NY.

Goldberg, C. (2000b). "Vermont Gives Final Approval to Same-Sex Unions." *New York Times*, New York, NY.

Goldberg, C. (2000c). "Maine Will Cap Drug Prices With a Groundbreaking Law." *New York Times*, New York, NY, A18.

Goldberg, C. (2000d). "Maine Enacts a Law Aimed at Controlling Cost of Drugs." *New York Times*, New York, NY, A30.

Gore, P. (2001). "Interview on Work of Maine Chamber of Commerce on LD 2599", Maine Chamber of Commerce.

Graham, D. (2004). "Vioxx, Heart Attacks, and the FDA" , US Senate, Washington, DC.

Green, J. (2005). "It Isn't the Message, Stupid." *Atlantic*.

Grotke, C. (2004). "Interview: Cheryl Rivers." *iBrattleboro*, Brattleboro, VT.

Hacker, J. (2006). *The Great Risk Shift: The Assault on American Jobs, Families, Health Care, and Retirement--And How You Can Fight Back*, Oxford University Press, New York, NY.

Hansel, P. (2003). "Interview on Prescription Drug Policy Options", California Senate Office of Research.

Haviland, S. (2002). "Interview on Summer 1999 Work with Vermont Public Interest Research Group." Connecticut Citizen Action Group.

Health and Human Services Committee. (2000). "LD 2599 Sign In Sheet", Maine Legislature, Augusta, ME.

Health and Human Services Committee. (2003). "AB 1739: Committee Analysis", California State Senate.

Health Consumer Alliance. (2004). "Sick and In Debt", Los Angeles, CA.

Hempling, S. (1999). "State Price Regulation", Health Access Oversight Committee, Montpelier, VT.

Henderson, D. (2006). "Calif. price curbs alarm drug makers." *Boston Globe*, Boston, MA.

Henderson, M. (2001). "Interview on Task Force on Improving Access to Prescription Drugs", Maine Equal Justice Partners.

Hendrickson, S. (2005). "Pharmaceuticals: State Departments That Purchase Prescription Drugs Can Further Refine Their Cost Savings Strategies." *Report No. 2004-033*, California State Auditor, Sacramento, CA.

Higgins, A. J. (2000). "Drug Bill Deal Reached." *Bangor Daily News*, Bangor, ME.

Hiltzik, M. (2005). "Drug Firms Try to Fool Voters." *Los Angeles Times*, Los Angeles, CA.

Himelfarb, R. (1995). *Catastrophic Politics: The Rise and Fall of the Medicare Catastrophic Coverage Act of 1988*, Pennsylvania State University Press, University Park, PA.

Hinch, J. (2004). "His coattails are long and bipartisan." *Orange County Register*, Santa Ana, CA.

Hirschler, B. (2010). "World's top-selling drugs in 2014 vs 2010." Reuters, New York, NY.

Hoadley, J. (2005). "Cost Containment Strategies For Prescription Drugs." *Publication No. 7295*, Kaiser Family Foundation, Menlo Park, CA.

Holzman, D. (2000). "Maine Drug Discount Program Spurring Interest in Other States." *Drug Topics*, North Olmsted, OH, 82-87.

Initiative and Referendum Institute. (2002). "Basic Steps To Do An Initiative Petition In California", University of Southern California, Los Angeles, CA.

Institute of Governmental Studies Library. (2004). "Recall in California", University of California, Berkeley, CA.

Integrity in Science. (2003). "Non-Profit Organizations Receiving Corporate Funding", Center for Science in the Public Interest, Washington, DC.

Ismail, M. A. (2005). "Drug Lobby Second to None", Center for Public Integrity, Washington, DC.

Ismail, M. A. (2006). "Deep Pockets Contribute to Success", Center for Public Integrity, Washington, DC.

Jack, A., and Williams, F. (2006). "WHO demands early disclosure of drug trials." *Financial Times*, London, UK.

Jasper, J. M. (2004). "A Strategic Approach to Collective Action." *Mobilization*, 9(1), 1-16.

Joint Standing Committee on Appropriations and Financial Affairs. (1998). "Committee Amendment "A" (H-1098)." , Maine Legislature, Augusta, ME.

Just the Facts. (2009). "California Voter and Party Profiles", Public Policy Institute of California, Sacramento, CA.

Kaiser Daily Health Policy Report. (2005). "Federal Judge Dismisses Lawsuit Against Maine Law", Kaiser Family Foundation, Menlo Park, CA.

Kaiser Family Foundation. (2005). "Trends and Indicators in the Changing Health Care Marketplace." *7031*, Menlo Park, CA.

Kane, R. L., Ladd, R. C., Kane, R. A., and Nielsen, W. J. (1996). "Oregon's Long Term Care System", Institute for Health Services Research, University of Minnesota, Minneapolis, MN.

Kasprak, J. (2001). "Vermont Prescription Drug Program Court Decision." *Report No. 2001-R-0535*, Office of Legislative Research, Hartford, CT.

Kasprak, J. (2003). "Prescription Drug Programs - Maine and Vermont (Update)." *Report No. 2003-R-0029*, Connecticut Office of Legislative Research, Hartford, CT.

Kaufman, W. (2002). "Ohio voters demand affordable medicine." *People's Weekly World*, Chicago, IL.

Kelley, K. J. (2004). "The Prog Prognosis." *Seven Days*, Burlington, VT.

Kerr, P. (1992). "A Showdown on Workers' Compensation in Maine." *New York Times*, New York, NY.

Kesich, G. (2000a). "GOP "arm-twisting" erodes support for drug-pricing bill." *Portland Press-Herald*, Portland, ME.

Kesich, G. (2000b). "Prescription drug plan OK'd." *Portland Press-Herald*, Portland, ME.

Kesich, G. (2000c). "Prescription drug price controls gain momentum." *Portland Press-Herald*, Portland, ME.

Kitchman, M., Neuman, T., Sandman, D., Schoen, C., Gelb Safran, D., Montgomery, J., and Rogers, W. (2002). "Seniors and Prescription Drugs." *Publication No. 6049*, Kaiser Family Foundation, Menlo Park, CA.

Lawrence, S. (2005). "Calif. NAACP catches flack for drug initiative." *Bay State Banner*, Boston, MA.

Lazos, A. (2000). "Interview on Public Law 786." Office of Maine Senate Majority Leader.

Learner, N. (2008). "PBMs Allegedly Manipulate Definition of 'Brand' and 'Generic' Rx at Payers' Expense." *Drug Benefit News*, Washington, DC.

LeDuff, C. (2003). "An Outsider Candidate Who Favors Insider Advice." *New York Times*, New York, NY.

Leibovich, M. (2007). "The Socialist Senator." *New York Times*, New Y ork, NY.

Leibowitz, J. (2006). "Exclusion Payments to Settle Pharmaceutical Patent Cases: They're B-a-a-a-ck!" *Second Annual In-House Counsel's Forum on Pharmaceutical Antitrust*, Philadelphia, PA.

Leinonen, C. (2006). "Interview on MSEA Work on Maine Rx." Maine State Employees Association.

Levey, N. N. (2005). "Black Politicians Say Mailer Distorts Support." *Los Angeles Times*, Los Angeles, CA.

Lewiston Sun Journal. (2000). "Prescription cost-cutting plan arises", Lewiston, ME.

Lisberg, A. (2000). "Anti civil union mail blitzes Vermont." *Burlington Free Press*, Burlington, VT.

Mackey, S. (2001). "New Directions for Vermont." State Legislatures, National Conference of State Legislatures, 40.

MacLean, A. (2000). "Neither for nor against", Maine Medical Association, Manchester, ME.

Maine State Employees Association. (2000). "Is the High Cost of Prescription Drugs Making You Sick?" , Augusta, ME.

Market Decisions. (2000). "Poll on Drug Price Policy." *Maine Times*, Portland, ME.

Markowitz, D. (2000). "Elections: Primary and General Election", Vermont Secretary of State, Montpelier, VT.

Marvin, J. (2000). "Interview on Maine State Employees Association Support of Maine Rx." Maine Council of Senior Citizens.

Marvin, J. (2001). "Interview on MSEA support of Maine Rx II." Maine Council of Senior Citizens.

Mathews, J. (2003). "Little-Known Activist Is Recall Powerhouse." *Los Angeles Times*, Los Angeles, CA.

Matier, P., and Ross, A. (2005). "Drug industry gives $450,000 payday to Willie Brown." *San Francisco Chronicle*, San Francisco, CA.

McAdam, D., McCarthy, J. D., and Zald, M. N. (1996). "Introduction." *Comparative Perspectives on Social Movements*, D. McAdam, J. D. McCarthy, and M. N. Zald, eds., Cambridge University Press, New York, NY.

McAdam, D., Tarrow, S., and Tilly, C. (2001). *Dynamics of Contention*, Cambridge University Press, New York, NY.

McCloskey, A. (2000). "Still Rising." *Publication No. 00-103*, Families USA, Washington, DC.

McGorrian, C. (2000). "Testimony before Vermont House Health and Welfare Committee", Health Law Advocates, Boston, MA.

McKinnell, H. (2002). "Press Release: California Governor Gray Davis, Pfizer CEO Hank McKinnell, and Vice Chairman, John Niblack, Open Major Life Science Research Campus", Pfizer, La Jolla, CA.

Meier, C. F. (2001). "Drug Wars in Maine." *heartlander*, Heartland Institute, Chicago, IL.

Minnesota Department of Human Services. (2004). "Minnesota's plan to access affordable prescription medication", State of Minnesota, St. Paul, MN.

Mishel, L., Bernstein, J., and Shierholz, H. (2010). *State of Working America 2008/2009*, Economic Policy Institute, Washington, DC.

Mishra, R. (2000). "Trailblazers elders' effort led to Maine drug law." *Boston Globe*, Boston, MA, A1.

Molotsky, I. (1987). "Critics Say FDA Is Unsafe in Reagan Era." *New York Times*, New York, NY.

Moon, M., Smith, B., and Gustafson, S. (2008). "Creating a Center for Evidence-Based Medicine." *Study No. 08-1*, American Institutes for Research, Washington, DC.

Mortimer, R. O. (1998). *Demand for prescription drugs: the effects of managed care pharmacy benefits*, University of California, Berkeley, Berkeley, CA.

Murphy, T. (2000). "House GOP Concerns Answered in New Rx Plan", Maine House Republican Leadership, Augusta, ME.

Myers, J. (2005). "Capital Notes: Prescription Drug Negotiations." *KQED News*, San Francisco, CA.

National Center for Health Statistics. (2009). "Health, United States", Centers for Disease Control and Prevention, Atlanta, GA.

National Conference of State Legislatures. (2009). "Prescription Drug Discount, Price-Related and Bulk Purchasing Legislation, 1999-2000.", Denver, CO.

National Governors Association. (2001). "Addendum to State Pharmaceutical Assistance Programs: The Maine Rx Program", Washington, DC.

National Institute on Money in State Politics. (2011). "Investigate Money in State Politics", Helena, MT.

Neuman, P., Strollo, M. K., Guterman, S., Rogers, W. H., Li, A., Rodday, A. M. C., and Safran, D. G. (2007). "Medicare Prescription Drug Benefit Progress Report." *Health Affairs*, 26(5).

Neumann, P. J. (2006). "Emerging Lessons From The Drug Effectiveness Review Project." *Health Affairs*, 25(4).

New York Times. (2008). "Election Results 2008", New York, NY.

Nicholas, P. (2004). "Schwarzenegger deems opponents 'girlie-men'." *San Francisco Chronicle*, San Francisco, CA.

Noonan, D. (2000). "The Real Drug War." *Newsweek*, 28.

Office of Health Care Ombudsman. (2011). "Overview of Green Mountain Care Programs", Vermont Legal Aid, Burlington, VT.

Olson, H. (1999). "Prescription Drug Report", Health Access Oversight Committee, Montpelier, VT.

opensecrets.org. (2004). "Pharmaceuticals / Health Products: Top Recipients", Center for Responsive Politics, Washington, DC.

opensecrets.org. (2004). "Race for the White House: Howard Dean", Center for Responsive Politics, Washington, DC.

opensecrets.org. (2010). "Barack Obama (D) Top Contributors", Center for Responsive Politics, Washington, DC.

Orbeton, J. (2000). "Interview on Public Law 786." Office of Policy and Legal Analysis, Maine State Legislature.

Oregon Office of Medical Assistance Programs. (2006). "Oregon Health Plan: An Historical Overview", Oregon Department of Human Services, Salem, OR.

Orlando Sentinal. (1991). "Maine Makes Progress, Oks $3.2 Billion Budget", Orlando, FL.

Oshiro, M. (2002). "2002 Session is a Victory for Consumers, Electorate", Hawaii State Legislature Website, Honolulu, HI.

Padgett, J., Olabisi, O., and Young, M. (2006). "Medicaid Report: New Hampshire and Vermont." *Policy Brief No. 0506-09*, Rockefeller Center at Dartmouth College, Hanover, NH.

Page, L. (2000). "The mice that roared." *American Medical News*, Chicago IL.

Pammolli, F., and Riccaboni, M. (2004). "Market Structure and Drug Innovation." *Health Affairs*, 23(1), 48-50.

Pear, R. (2002). "Republicans Plan to Push Through Prescription Drug Coverage for the Elderly." *New York Times*, New York, NY.

Pearce, D., and Brooks, J. (2003a). "Self-sufficiency Standard for California", National Economic Development and Law Center, Oakland, CA.

Pearce, D., and Brooks, J. (2003b). "Self-sufficiency Standard for Massachusetts", National Economic Development and Law Center, Oakland, CA.

Peterson, K., McDonagh, M., Thakurta, S., Dana, T., Roberts, C., Chou, R., and Helfand, M. (2010). "Drug Class Review Nonsteroidal Antiinflammatory Drugs (NSAIDs)", Drug Effectiveness Review Project, Portland, OR.

Peterson, M. (2002). "Vermont to Require Drug Makers To Disclose Payments to Doctors." *New York Times*, New York, NY.

Peterson, M. (2008). "A bitter pill for Big Pharma." *Los Angeles Times*, Los Angeles, CA.

PhRMA. (2000). "Advertisement: She'll Just Have to Wait", Bangor, ME.

PhRMA. (2010). "PhRMA Statement on Health Care Reform", Washington, DC.

Pingree for Congress. (2008). "Official Biography", Portland, ME.

Pingree, C. (2000a). "Emergency Forum on Prescription Drugs", Office of Maine Senate Majority Leader, Augusta, ME.

Pingree, C. (2000b). "Interview on Enactment of LD 2599." Office of Maine Senate Majority Leader.

Pingree, C. (2000c). "Low Cost Drugs for the Elderly", Maine State Senate, Augusta, ME.

Pingree, C. (2000d). "Maine needs tough drug-price law." *Portland Press-Herald*, Portland, ME.

Pingree, C. (2000e). "Prescription Drug Price Fairness Action Plan", Augusta, ME.

Pingree, C. (2001a). "Interview on enactment of LD 2599 III." Office of Maine Senate Majority Leader.

Pingree, C. (2001b). "Interview on enactment of LD 2599 IV." Office of Maine Senate Majority Leader.

Pingree, C. (2001c). "Interview on Pharmaceutical Lobbyists." Office of Maine Senate Majority Leader.

Pingree, C. (2005). "Canada Cozies Up to Big Pharma." *Huffington Post*, New York, NY.

Poirier, P. (2000). "March 2000 Status of Vermont Efforts on Prescription Drug Prices." *Northeast Legislative Association on Prescription Drug Prices Meeting*, New York, NY.

Political Campaigns. (2005). "Election's lessons/ An advertising war." SFGate.com, San Francisco, CA.

Pollina, A. (2000). "Interview on Defeat of S. 300." .

Pollina, A. (1999). "Vermont Prescription Drug Price Control Legislation." *Meeting of National Council of Senior Citizens - New England*, Sturbridge, MA.

Powell, M. (2000). "Letter to Timothy Westmoreland, Health Care Financing Administration Medicaid Director", PhRMA, Washington, DC.

Prescription Project. (2008). "Prescription Data Mining", Community Catalyst, Boston, MA.

Ptashnik, B. (2000). "S. 300", Vermont Legislature, Montpelier, VT.

Quinn, F. (2000a). "Compromise unveiled on prescription drug plan." Associated Press, New York, NY.

Quinn, F. (2000b). "Drug pricing compromise reflects varying views on controls." Associated Press, New York, NY.

Quinn, F. (2000c). "Prescription drug price-cap bill goes to governor." Associated Press, New York, NY.

Rankin, K. (1996). "More litigation is likely for pharmaceutical firms." *Drug Store News*, New York, NY.

Remsen, N. (2000). "Drug price controls reconsidered." *Burlington Free Press*, Burlington, VT.

Repeal Prop 8 in 2010. (2010). "The Countdown to Equality Starts Now", Studio City, CA.

Rich, A. (2000). "Bringing Down The Cost Of Prescription Drugs." *Nor'Easter Monthly*.

Richards, P. (2003). "Drug Firms Prescribe Cash for Political Ills", National Institute on Money in State Politics, Helena, MT.

Richardson, K. (2002). "The Public Health Service (PHS) Section 340B Drug Pricing Program", Health Resources and Services Administration Pharmacy Services Support Center, Rockville, MD.

Rivers, C. (2000a). "Interview on S. 300." Office of Vermont Senate Majority Leader.

Rivers, C. (2000b). "Keys to Defeat of S. 300", *Northeast Legislative Association on Prescription Drug Prices Meeting*, South Portland, ME.

Rivers, C. (2000c). "March 2000 status of Vermont efforts on prescription drug prices." *Northeast Legislative Association on Prescription Drug Prices Meeting*, New York City.

Rivers, C. (2002). "Interview on S. 88." National Legislative Association on Prescription Drug Prices.

Rivers, C. (2004). "Executive Director's Report", National Legislative Association on Prescription Drug Prices, Burlington, VT.

Rivers, C. "Promoting Access to Prescription Drugs: 2003." California Program on Access to Care Briefing: California's 2004 Options to Improve Access to Medicines, Sacramento, CA.

Rochford, E. B. (1997). "Factionalism, Group Defection, and Schism in the Hare Krishna Movement." *Social Movements Readings on Their Emergence, Mobilization, and Dynamics*, D. McAdam and D. A. Snow, eds., Roxbury Publishing Company, Los Angeles, CA, 450-60.

Rojas, A. (2005). "A Powerful Partner." *Sacramento Bee*, Sacramento, CA.

Rosch, J. T. "Wading Into The Thicket of The Antitrust/Intellectual Property Law Overlap." *Innsbruck Symposium on Innovation and Competition Law*, Innsbruck, Austria.

Rosenthal, M. B., Epstein, A. M., Berndt, E. R., Donohue, J. M., and Frank, R. G. (2003). "Impact of Direct-to-Consumer Advertising." *Publication No. 6084*, Kaiser Family Foundation, Menlo Park, CA.

Ross, S. (2008). "Mom Q & A - Chellie Pingree." *RaisingMaine*, Portland, ME.

Rowe, S. (2000). "Press Release: Democratic Leaders Urge Legislature to Pass Fair Drug Price Bill", Office of the Speaker of the House, Augusta, ME.

Rowland, C. (2006). "US steps up seizures of imported drugs." *Boston Globe*, Boston, MA.

Salladay, R. (2007). "How Schwarzenegger Won." *Los Angeles Times*, Los Angeles, CA.

Sanchez, L. (2000a). "Interview on final version of S. 300." Office of Vermont Senate President Pro Tempore.

Sanchez, L. (2000b). "Interview on S. 300." Office of Vermont Senate President Pro Tempore.

Sanchez, L. (2001). "Interview on Interest Groups and S. 300." Office of Vermont Senate President Pro Tempore.

Scholz, L. (2008). "The 340B Drug Pricing Program." *National Conference of State Legislatures Legislative Summit*, New Orleans, LA.

Schweitzer, S. (2007). *Pharmaceutical Economics and Policy*, Oxford University Press, New York, NY.

Shaheen, J., King, A., and Dean, H. (2000). "Meeting of Quebec Health Minister and Northeast Legislative Association on Prescription Drug Pricing", Office of the Governor of Vermont, Montpelier, VT.

Sharp, D. (2000). "Groups embark on last-minute bid to stop prescription drug bill." Associated Press, New York, NY.

Shumlin, P. (2000a). "Interview on Defeat of S. 300." Office of Vermont Senate President Pro Tempore.

Shumlin, P. (2000b) "Keys to Defeat of S. 300." *Northeast Legislative Association on Prescription Drug Prices Meeting*, South Portland, ME.

Shumlin, P. (2000c) "March 2000 Status of Vermont Efforts on Prescription Drug Prices." *Northeast Legislative Association on Prescription Drug Prices Meeting*, New York, NY.

Shumlin, P. (2011). "Gov. Shumlin Signs Historic Health Care Reform Bill", Executive Office of Governor Peter Shumlin, Montpelier, VT.

Sifry, M. (2004). "What about campaign finance at the state level?" , Nieman Foundation for Journalism at Harvard University, Cambridge, MA.

Simon, H. A. (1987). "Bounded Rationality." *The New Palgrave : a Dictionary of Economics*, J. Eatwell, M. Milgate, and P. Newman, eds., Macmillan Press Ltd, London, UK, 266-68.

Singer, N., and Wilson, D. (2009). "Menopause, as Brought to You by Big Pharma." *New York Times*, New York, NY.

Smallheer, S. (2000). "Cut drug prices? It's a no-brainer." *Rutland Herald*, Rutland, VT.

Smith, D. (2002). "Medicaid Supplemental Drug Rebate Agreements." *State Medicaid Director Letter No. 02-014*, Centers for Medicare & Medicaid Services, Baltimore, MD.

Sneyd, R. (2000a). "Lawmakers maneuver toward adjournment." Associated Press, New York, NY.

Sneyd, R. (2000b). "Lawmakers seek ways to cut prescription costs." *Portsmouth Herald*, Portsmouth, NH.

Sneyd, R. (2000c). "Lobbyists work overtime on drug issue." Associated Press, New York, NY.

Sneyd, R. (2000d). "New England governors back drug-buying pool." Associated Press, New York, NY.

Sneyd, R. (2000e). "Pharmaceutical industry sues government." Associated Press, New York, NY.

Sossei, S., Emminger, S., Alois, P., Krawiecki, B., and Commisso, F. (2009). "Medicaid Reimbursement of Synagis." *Report No. 2008-S-153*, New York Office of Comptroller, Albany, NY.

Speier, J. (2007). "Interview on California Prescription Drug Politics in the Early 2000's." Office of California Senator Speier.

Stagnitti, M. (2007). "Trends in Outpatient Prescription Drug Utilization and Expenditures, 1997 to 2004." *Statistical Brief 168*, Agency for Health care Research and Quality, Rockville, MD.

Staton, T. (2010). "Reform Sets Big Budget for Comparative Research." *FiercePharma*, Washington, DC.

Stop Medicaid Fraud. (2009). "Pfizer Fact Sheet", US Department of Health and Human Services, Washington, DC.

Strongin, R. J. (1999). "Providing Outpatient Prescription Drugs through Medicare", National Health Policy Forum, Washington, DC.

Suarez, R. (2003). "Pricing Drugs." *NewsHour*, Arlington, VA.

Sweet, A. (1998). "Press Release: Senator Pingree to Join Seniors on Bus Trip to Canada for Medicines", Augusta, ME.

Sweet, A. (1999). "Memo on Northeast Prescription Drug Conference", Office of Maine Senate Majority Leader, Augusta, ME.

Sweet-Lazos, A. (2000). "Memo on LR 3636, Fair Pricing of Prescription Drugs", Office of Maine Senate Majority Leader, Augusta, ME.

Thomas, C. P., Wallack, S. S., Lee, S., and Ritter, G. A. (2002). "Impact Of Health Plan Design And Management On Retirees' Prescription Drug Use And Spending, 2001." *Health Affairs*, 21(6), Web Exclusives:W408-419.

Thomas, L. G. (1983). *The Competitive Status of the U.S. Pharmaceutical Industry: The Influences of Technology in Determining International Industrial Competitive Advantage*, National Academy Press, Washington, DC.

Thomason, R. (2007). "Interview on Assemblyman Frommer's work for Access to Prescription Drugs." Office of California Assembly Majority Leader.

Treat, S. (2007). "Interview on mid-decade state prescription drug bills." Office of Maine Representative Treat.

US Census Bureau. (2008). "Statistical Abstract of the United States: 2009." *128th Edition*, US Department of Commerce, Washington, DC.

US Department of Veterans Affairs. (2009). "Drug Pharmaceutical Prices", Washington, DC.

US Food and Drug Administration. (2005). "Thalidomide: Important Patient Information." *Publication No. (FDA) 96-3222*, United States Department of Health and Human Services, Washington, DC.

US General Accounting Office. (1991). "Changes in Drug Prices Paid by VA." *Report No. HRD-91-139*, Washington, DC.

US General Accounting Office. (2002). "FDA Oversight of Direct-to-Consumer Advertising Has Limitations." *Report No. GAO-03-177*.

Vermont Legislative Bill Tracking System. (2000a). "Conference Committee for S. 300", Vermont State Legislature, Montpelier, VT.

Vermont Legislative Bill Tracking System. (2000b). "H. 365", Vermont State Legislature, Montpelier, VT.

Vermont Legislative Bill Tracking System. (2000c). "Rollcall Votes for S. 300", Vermont State Legislature, Montpelier, VT.

Vermont Legislative Bill Tracking System. (2000d). "Status of S. 300", Vermont State Legislature, Montpelier, VT.

Vermont NEA Today. (2004). "Vermont NEA Recommendations for Lt. Governor", Montpelier, VT.

Vermont PIRG. (1999). "Prescription Drug Pricing Proposal", Montpelier, VT.

Voice of the ILWU. (2002). "New laws benefit working families", Honolulu, HI.

von Oehsen, W. (2001). "Pharmaceutical Discounts Under Federal Law.", Public Health Institute.

Wallace, M. (1999). "Why So Expensive?" *60 Minutes*, CBS News.

Washuk, B. (2000a). "Bill's Aim: Controlling Drug Prices." *Lewiston Sun Journal*, Lewiston, ME.

Washuk, B. (2000b). "Drug bill passes easily." *Lewiston Sun Journal*, Lewiston, ME, A1.

Washuk, B. (2000c). "Lawmakers: Cut costs of prescriptions." *Lewiston Sun Journal*, Lewiston, ME, A1.

WCAX.com. (2008). "Three Big Endorsements for Pollina", South Burlington, VT.

Weber, D., Reddan, J., and Keegan, M. (2001). "Study of Pharmaceutical Benefit Management." *HCFA Contract No. 500-97-0399/0097*, Health Care Financing Administration, Baltimore, MD.

Weber, H. (2001). "Governors announce tri-state prescription buying plan." Associated Press, New York, NY.

Weil, E. (2004). "Grumpy Old Drug Smugglers." *New York Times*, New York, NY.

Weiner, J., Lyles, A., Steinwachs, D., and Hall, K. (1991). "Impact of Managed Care on Prescription Drug Use." *Health Affairs*, 10(1), 140-154.

Weinstein, J. (2001). "Court Upholds Maine Rx Program." *Press Herald*, Portland, ME.

Weintraub, A. (2009). "The Fight Over Drug Data Mining." *BusinessWeek*.

Weisenthal, J. (2009). "Goldman: Prepare For The De-Stimulus." *Business Insider*, New York, NY.

Wildermuth, J. (2005). "Drug firms arming for battle at ballot box." *San Francisco Chronicle*, San Francisco, CA.

Wilson-Coker, P. A. (2006). "ConnPACE: Celebrating 20 Years", Connecticut Department of Social Services, Hartford, CT.

Wolfe, J. (2001). "Director at Waldron Group of Companies Tapped to Lead South Portland Golf Club" Wolfe News Wire, Portland, ME.

Woloson, A. (2008). "Interview on IMS lawsuit Against LD 4." Prescription Policy Choices.

Woodruff, B. (1999). "Prescription Drugs Are Cheaper in Canada." ABC News, New York, NY.

Wright, A. (2005). "Drug Company Domination by Dirty Tricks and Deception", Health Access, Sacramento, CA.

Wu, K. (2003). "Income and Poverty of Older Americans in 2001", Public Policy Institute, Washington, DC.

Wyckoff, P. T. (2007). "Minnesota-Canadian Prescription Drug Bus Trips." Minnesota Senior Federation.

Yi, D. (2006). "Savings Ahead in Generic Medicines." *Los Angeles Times*, Los Angeles, CA.

York, A. (2009). "Interest groups' lobbying tally tops $500 million." *Capitol Weekly*, Sacramento, CA.

Zeleny, J. (2003). "Dean abandons public financing system in presidential bid." *Chicago Tribune*, Chicago, IL.

Index

60 Minutes, 60-61
AB 2911 (Nuñez), 128 129; see also California Discount Prescription Drug Program
ACA. See Affordable Care Act
Affordable Care Act (ACA), 145: Independent Payment Advisory Board (IPAB), 145-146; Patient-Centered Outcomes Research Institute (PCORI), 146
AFL-CIO. See Labor federations
Allen, Tom, 29, 57-58, 79
American Association of Retired People: California 119, 129; Vermont 42
AMP. See Prices, Prescription Drugs: Average Manufacturer Price
Angelides, Phil, 123-124
AstraZeneca (drugmaker), 89
Baldacci, John, 78-79
Bristol-Myers Squibb (drugmaker), 40, 50, 90
Brown, Willie, 118-119
Bruno, Joseph, 63, 65, 72, 79
Burlington Drug Company, 38-39
Burlington Free Press, 38
Bush, George H.W., 11
California Alliance of Retired Americans (CARA), 107, 109-110, 111
California Chamber of Commerce, 107, 112
California Discount Prescription Drug Program (CDPDP), 129, 130, 131, 132; see also AB 2911 (Nuñez)
California Proposition 79; 114, 116, 117, 120
CALPIRG. See California Public Interest Research Group
Capell, Beth, 122, 124, 125, 126, 127, 131
CARA. See California Alliance of Retired Americans

Carson, Dan, 112, 114
CCS. See Congress of California Seniors
CDPDP. See California Discount Prescription Drug Program
CER. See Evidence-Based Health Care: Comparative Effectiveness Research
Concannon, Kevin, 47, 53, 57, 63, 66, 72-73, 77, 78, 79, 95, 112
Congress of California Seniors (CCS), 100
Critical hardships, 141: restrictions to access to essential medicines, cost-based, 23, 70
Currier, Leon, 58
Davis, Gray, 99, 100, 102-103, 104-105, 134
Dean, Howard, 37, 38, 41, 44, 46, 47, 48, 51, 66, 82
DEL. See State Pharmaceutical Assistance Programs: Low-cost Drugs for the Elderly
DERP. See Evidence-Based Health Care: Drug Effectiveness Review Project
DTC advertising. See Marketing: Direct-to-consumer advertising
Evidence-Based Health Care, 83-84, 104, 106, 107: Academic detailing, 93; Comparative Effectiveness Research (CER), 84, 101, 145; Drug Effectiveness Review Project (DERP), 84; New York State Medicaid Prescriber Education Program, 93; Oregon Health and Science University (OHSU), 84, 101; Website, 109
Farrell, Jim, 111, 115
FDA. See US Food and Drug Administration
Flaherty, Michael, 40, 45
Frommer, Dario, 101-102, 103-104, 113, 125, 129

FSS. See Prices, Prescription Drugs:
    Federal Supply Schedule
FTA. See Free Trade Agreement
GlaxoSmithKline (drugmaker), 40
Gretkowski, Hank, 40, 45
HR 4627, the Prescription Drug
    Fairness for Seniors Act of 1998,
    29, 50, 58
IMS Health (pharmaceutical data
    vendor), 91-92
Independent pharmacies, 40, 63, 71-
    72, 74
IPAB. See Affordable Care Act:
    Independent Payment Advisory
    Board
Issa, Darrell, 103
King, Angus, 43, 65, 66, 67, 71, 72,
    74, 75, 139
Kitzhaber, John, 83
Labor federations: California Labor
    Federation, 104, 105-106, 116;
    Maine American Federation of
    Labor-Congress of Industrial
    Organizations (AFL-CIO), 63;
    Ohio AFL-CIO, 85; Vermont
    State Labor Council, 48
Labor organizations, 143, 148:
    Alliance for a Better California,
    116, 117; International Longshore
    and Warehouse Union, 85; Maine
    State Employees Association
    (MSEA), 53, 59, 60, 63, 64-65,
    68, 80, 138; Service Employees
    International Union (SEIU), 53,
    97, 105, 114, 116, 120, 122, 124,
    125-126, 139; Vermont State
    Employees Association, 29, 39
LD 2599 (Pingree), 66; see also
    Maine Rx
Legislative leadership, powers, 33,
    62, 95, 106, 111, 122: calling
    press conferences, 65, 113
Leinonen, Carl, 60, 61, 64
Lingle, Linda, 85
Maine Chamber of Commerce, 55, 67
Maine Council of Senior Citizens
    (MCSC), 59, 68
Maine Equal Justice Partners, 56-57
Maine Rx Plus, 78

Maine Rx, 53, 73-74, 113, 115; see
    also LD 2599
Marketing tactics, pharmaceutical:
    Data-mining, 21, 91; Detailing,
    12; Direct-to-consumer (DTC)
    advertising, 20, 90; Gifts to
    physicians, 47, 108, 145
Marvin, John, 34, 55, 59-60, 61, 63,
    75, 80
MCSC. See Maine Council of Senior
    Citizens
Medicaid: waivers, 130-131;
    Supplemental rebates, 14, 46-47,
    77, 98, 133; Unpaid supplemental
    rebates, 89
Medicare managed care, 23
Medicare Modernization Act, 6, 86,
    135: Nonintervention clause, 87,
    132-133, 145; Part D, 86, 121-
    122, 132; Part D doughnut hole,
    87, 145
Merck (drugmaker), 4, 19, 21, 40
MSEA. See Labor Organizations:
    Maine State Employees
    Association
National Legislative Association on
    Prescription Drug Prices
    (NLARx), 47, 49, 83; see also
    Northeast Legislative Association
    on Prescription Drug Prices
New York Times, 68
NLARx. See National Legislative
    Association on Prescription Drug
    Prices
Northeast Legislative Association on
    Prescription Drug Prices, 27, 46;
    see also National Legislative
    Association on Prescription Drug
    Prices
Nuñez, Fabian, 118, 122-123, 124-
    125, 125-126, 128, 129
OHSU. See Evidence-Based Health
    Care: Oregon Health and Science
    University
Ortiz, California State Senator
    Deborah, 104, 112, 113-114, 116,
    118, 128
OURx Coalition, 107, 109, 113, 127,
    130, 131, 132

PBM. See Pharmacy Benefit
    Manager
PCORI. See Affordable Care Act:
    Patient-Centered Outcomes
    Research Institute
PDL. See Preferred Drug List
Pelosi, Nancy, 132
Perata, Don, 122-123, 124-125, 126,
    128
Pfizer (drugmaker), 78, 89, 134
Pharmaceutical industry status:
    Fortune 500 ranking, 21-22, 25,
    94; Share of US health care costs,
    23-24
Pharmaceutical Research and
    Manufacturing Association
    (PhRMA), 40, 46-47, 69, 75-76,
    81, 86, 101, 111, 112, 116, 118,
    128, 139, 147
Pharmacy Benefit Manager (PBM),
    15, 21, 82-83, 91, 92, 104, 105,
    107
PhRMA v. Concannon, 76-77, 103
PhRMA. See Pharmaceutical
    Research and Manufacturing
    Association
Pingree, Chellie, 36, 43, 56-57, 58,
    61, 62-63, 66, 71, 72, 74, 78, 79,
    117
PMPRB. See Prices, Prescription
    Drugs: Patented Medicine Prices
    Review Board, Canadian
Political sociology literature:
    Bounded rationality, 148;
    Eckstein, Harry, 148; Framing,
    140-141; Hacker, Jacob, 148;
    Himelfarb, Richard, 148; Jasper,
    James, 140; Resource
    Mobilization Theory (RMT), 140,
    148; Simon, Herbert, 148
Political tactics, access to
    prescription drug advocates:
    Capitol offices visits, 68, 109-
    110; Demonstrations for elected
    officials, 75; Petitions to elected
    officials, 59; Postcards to elected
    officials, 111; Small political
    arenas, 143-144; Town hall
    meetings, 39, 63, 64-65; phone
    calls to elected officials, 71

Political tactics, pharmaceutical
    industry: Ad campaigns, 69-70,
    75, 118, 119; Astroturf lobbying,
    17, 69, 86; Campaign
    contributions, 16, 81-82, 86, 95;
    Counter initiatives, 117, 120,
    135; Lawsuits, 76-77, 85, 117;
    Meetings with legislative and
    executive branch leadership, 17,
    69, 81-82; Pharmaceutical
    Assistance Programs, 18, 69
Pollina, Anthony, 30, 33, 45, 46, 47-
    48, 50, 60
Portland Press Herald, 67, 69
Preferred Drug List (PDL), 14, 26,
    72-73
Prices, Prescription Drugs: 340(b)
    price, 15, 25, 28; Average
    Manufacturer Price (AMP), 125,
    127; Medicaid price, 14;
    Canadian Patented Medicine
    Prices Review Board (PMPRB)
    price, 13; Federal Supply
    Schedule (FSS) price, 13; Market
    share, impact, 95-96, 109
Private interest groups, 4
Profit-maximizing tactics,
    pharmaceutical industry:
    Blockbuster drugs, 3,10; Clinical
    trials, drugmaker-run, 18-19; Free
    Trade Agreement (FTA)
    restrictions, 88-89, 94;
    Oligopolistic prices, 10; Patents,
    9-10; Pay-for-delay, 90
Public interest groups, 5
Public interest research groups:
    California Public Interest
    Research Group (CALPIRG), 97,
    100-101; Vermont Public Interest
    Research Group (VPIRG), 29
Publicity, access to prescription drug
    advocates: alternative media, 70;
    prescription drug-buying bus
    trips, 31, 50, 58, 60
Rescue California, 103
Righteous indignation, 2, 12, 34, 58,
    138, 141, 142
Rivers, Cheryl, 27, 30, 42, 44, 45, 46,
    47, 50

RMT. See Political sociology
    literature: Resource Mobilization
    Theory
Rosenstein, Stan, 103, 126-127
Rowe, Steve, 64, 67, 75, 78
S 300, 27-28, 36-37, 38, 39
SAN. See Senior Action Network
Sanders, Bernie, 28, 30, 50
Schondelmeyer, Stephen, 35, 51, 125
Schwarzenegger, Arnold, 105, 106,
    109, 110-111, 111-112, 113, 115,
    121, 123-124, 128, 129, 130, 139
SEIU. See Labor Organizations:
    Service Employees International
    Union
Senior Action Network (SAN), 107,
    109, 111
Shumlin, Peter, 27, 32, 35, 42, 44, 45,
    46, 47-48, 65
Soto, Nell, 101
SPAP. See State Pharmaceutical
    Assistance Programs
Speier, Jackie, 98-99, 100, 113, 133
Stark, Pete, 132
State Pharmaceutical Assistance
    Programs (SPAP), 15:
    ConnPACE, 7; Golden Bear, 100,
    109-110; Low-cost Drugs for the
    Elderly program (DEL), 56;
    Vermont Health Access Program
    (VHAP), 34, 37; VScript, 34
Takumi, Roy, 85
Tauzin, Billy, 87, 118, 124-125, 126,
    147
Thomason, Richard, 128
Treat, Sharon, 82, 83, 92, 115, 125
US Court of Appeals for the First
    Circuit, 76-77, 92
US Food and Drug Administration
    (FDA), 11, 20-21
US House Committee on
    Government Reform, 29, 58
Vermont Prescription Drug Cost
    Containment and Affordable
    Access Act of 2002, 47
Vermont Civil Unions Act, 36, 39-
    40, 41, 42-43
Vermont Consumers Campaign for
    Health, 30, 39

VHAP. See State Pharmaceutical
    Assistance Programs: Vermont
    Health Access Program
Viguerie, Richard, 69, 86
VPIRG. See Vermont Public Interest
    Research Group
Wilson, Pete, 105, 134
Wyeth (drugmaker), 17-18, 40
Young, Casey, 124, 125
Zingale, Daniel, 120, 124

About the Book

How can health-access advocates beat the wealthy pharmaceutical industry, which has the biggest spending lobby in Washington? Ramón Castellblanch provides a ringside seat at the battle as he reveals how activists in Vermont, Maine, and California took on Big Pharma in their state legislatures to promote better and cheaper access to prescription drugs—and ultimately pushed Congress to enact a Medicare prescription drug benefit. He also draws lessons from these cases about the possibilities for success elsewhere in the health policy arena, highlighting the crucial role that voters' righteous indignation plays in fueling popular support for grassroots political leaders who are taking on powerful business interests.

Ramón Castellblanch is associate professor of health education at San Francisco State University. Previously, he has been a health policy consultant for the California State Employees Association, health policy analyst for the American Federation of State, County, and Municipal Employees, and political action director for the Bazelon Center for Mental Health Law.